SOLOMONI

Times and tales from Solomon Islands

SOLOMONI

Times and tales from Solomon Islands

Roger Webber

Matador
5 Weir Road
Kibworth Beauchamp
Leicester LE8 0LQ, UK
Tel: (+44) 116 279 2299
Fax: (+44) 116 279 2277
Email: books@troubador.co.uk
Web: www.troubador.co.uk/matador

ISBN 978 1848765 474

British Library Cataloguing in Publication Data.
A catalogue record for this book is available from the British Library.

Typeset in 12pt Perpetua by Troubador Publishing Ltd, Leicester, UK
Printed and bound in the UK by TJ International Ltd, Padstow, Cornwall

Matador is an imprint of Troubador Publishing Ltd

To Bridget
(1944 - 1972)

Contents

List of illustrations

Maps:
1. Southwest Pacific.
2. Solomon Islands.

Figures:
01. Volcanoes of Western Solomons; Kolombangara cover, Rendova above.
02. On tour on Malaita, Bridget with Sophy.
03. "Who now pikanini?" waiting for the doctor.
04. Married and unmarried woman in Kwaio, Malaita. Only when a woman is married does she wear a loincloth or skirt. The small hut on the left is where a woman has to stay when she is menstruating.
05. A Polynesian family cutting copra on Ontong Java. Both men and women are tattooed, but more so the women with most of the tattoo between the waist and the knees, and therefore hidden from view. Note the booby chick kept as a pet and source of food.
06. The picture that was seen around the world. Lucy receives treatment in hospital immediately after the aircrash. (With permission of Associated Press).
07. Lucy and Sophy after the accident with Heti Bea.
08. Royal visit to Gizo. War canoes getting ready to escort the launch back to the Britannia.
09. Choiseul dancers. Note the pan pipes and the large number of arm rings worn by the dancer in the front, indicating his chiefly status.

10 a & b. Chiefs' skull place on Vella Lavella.

11. Yam house in the Trobriand Islands, Papua New Guinea.

12. Interior Guadalcanal, Tetekanji.

13. Na Poli village in Tetekanji. Grass skirts were always worn by the women before being superseded by material.

14. On the summit of Makarakomburu (2447 m), highest point in Solomon Islands. The trees are gnarled and moss covered in the mountain forest.

15. Crossing a flooded river on Guadalcanal, John Tagabosoe on the right.

16. Tikopia.

17. Anointing the food bowl in Tikopia.

18. Custom queen contestant draped with strings of shell money.

Acknowledgements

Working in the Solomon Islands was a unique opportunity that I will always treasure, one of the most interesting places in the world and some of the nicest people anywhere. They accepted me as one of them, taking me into their villages and treating me with the abundant hospitality that is so characteristic of these islands. It was during these times that I would hear stories of what the islands were like in the early days while much of what happened is of events that took place while I was with them. They were my guides and helpers, I learnt so much from them and I thank them all for their considerable contribution.

I will not single out any particular person, some of them are mentioned by name in the text, while others will know who they are, but however big or small their contribution, none of this could have taken place without them.

There has understandably been a considerable literature written about this fascinating part of the world, much of which I have listed under "Source material and further reading." This has been an invaluable store of reference from which I have freely taken and I would like to thank the many authors of these works for their help.

I wish to thank Associated Press for the use of Figure 6.

Note on use of words

There was no written language in the islands until comparatively recent times, initiated by the missionaries who wanted to translate their religious books. Even so there is little conformity of spelling and attempts to spell words in a phonetically suitable way, such as Ngella, have generally not been followed and a shortened version, Gela, is more commonly used. Also *r* and *l* are often interchanged, such as Sinerango or Sinalanggu, so I have used *r* whenever this occurs.

A grammar and spelling is developing for Pidgin but no conformity has yet been reached so where I have found it useful to express a passage in Pidgin I have used a version which makes it more easily understood by the English speaker.

The islands are officially known as Solomon Islands, without *the* in front, but when they are described in a comparative way, such as discussing the people, then *the* is placed in front, or the alternative, *the Solomons,* is used. The Solomon Islands would therefore apply to the geographical group, which includes Bougainville and Buka in present day Papua New Guinea, whereas just Solomon Islands refers to the country on independence.

Introduction

The war had just finished and I had been told that my brother and I would travel out to be with my father. He was however a father I hardly knew for when the war started he signed up and I never saw him again. I was now six and my world extended to the small area of South London where we lived and Minehead in Somerset where we had spent the war years. Where were we going to and what was it going to be like, at that age I had no concept of this strange new land?

Even the journey out was a great adventure as we were herded into one vast cabin of a troop carrier, the only vessel available at that time in 1946. To young eyes everything was new and strange, seeing people with black skins as we berthed at Port Sudan, then to arrive at Mombassa with its Arab dhows and Portuguese fort, it was all an intriguing world. Here we transferred to a smaller ship, the *Al Said,* an old fashioned craft with tall funnel and cutaway stern, that would take the three of us to Zanzibar. My mother was relieved to see her husband again, she had never been abroad before, then having gone through the rigours of the war, to have to travel all the way to East Africa in charge of two troublesome brats.

Zanzibar was everything anyone could ever have asked for; we had a big house and endless garden, where monkeys would come down from the trees and if the opportunity arose scamper in through an open door and steal some bananas. I made a bow and arrow and pretended to hunt them and the other strange animals that I would imagine were there. Wild boar lived in the forest and leopards hunted the monkeys, adding excitement to my childhood world, but in reality there was little chance of them coming anywhere near our garden.

My father was the headmaster of the government secondary school, which had fought a constant a battle with termites to keep the buildings from falling down. The phase of reconstruction that was taking place after the war in Europe had overflowed to the colonies as well, but instead of constructing new buildings on the present site it was decided that the school should move down to the coast. So we left the house with the forested garden to move into an entirely new one right on the beach. It was like giving a child everything he could ever want.

Sadly it had to come to an end for despite the education system of which my father was a part there was no suitable school for us to go to in Zanzibar, it was considered that we would have an unfair advantage over the local children, so we were sent to boarding school in Nairobi. It was a traumatic experience, at the tender age of seven to leave family and that wonderful life in Zanzibar to be thrust into a primary school that was to not only cater for the likes of my brother and I, but the sons of up-country farmers who treated the African and everybody else with disdain, and re-settled Italian prisoners-of-war who brought their families from the slums of Naples to start a new life in East Africa. It was a tough upbringing, for the more you succeeded academically, the more you brought on the jealousy and bullying of these unpleasant types.

When the holidays came and we returned to our beautiful island it was like entering a fairyland once more. There was the sea and picnics, friends and parties, why did we have to go back to school again? The dichotomy continued for six years until a more sinister threat came to the school in Kenya. Talks of secret societies had been rumoured and then the murders started, the Mau Mau had come into existence.

Bars were put on the dormitory windows and we could no longer go out for walks or even cross the road to the playing fields. Africans who worked in the kitchens, did the cleaning or managed the school grounds could have taken the secret oath, so you did not know who might be a member of the organisation. Amongst schoolboys the stories were magnified, the fear increased and for my father it became the time of decision. He had been looking at secondary schools in England and this finally made up his mind.

It was a new experience, I did not know England, although I had been brought up there during the war years, I was too young to remember much about it. I was tested academically for although I had always been near the top of the class in Nairobi, I found myself more often near the bottom in my new school. I was also used to defending myself against the constant assaults at my old school that I had to stop myself from becoming the bully in my new environment. We stayed with our grandparents in a flat in Balham during the holidays as visits for children to their parents abroad were few and far between. We had entered a new world of peace and academic excellence, but at the same time had lost that perfect childhood that we had known in Zanzibar. Somehow the trials of the school in Kenya did not matter, because come the holidays we would always go back to Zanzibar, but now we could not even do that.

The memories never waned though, they became a powerful part of my inner feelings, some day I would find it again, return to those tropical climes. I wanted do something in life that would take me back to the life I had known before.

Initially it was not Africa but Solomon Islands where I would work. It was to be just a single contract of two years, but such was the fascination and interest that I returned again and again until it was ten years before I finally left. This then is the story of these years, life as a doctor and a description of most of the islands, remote areas of which few people ever get to see. It is also the story of the last days of Protectorate as these islands followed the path to independence. Many things happened during this time, such as the earthquake on Guadalcanal, which was to change this island as much as the shattering events of the Second World War. But the Solomon Islands have been more than an isolated entity, historically they have been a bridge to different peoples as they made their way into the vast expanse of the Pacific.

First though were the trials and tribulations of becoming a doctor, especially one that wanted to work in tropical countries.

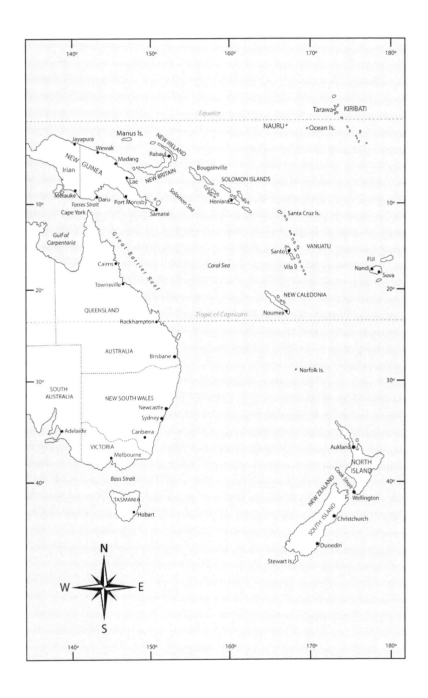

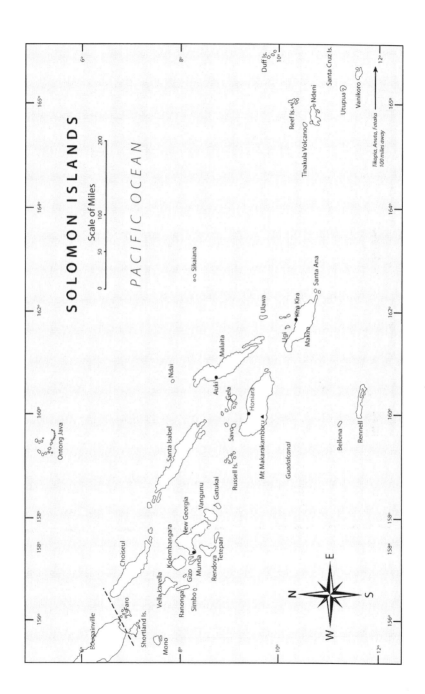

SOLOMON ISLANDS

Scale of Miles

0   50   100   200

PACIFIC OCEAN

Ontong Java

Santa Isabel

Choiseul

Vella Lavella

Ranonga
Simbo
Gizo
Munda
Kolombangara
New Georgia
Vangunu
Rendova
Tetepari
Gatukai

Mono
Shortland Is.
Faro
Bougainville

Russell Is.
Savo
Honiara
Mt Makarakambou
Guadalcanal

Ndai
Auki
Gela

Malaita

Sikaiana

Ulawa

Ligi
Makira
Kira Kira

Santa Ana

Bellona
Rennell

Reef Is.
Tinakula Volcano
Ndeni

Duff Is.

Santa Cruz Is.

Utupua
Vanikoro

Tikopia, Anuta, Fotaka
100 miles away

N
W   E
S

6°   8°   10°   12°

156°   158°   160°   162°   164°   165°

CHAPTER ONE

The Persian Carpet

It was an incredibly long room and at the far end was an enormous table with high back chairs around three sides. These were so immense that the back came up much higher than the top of any person sitting in them.

Having walked the length of the room, like it was some trial I had to do first, I was asked to sit down at the very far end of the table. Five or six figures tried to make themselves as tall as the chairs they sat in, turning over pieces of paper with details of the person sitting in front of them. After a few basic questions came the standard poser,

"And now Mr Webber will you please tell us why you want to do Medicine?"

I was prepared for this and without any hesitation replied,

"Because I want to work abroad."

The interviewers having made themselves as large as possible to show their importance in the task at hand, now looked as though they were going to explode in disbelief.

"Work abroad? What is wrong with this country?"

So I explained that I thought there was a greater need for doctors in developing countries as the standard of medicine in this one seemed to be well cared for.

Having recovered themselves from the shock of this unlikely response, they being more used to the potential doctor talking about wanting to become a consultant in this or that speciality, they persisted with the interrogation.

"Where would you work abroad, I take it that it would be in a Commonwealth country?"

I had become attracted to the Amazon and wanted to work in South America where there was actually only one Commonwealth country, so I said,

"There seems to be a great need in many countries that are not in the Commonwealth and I might well work in one of these."

I left the room knowing that I would not get offered a place there, in fact if by some strange chance they had done so I wouldn't have accepted it. They didn't seem to like people who were not going to fit into the mould, and especially if they were going to waste their wonderful training on a bunch of primitive people. Fortunately King's College were not so narrow minded and offered me a place provided I passed my "A" levels.

Unsettled by the death of my father in Zanzibar and the uncertainties of whether I wanted to continue studying after so many years at school my "A" level results were a disaster, and I lost the place at King's. So I went off on a great wander through Africa which gave me the necessary break, but also the conviction that medicine was really what I wanted to do. I set about doing my exams again and having passed them, now tried to get into Medical School once more.

With such a poor examination record most medical schools wouldn't even give me an interview and King's only did so because they had offered me a place in the past. It was as though they felt under some sort of obligation to see me again but had decided almost before I went in that that they were not going to give me a chance. After their previous pleasantness the interview was a depressing affair, leaving me demoralised and somewhat stunned. I was beginning to think that I would never get into medical school when amongst all the rejection letters was one for an interview at the Royal Free. I knew all hope rested on it and was already thinking of other alternatives to do in life if I failed.

On returning to England I had found a job working as a laboratory technician in the Maida Vale Hospital for Nervous Diseases. I was taken on to do the histology, working my way up from preparing the tissues, to cutting and making slides. The work appealed to me, and I wondered whether I could do it for the rest of my life, but I really did want to become a doctor. The junior pathologist was married to a psychiatrist at the Royal Free and as to whether she put in a word for me I was never to know, except that I did get an interview there.

After my experiences at Kings I was not particularly hopeful, especially when I found there were 20 candidates for each place and many of them were bright young school leavers who had achieved brilliant results in their A levels. However there was much talk in the press at the high drop-out rate and so medical schools were keen to make sure that they selected candidates who would survive the course. The Royal Free had been successful at this due to their policy of taking a proportion of mature students and as I was several years older than most of the competition, had done two jobs and travelled, I thought this might be my chance. All depended upon the interview.

This time the interview was a much friendlier affair, in a comparatively small room at the old medical school building in Hunter Street. There were four people, two men and two women and I was straight away made to feel at ease. The Dean, who was due to retire, was making her last selection of candidates and clearly was very much in charge of the proceedings. She asked me what I had done since leaving school and I told her about my travels, how I had made my way overland to East Africa, and how the experience had convinced me of the necessity to get qualified. Most of the other candidates had only been able to talk about the sports and interests they had done at school, so she sat back intrigued with the story I could tell. She then passed me on to the other members of the board and one in particular, a rather serious man, who had sat unmoved at my travel stories. His question was straight to the point.

"I notice Mr Webber that you have had difficulty with passing your chemistry, don't you think chemistry is important in medicine?"

Chemistry had always been a problem, I really didn't like the subject, but it was an essential entry requirement. I felt I had to be truthful and replied,

"Chemistry might be required to start with but once qualified one was unlikely to want to know the chemical composition of the medicines used; also there were other ways of treating people such as surgery."

Out of the corner of my eye I could see the Dean smile to herself as she tried to suppress her laughter. I later found out that my doer interviewer was the Professor of Chemistry, but despite my gaff, I was accepted.

I started Medical School in October 1962 with the determination to get through, but my absence from academic life and greater age than my class mates made it much more of a struggle to get down to serious study again. As expected the biochemistry was the hardest subject, but in contrast anatomy fascinated me and I would spend hours dissecting in the Long Room. This ran the entire length of the top floor of the medical school and contained some 30 bodies. It was alright in the daytime but doing extra work in the evenings I would sit there alone surround with the corpses of all those unknown people. I wondered who they had been in life and imagined their ghosts returning to see what was being done to them.

I had left my job as a laboratory technician in June, taking myself off to explore England by bike, a country I didn't really know, but got as far as York only to suffer a cartilage injury, that was to plague me for the rest of my life. I had also arranged to go on a work camp in Harlow New Town run by the Quakers, and although the work aspect was not very challenging the personal relationships that developed were of considerable importance. This was particularly so because of prisoners from Pentonville that worked with us on day release as part of their re-orientation into society. It was intriguing to discover what nice people they were with many stories to tell, not the mindless ruffian that we expected. By coincidence there was a girl there called Myfanwy, who was starting at the Royal Free as well, but in the pre-clinical year. She knew the girlfriend of the brother of a girl that would be in my year and asked me to locate her when I began.

I thought little more about this until the term started and we were all a large group of boys and girls who had never met each other before, but would be spending the next five years together. One talked to the person you happened to be sitting next to or the others dissecting a body with you, but it took some time before I got to know the whole group. Eventually I tracked down the girl I had been asked to find by Myfanwy and the three of us had our first meeting.

She was called Bridget and Myfanwy found a good friend in her, the three of us often meeting together. I hardly noticed her at first and it wasn't until some three weeks later that I began to realise that something was happening to me, there was a sense of affection developing, was I falling in love?

Bridget had only just turned 18, so was the youngest in our class, but had such a brilliant academic record that she was accepted at a younger age than the others. She still had the schoolgirl manner about her and this was why I had hardly noticed her at first. Some of the other girls were similar to me having done something else in life since leaving school and I initially found them more interesting. But once I met Bridget I realised that she had many ideas on life that seemed very advanced for her years and a desire to work abroad similar to mine. She had a very pretty face and long blond hair, as well as an attractive figure, so how could I resist such a charming person. In fact Myfanwy had done me a great favour by getting me to search her out first, as after a few weeks of our year starting it was not difficult to notice that there was a general exploration going on. Some of the men seemed to have set themselves the task to try out each girl in turn, but I had a head start with them over Bridget, who was by far the most attractive girl there.

It had been such a hard struggle to get into medical school that I had vowed I would not have any girl friends, concentrating my entire efforts on studying, but I soon found this difficult to keep. Something very strong was welling up inside me and I knew that I had to do something about it. Although I saw a lot of Bridget I kept up a certain aloofness to try and protect myself from becoming too friendly, but finally my resistance broke and one day as we were about to go our separate ways home I said to her rather hesitatingly,

"Would you like to go out somewhere?" I hadn't really thought about where we would go or what we should do, I just wanted to sound out her feelings as she had not shown any obvious interest in me, and I half expected her to refuse.

She agreed so we went to the small gardens at the back of the Medical School and sat and talked for a while. To my surprise she then admitted,

"I thought you were never going to ask me."

Far more gradually and genuinely our attachment grew, not like the fast affairs that I had been through in the past few months. We both knew that the objective was to get through medical school so had to restrain ourselves, finding that we could help each other with our studies. Discussing the insertion of muscles on a couple of bones might not seem the most romantic way to carry on a courtship, but to two medical students it was inspiring. Life was not all like this though, we went out to concerts and spent time walking in the park, frustrated by the lack of a place where we could express our desire to just be one with each other. Bridget stayed with relations in Kensington and I had digs in Harringay, so we couldn't have lived further away from each other.

Our first year was coming to a close and soon we would have the only long holiday in the whole five years of the medical course. We envied other university graduates who had two long holidays and only had to study for three years, so we were determined to make the most of the one opportunity we had. Bridget had arranged to do some voluntary work in Greece so I was to go that far with her and then continue on by myself. Unfortunately these plans fell through so instead she went to Switzerland to be with a group of voluntary workers and I went off by myself as I had a complex problem to solve.

I had learnt how to be self-sufficient on my overland journey through Africa, surviving the difficulties of long periods on my own. What is more I had so thoroughly enjoyed my travel that I shunned the opportunity of returning all the way back to England by ship, continuing overland to South Africa. Travel and seeing the world had become very important to me, so studying medicine could be a means to doing this, as well as being a worthwhile profession to follow. I had seen at first hand the plight of people in disease-ridden Africa, and I wanted to be able to do something about it. Now I had met somebody very special to share my life with, but by doing so I would not be able to lead that life of singular exploration that I had begun.

The question was not, "Was Bridget the right person for me, but rather should I get married?"

I knew I had found the person I wanted to be with, but was I prepared to give up all that I had planned in order to marry her. This was why we went our separate ways instead of sharing this long holiday, I needed time to be by myself to think all these things over, and what better way to do this than travel. It was 1963 and following the road to India was the way to go, so this was the journey I planned to make.

* * * * *

As I set off I wondered whether I was doing the right thing. Bridget had been so sad yesterday and now I was back to the difficulties of trying to get a lift on the road to Dover. Also it was a fine day, which made it all the more difficult for me to leave than when it was a gloomy and depressing one, but this was the first day travel blues that I always have.

By that night I had crossed the Channel and reached Oostende, and by the next day traversed the whole of Belgium and was into Germany. I travelled through Germany to Austria, the way I would have gone with Bridget if her original plans had come to fruition, but now I was alone. At quiet moments all the memories would come flooding back, there were those thoughts of our parting, of how we had planned to be together for at least part of the time, what was she doing and thinking? I questioned again why I had gone off on my own and hoped that we would both gain from our separation.

I was glad when I reached Vienna as this indicated the end of my hitchhiking for some time. I hated standing on the road and asking for lifts, but the little money that I had saved from my grant would not allow me to travel any other way. Remarkably it had cost me only £4 and ten shillings to get this far, which included the Channel crossing and my accommodation for a week, but now I had come to the Iron Curtain and the only way through was by train.

Our small train set out from the main station in Vienna passing through the last of the mountain scenery before we came to the barbed wire of the frontier. Two high fences separated a length of no-mans land that was probably mined, forming a very uninviting welcome to Hungary. The train came to a halt and they disconnected the engine, mounting a machine gun at either end, while armed guards stood along either side. First all our passports were taken then our baggage was searched, as though they were looking for specks of gold dust. It was while we were waiting that I noticed this agitated lady with her young son, who as soon as she realised I was English, began talking to me.

"Please can I stay with you as I am frightened?" She explained that she had escaped from the country during the 1956 Hungarian uprising and was returning for the first time in an amnesty that had been declared.

"Where have you come from and how have you managed since leaving your country?" I asked.

So she told me how she had got to England, later marrying an

Englishman, so changing her nationality, but even so was still terrified that the amnesty was just a ploy. She thought she might be arrested, the more we waited the more she became worried, then to my surprise she then asked.

"Will you pretend to be my husband if the immigration people start questioning me?"

Fortunately nothing more happened, another engine was put on the front of the train and we slowly chugged our way to Budapest. The lady's sister was there to meet her and she began to relax a little, but my problems were just beginning. Where was I to stay, there were no youth hostels and I couldn't afford a hotel? People from the train tried to help me, but accommodation was at a premium, when someone suggested I try the university hostel. When I got to the University I explained to the porter what I wanted but he refused to help, so I stopped some students who found one amongst them who spoke English and he tried to bargain with the porter to let me in. The porter though was quite unrelenting so they smuggled me in round a back entrance and let me sleep on the floor of their room.

Budapest was a city of contrasts, from the fine buildings of Buda and the wonderful views out over the two parts of the city, to the scruffy unkempt state of the buildings in Pest, still with bullet holes from the 40/45 war, added to by those of the 1956 uprising. Everything seemed to be about 20 years behind the rest of Europe, with old rickety trams like those that used to rattle along Balham High Street, to the way people were dressed. My student friends seemed to think they had a good life with learning Russian and going to Moscow as their main ambition, but when I told them about the West and the freedom to pursue studies wherever you wanted, they were surprised. They pressed me with questions and I gave them straight answers with the result that there was soon a fierce discussion in Hungarian that I could not understand. There were the hard-liners and the more progressives amongst my little group of friends, and I soon realised that a doctrinal row was taking place.

I was certainly grateful for a place to stay but the Hungarian State University of Technics was not a place I would like to have lived in for the duration of my studies. The building looked very grand on the outside, with huge staircases and a massiveness to impress, but the students slept on bunk beds, six to a room with no shower and only cold water to wash in. There were no meals organized and they all contributed to getting something to eat, so I managed to sneak out unnoticed and buy some food to add to their larder. It was quite a cat and mouse game slipping out past the porters and then back again and I quietly mused if I could become a spy!

I only had a transit visa which I managed to stretch out to almost two days in Budapest and then at some ungodly hour in the morning made my way to the station to catch the train to Beograd. Of course the train was late so I was then confused as to which train I should take, but eventually found myself on the right one. When the immigration people boarded the train they said nothing about my extra day's stay, but kept my passport until the border, just in case I should have any strange ideas of not wanting to leave. It was a dull journey through uninteresting scenery of endless fields of wheat until we reached the Yugoslav border. The authorities boarded the train at Subotica, where in contrast to the walls of barbed wire at the Austrian border there was just a strip of sandy soil with well spaced sentry posts. However I had crossed the Iron Curtain and was now in the more forward looking Yugoslavia.

Belgrade was a modern city with skyscrapers, new roads and bridges, in an attractive situation. What was more was there was an information place at the station that told me about a cheap hostel where I was able to have a hot shower and wash some clothes. It was quite a contrast, they were both communist countries, but Russia dominated Hungary, while Yugoslavia had fought for its freedom and adopted its own form of communism. Everything seemed to depend upon Tito, who's benevolent despotism held the divergent peoples together, with the result that when he died it tore itself apart in the violent events of the early1990's. But in the 1960's it was a nice country to visit, with fine museums, an active church and a people who had everything to live for.

If Hungary had been a shock then Bulgaria was an even bigger one. I continued on my train journey on what had once seen the Orient Express, but was now replaced by a series of overcrowded, scruffy carriages; this however was compensated for by a change in scenery. We had entered the mountains and were soon in a spectacular gorge that barely seemed to have room for the river, let alone a railway line. This widened out as we crossed the border, the walls of the gorge now made of a gentle pink stone. As we neared the end of our journey a few rough houses came into view, one or two chimneys and a low platform that you had to climb down to. I had arrived in Sofia.

Just this little piece of Bulgaria told me more than I wanted to know about the country. The children were filthy, often clothes-less, playing amongst a scattering of state-built houses. Even more surprising was to see amongst these utilitarian constructions one or two huts built of mud, looking like they should have been in Africa. These were joined by a road that had pavements and street lamps, but the surface was just grass. This probably didn't matter though, for while Budapest might not have had much traffic and Belgrade even less, Sofia had none at all. I could walk down the middle of a main road and have no fear of being knocked down by anything.

There was nowhere to stay except in the station, but as in Budapest some students came to my rescue and invited me to share their room with them. In this I was amazed that despite the poverty they were so generous in helping me. I had grown a beard and one of the guards on the train checking my passport photograph against what he saw before him jokingly called me Fidel Castro, so perhaps I was beginning to look the part as well.

Sofia had neither the history nor the interest of Budapest or Belgrade, with museums and art galleries that glorified a communist regime rather than anything interesting that might have happened in the past. Only when I took a tram out to Boyana and climbed up to the monastery on Vitoshka did I find anything really worth visiting. The mountain was a great spring for the city, feeding its numerous drinking fountains with icy cold water that was so refreshing in the hot weather. It was a land of plenty with so many peaches I could make a meal out of them, so why was there so much poverty?

The people were noticeably unhappy with their lot. I would occasionally see a woman in tears, but why was she crying? They were poor, very poor and what little money they had was spent on the Toto Loto; living in hope that they would be lucky some day. I couldn't help notice how the hospital had been built next to the station so that all the fumes and noise from the trains permeated the place. It looked like some monstrosity from the days before antisepsis had come on the scene, with patients in pyjamas wandering round the black grass, stared at by passers-by, as though that was their reason for being there. It was a depressing site and I was glad when the old steam engine, looking like something out of *Anna Karenina,* came into the station and slowly pulled out the train I was now on.

There was perhaps just as much poverty as we entered Turkey. Miserable fields of wheat, bony cattle and goats being herded by ragged children, then the shanty suburbs of Istanbul, but the place was alive with activity, everything was on the move, it was a different world. This was the transition, I was on the threshold of Asia, the first time I had ever been to this continent. It was a new experience but one that was to absorb me for the next few months and many more times in the future.

In the centre of Istanbul was the great mosque of Hagia Sophia, with its immense dome and circular design, once Constantine's great cathedral. By placing minarets at each corner it then became the model for the Blue Mosque and a succession of others. The Mosque is built on ancient foundations as the remains of Roman buildings can be seen jutting out from under it. Constantinople, as it was previously, was the last bastion of the Roman Empire until it fell to the Ottomans in 1453. It then became the capital of a vast empire, including the three European countries I had just come through. With the collapse of the Turkish Empire during World War I it was no longer central to the new Turkey and Kemal Atatürk (the founder of modern Turkey) moved the capital to Ankara. However its strategic position at the entrance to the Black Sea and as the gateway to Asia ensured that it would always be a city of considerable importance.

Istanbul is a crossroads of travel to Asia and several wanderers who had been to India were in town while I was there. For some India had been a big disappointment, the poverty and petty thieving had marred their stay, and the spiritual goal they had set out to find had eluded them. They were returning disillusioned, but perpetual wanderers. They would work somewhere for some money then go off again to seek what they were looking for in another part of the world. I could see this happening to me, especially as one of them had been a university student and abandoned his studies so he could complete his journey. It was still a long way to India and I would soon find myself having to make a similar decision. But doing medicine was more important to me and there was the added incentive to get back again and see Bridget, so I decided that I would just go as far as Tehran and then return by a different route. This would be something achieved, but be obtainable in the time available, rather than go on ever hopeful of getting to India, but fail to return in time for the next term.

Train travel had been successful through the communist countries and was incredibly cheap in Turkey, so I decided to continue by this means until the end of the railway line. I had however reached the end of the railway line in a way, for the route travelled by the Orient Express finished in Istanbul and I had to cross the Bosphorus to find the start of the Turkish railways. This was run by a different authority, which seemed to relish its inefficiencies, letting you have as little information as they possibly could let out. Eventually though I managed to secure a ticket for onward travel to Ankara.

As the train started off there seemed to be plenty of room in the third class, but I soon realised why, we were stopping at every station. I had caught the slow train, so not only were we scheduled to take twice as long, but we had a string of goods wagons attached as well. As it was a single line we had to wait for any train coming in the opposite direction and for expresses to overtake us, meaning that some of our stops were for an hour, two hours and even three in one case, so that by the following morning we were still only slowly making our way forwards. As we passed along the attractive coast it began to rain, but up in the mountains there had been such a deluge that in places the line was washed away. This had been hurriedly repaired and as the train gingerly passed over, the lines were pushed into the mud and disappeared from view. So perhaps this was an advantage of being on a slow train. This also gave me ample chance to absorb the breathtaking scenery of deep gorges, thundering rivers and huge mountains towering up on both sides. By nightfall we had climbed onto the plateau and 24 hours after leaving, finally reached our destination.

In the early morning sun there was a golden landscape, the horizontal rays of light picked out the rocky mounds and ridges amongst the fields of wheat, while dotted here and there were Angora sheep, tended by children in colourful dress. The train was a microcosm of Turkish life and although by now crowded, it brought out a friendliness in my carriage companions, intrigued to have a foreigner in their midst. I was offered food, while conversation was in a charade of gesticulations and the odd word of English. Early on in the journey though there was an incident I would rather never happened.

I got up from my seat to go outside so put my map there in an attempt to keep my place. This did not seem to be a Turkish custom however and very soon there was a moustachioed man sitting in my place, who took a fancy to my map. When he moved off he took it with him so when I came back I asked where it was and a guard was called. He went off in the direction the man had been seen to go and soon this poor character was dragged back by the scruff of his neck with an occasional wallop to the back of the head. I pleaded with the guard not to hurt him, but this made no difference and after a few more blows, which I can't help feeling the guard enjoyed an excuse to execute, the poor chap was sent on his way.

I was surprised at the variety of types there were on the train, ranging from fair skinned people with bluer eyes than mine, to the swarthy person with heavy features that one associates with a Turk, while others were so dark you wondered what part of Africa they might have come from. I was more impressed with them than other Moslems I had come across in the way they cultivated their land and looked after each other, including their beggars. But women were a rarity, you really had to look hard to find them, working in the fields or peeping out from behind curtains. They wore baggy trousers with little red waistcoats and wound a white scarf around their neck and head, so as to hide their face.

Ankara, the capital of modern Turkey, was the resistance base of Kemal Atatürk (1881-1938), who is enshrined in a huge mausoleum in its midst. He had been the hero of World War I, especially in resisting the attempt by the Allies to take the Dardanells. He was not only a good general in war but also a far-sighted statesman, who realised that the ailing Turkey had to be completely re-organized. His mausoleum was interesting as an illustration of what similar structures in Greece or Rome might have looked like, but differing from them in containing all his cars, gifts of state, the suits he wore, his hair brush and even his comb. I didn't see his toothbrush though so I wonder whether he cleaned his teeth, or just took them out every night and put them in a glass!

His legacy was a fine one, but his city, although founded in ancient times, lacked the character of Istanbul. Inside its museum were the remains of perhaps one of the greatest civilizations of the ancient world, the Hittites. I was becoming interested in all the places I was visiting and wanted to explore more, but since the objective of my journey was to travel much further east than this, I had to save this for a later occasion.

The train left in the early morning and although it was crowded I was soon invited into one of the compartments and squeezed in between two well-padded backsides. Also ensnared was a German girl, called Anna-Marie, whose pluck I admired. No more than 19 and hardly 5 feet in height she was travelling alone in a Moslem country. She planned to visit most of the Middle East and to be away for five months. Women are a rarity on trains and never travel alone so I felt some responsibility for her, but she was more than capable of looking after herself. Our journey developed into a sort of a party as they insisted on sharing their food with us, later on fuelled by the consumption of Racki. This surprised me as alcohol is normally forbidden in Islamic countries, yet here it was consumed in greater quantities than it should have been, with the result that soon all of my companions were in an inebriated state.

The scenery was impressive with snow-covered mountains, fast flowing rivers and spectacular gorges. Where the railway line could not be squeezed along the side of a river then tunnels were cut through the mountain to find another valley, which we then followed to its conclusion. This was Erzurum, in the east of Turkey and as far as the train would take us.

We now had to find our way to the border with Iran. There was a bus but it seemed uncertain as to when it would leave and exactly where it was going to, so Anna-Marie and I decided to hitchhike. As we made our way towards the main road we were joined by two more Englishmen, so we made a worthwhile stop for the first lorry that came along. Hitchhiking is not understood in the same way as Europe, but rather a lorry agrees to take you for a small fee. This one said it was going to the border town, but after taking our money dropped us off short. However we were helped by a soldier guarding some lonely installation that would have been of no interest to any enemy. He stopped a small bus that somehow managed to pack us all in and take us to Dogubayazit, our destination.

When we had travelled in the back of the open lorry we were at the mercy of the sun, but this was compensated for by grand scenery. Like the train we started in a gorge and then climbed steadily, almost to the snow line (and this was mid-summer) until we reached the saddle between two hills, from where we descended ever downwards to the hot plain. The sun beat down on us all the time and it was difficult to keep up anything like a sufficient fluid intake. I had certainly become very dehydrated by the time we reached the border town and never really made up the deficit.

We knew the next part of the journey would be the most difficult as there was no regular traffic towards the border and we were at the mercy of unscrupulous lorry drivers. The journey yesterday, for all its discomfort had cost us more than the train journey across the entire country so we said we would do better today. We bargained with several lorries, but they would not take us for what we considered a reasonable price, so we waited. It was dry and hot, the only compensation being the fine view of Mount Ararat, a volcanic peak that rose 5122m (almost 17 thousand feet) from the plain, attracting snow on its upper reaches. This was the place that Noah's Ark was meant to have settled after the great flood. Certainly the hot dry plain looked as if it had once been the bottom of the sea, while the mountain was a refreshing sight as we waited for a reasonable lift.

We eventually found a ride in the back of a crowded lorry, with people spitting on us and flies and dust everywhere. We seemed to spend as much time off the road as on it, but eventually got to the frontier. Anna-Marie had not been prepared to wait with us, going with some Turks who said they were travelling as far as Tehran. Later we passed her lorry broken down near the frontier, so we could only think what might have happened to her? We just hoped she had been with some reasonable people.

Iran was still under the control of the Shah, so westerners were welcomed and there was no difficulty in crossing the border. In fact one of the first things I noticed was that the women were not all covered up like sacks of potatoes, but wore clothes that allowed them to show something of their femininity. Even the scenery seemed pleasanter, but before we could completely settle to Iran we had one last hurdle with an unscrupulous bus driver.

We needed to get as far as Maku, the first town across the border for which we had to bargain once again. Eventually we were across and were rewarded with the impressive site of Maku, half built into the side of a cliff face, as it clung to its precarious position on the side of a ravine. From here we could buy a bus ticket for a standard price as far as Tabriz, there was a pleasant hotel, so we settled back into what we hoped would be an easier time in Iran.

Sadly the hotel was a misconception as we were kept awake by fleas, bed bugs and every other conceivable biting thing. Also, whether from all the sun or something I had eaten, I developed severe diarrhoea that woke me at frequent intervals during the night. The bus journey then became agony as I held myself in until the next stop, where I would rush off to find some horrible fly infested hole in the ground that served as a public toilet. The road was atrocious, hurling us into the air as the bus hit one pothole after another, all adding agony to my delicate insides. On learning of my predicament some friendly Iranians suggested I eat yoghurt, so I downed a couple of bowls, as this was one food that seemed to be available everywhere. It had a remarkably quick effect, a cure I have often used on subsequent occasions.

Eventually we joined the tarmac road to Tabriz, and within a short while had reached the big city. By now I was better, but one of my travelling companions and a Frenchman we had met on the way were in the same state that I had been in the night before. They spent the next day resting while I went to explore the limited sites of Tabriz, the Blue Mosque and the Ark, a huge brick fortress, but more interesting was the bazaar. It was like entering a different world; large cool hallways full of Persian carpets, but everywhere I went I seemed to be more the attraction, especially when I went into any of the mosques. I had never come across any restriction to entering mosques before, as long as I removed my shoes, so I assumed that there would not be any problem in Iran. I had no difficulties in Tabriz, but later on I was to make a mistake that almost cost me my life.

I had presumed that Stewart and Keith, the two Englishmen I had met in Erzurum, were travelling companions, but Keith who had not succumbed to the dreaded diarrhoea, suddenly declared that he was going to go his own way down to the Caspian Sea, while we planned to take the train to Tehran. I felt rather let down as I was left looking after the other two, preparing oral rehydration fluid and trying to feed them yoghurt. So when we came to take the train that evening, with me hardly recovered from my ordeal and my two companions decidedly worse for wear, I hoped that we would have a reasonable journey. However Stewart went from bad to worse and the guard insisted on finding a doctor. He prescribed the same treatment I had been giving him, but this encouraged the guard to open a spare compartment, allowing us to have a decent sleep. Iranian trains were quite a different experience to those in Turkey.

By the morning we were passing a rocky ridge of mountains on one side and desert on the other, with villages of little mud houses amongst palm groves. My patients were better after the good sleep, courtesy of our friendly guard. On arrival our motley group made its way into Tehran to find somewhere to stay, but while we were looking round a huge dust storm plunged the city into darkness and panic. Bits of trees, loose roofing, sign posts and the odd lamp-post went flying around as we found some temporary shelter. This was followed by a few drops of rain, which soon turned into a force even stronger than what the dust storm had just been, so soon the streets were rivers. We couldn't move until the flood had abated somewhat.

By a strange coincidence Keith, after his wanderings along the coast of the Caspian Sea met up with us again in Tehran. Now all of us, recovered from our episode of dysentery, could consider our future travels. For me Tehran was a place of decision. I had come this far and confirmed my earlier thoughts to turn back, but I wanted to go a different way. I had reached my destination sooner than I expected and now had plenty of time, so decided to take a more southerly route, through Iraq and Jordan. Iraq had recently had differences with Britain and nationalised the oil industry so I was uncertain as to whether I would be able to travel there, however when I went to the Iraqi Embassy they gave me a visa without any difficulty. Surprisingly it was more of a problem to get a visa for Jordan as they required a letter from the British Embassy, certifying that I was not of the Jewish faith or Hebrew tongue. So with these valuable documents my way home was determined.

Tehran was the capital of modern Iran, but had few remains of the old Persia I wanted to see. If I could not get to India then at least I wanted to see as much of this country as possible, the greatest empire in the world at that time. Old Persia lay south in Shiraz and Esfahan (Isfahan), and this was the way I now planned to go. I could take a train as far as the holy city of Qom, but after that it was back to the road again.

I was surprised at how harsh the desert was in this central part of the country, completely arid with no sign of vegetation except at the few oases and river crossings; rivers that flowed into the desert and then disappeared completely. Where there was water there were curious domed mud houses, the only design that could ameliorate somewhat the unrelenting sun. A group of them was enclosed by a wall that made it into a small fortress, protection against both the elements and intruders. The only animals that could survive these conditions were goats, and these decimated anything that tried to grow.

Qom was dominated by its huge domed mosque, the front covered with immense sheets of silver, which gave a blinding light when the sun fell on it. It was as though it was signalling to everybody that this was where the light of the world came from, this was the most holy place. It was famous because Fatima, the sister of Mohamed, was buried there. It became a place of pilgrimage and the burial place of kings and saints.

I asked various people if I could go inside and as there seemed no restriction I wandered in. I went further, into the madrasah, where there was some excitement and various people came up to me and asked me what was my religion. There seemed not to be any problem and a priestly looking gentlemen took it upon himself to show me round. However we hadn't gone much further when a policeman came into the mosque and escorted me back to the police station, an interpreter was found and my passport studied with the thoroughness of a forensic scientist. They went through it time and time again as though something mysterious would suddenly leap out of the pages. Finally they explained to me that I was not allowed in the part of the mosque where I had been and was lucky that I had not taken any photographs. Apparently, not long ago an American had wandered in there and started taking pictures, infuriating the worshipers, who had killed him. I was lucky that the same fate had not befallen me!

In 1979, Qom was to be where the army surrendered to Islamic revolutionary militia and the Ayatollah Khomeini made his headquarters. This was the end of a liberal Iran when women were once more banished into the background and the country retrenched in upon itself.

I left Qom thankful that nothing more serious had happened and walked onto the road south, hoping for a lift. I had to wait for some time, but eventually a huge lorry pulled into the side and the driver said he was going to Esfahan. I was glad to be on the move again but although we climbed onto higher ground, everywhere was still a stony desert with the occasional ridge of red rock. In the distance were circular dust storms that I watched for some time. They would race across the ground as though they were some mysterious vehicle, then suddenly disappear, only to start up again somewhere else.

Esfahan is situated in a depression surrounded by low hills so that streams flowing down from the higher ground provided the city with an abundance of water. It was the major city of the Seljuk dynasty in the 11th – 12th century, but reached its heights in 1588-1629 with the

21

reign of Shah Abbas I. He designed the city around a vast central square (Meydan-I Shah) in which parades and great festivals were held. In the centre of the square is a pavilion where the King used to watch these great occasions, consisting of many small rooms rather like a series of matchboxes around a central gallery. On one side is the greatest of all Persian mosques, the Masjed-e Jame. It consists of the main mosque fronted with superb blue tiling, but perfection is found in the smaller Lotfollah or ladies mosque, with its lovely proportions. It was built in 1088 with a double dome so is completely soundproof. Despite the traffic outside none of this can be heard within, yet a whisper uttered inside is easily heard wherever you stand. Once inside the mosque it is the place "Where you feel closer to God than anywhere else", as its epitaph describes it.

Surrounding the square are shops making all sorts of goods and I was persuaded to buy a bowl made of seven metals that gave a particular note when it was struck. I was charged to always pass it on within my family and never give it away as a gift, but the man never explained why this was so. As instructed it is still with me so I have never found out what misfortune may come to me should it be given away.

Across the river from Esfahan is Jolfa, home to a community of Armenian Christians. Over the ages they had constructed a cathedral and twelve churches and were as industrious a community as in their heyday. Mount Ararat is their spiritual home, believing that they were the first people to occupy the world after the deluge.

By a strange coincidence I met up again with Anna-Marie who I had last seen in Turkey while we waited for a lorry to cross the border. There was no need for us to have been concerned about her, she had been well treated by her Turkish hosts and was now hand-in-hand with an Iranian boy.

As I was leaving Esfahan I was given a lift by some students who said that I should have stayed in the University and gave me an address of where I could lodge in Shiraz. They were only going as far as Shaheraz, but after that a mammoth lorry stopped and wedged me amongst the gears in the middle of the cab, between the driver and his mate. I seemed to be good at picking the slowest of lorries, this one going about as fast as a bicycle, only reaching top gear on a downward slope. I didn't realise when they stopped for me though that I would be with them for almost two days, for what was to be one of the most enjoyable parts of my journey.

As expected they kept on stopping for chai (tea), which although hot was the only water that you could trust to be safe to drink. The desert was endless and unforgiving and the temperature at some astronomical level I could only guess at. At one of our stops there was a commotion and all the drivers gathered round a man who had been picked up in the desert and brought in by one of the drivers. He was delirious and pale as a sheet and I thought was suffering from heat stroke. I tried to give him sips of water, but this only made him vomit, after which he felt better. My diagnosis might have been wrong but my treatment worked, I was certainly in need of proper medical training.

All along the route there were forts and outpost of soldiers as we passed ominous cliffs from which you could imagine gowned figures in their flowing robes galloping down to terrorise any passing vehicle. My imagination wandered, but I was later told that just three months ago this had been the case, and this was why the roads were now so heavily guarded.

We now entered Fars, the southern part of Iran and the heart of ancient Persia. Everything was different, the people more colourful and vigorous, working hard to produce crops from the sandy soil and change the scenery to one of trees and some greenness. We had climbed a steep pass, which took an interminable time in our slow lorry, then hurtling down the other side we entered a little valley that could have been in Spain or southern France. Here was a stopping place like so many others we had been to. Round the walls was a raised area covered with Persian carpets on which we lounged during the daytime to drink our chai, but now became our beds for the night.

After competing with the glaring lights, midges and the comings and goings of numerous vehicles during the night, we made an early start to get to Shiraz. My kindly lorry mates were going to make sure that nothing was missed though and they made a stop at Persepolis to visit the famous capital built by Darius the Great in 528 BC. Alexander in his war of revenge against the many attempts the Persians made to overcome Greece, burnt it to the ground. However its wonderful staircases with marching figures set into the side-walls, and the many columns with their decorative finales, still attest to the sumptuous nature of the royal palace.

The way to Shiraz was over a pass that excelled any that we had come over so far, passing between two walls of rock we could see the city stretched out on the plain below. Situated in the Zagros Mountains at 1,486 metres, we entered through the fine Khoram gate.

Shiraz was founded by the Seleucids in 312 BC, the Hellenistic culture that developed in the lands conquered by Alexander the Great. It continued to be an important city during the Parthian and Sasanid dynasties, which made Zoroastrianism the state religion and founded the famous fire temple. It became a Moslem centre after the Mongol invasion and that of Tamerlane (Timur), when so endowed was it with religious buildings that it rivalled Baghdad in importance. It was the birthplace of Sa'di and Hafez, two famous Persian poets, and the centre of Arabian medicine.

Zoroastrianism preceded Judaism and was the first religion to proclaim a monotheistic God, *Ahura Mazda*. He had two sons, one of which brought all goodness to the world, the other all evil. Zoroaster taught that the world would be consumed by a total conflagration and that only the followers of the good would rise from the dead to take part in the new creation. Darius the Great believed in the doctrine and made it the state religion of Persia where it was a driving force for many generations. Judaism, Christianity and Islam took many of its ideas in the formation of their religions. The main difference is the nature of the holy, which in Zoroastrianism is fire, hence their temples, of which there is a good example in Shiraz.

Entering a courtyard the temple has a central sanctuary with an eternal flame. As both the earth, which was created by *Spenta Mainyu* (the good son), and fire are holy a believer when they die can neither be buried nor cremated, so bodies are left to decompose, fed upon by holy crows. The Moslems first tolerated, then persecuted the Zoroastrians, many of them fleeing to the Bombay area of India where they are known as Parsees.

I followed up the address I had been given by the students from Esfahan and received the most wonderful hospitality. The Director of the Medical School knew my Professor of Anatomy and was delighted to have one of her students visit. Although somewhat scruffy and unannounced I was billeted in the interns' mess and given free board and lodge. The Medical School was a wonderful place, fully self-contained and next to the hospital. In the grounds was a swimming pool and Persian garden; I was in paradise. Everyone was so friendly and I wondered whether it would be Iran rather than India from which I would not return to England. I was tempted to stay here for some time and even continue my medical studies in such pleasant surroundings.

I was in the heart of old Persia, if I had not made it to India this was truly a marvellous substitute, the centre of an empire older than many in the sub-continent. It was like walking through history and soon I was totally absorbed in the old city as I wandered the bazaar. This was filled with Persian carpets like some oriental treasure house. They hung from the walls, lay several feet deep on the floors and made an excellent seat from which to admire the many colours and designs. There was something special about them, they were not just carpets, but each an individual work of art. Woven by a family group every carpet included certain motives that distinguished the area from which they came, but the final composition was their own. As they weaved their way, new batches of wool were dyed, so there were subtle changes in colour, which only added to the interest. I became quite absorbed as I wandered through this gallery of colour and opulence.

As a student with virtually no money left there was no way in which I could buy one and carry it back, but how could I leave this wonderful country without taking something so special as this with me?

I looked at carpet after carpet, wishing I could somehow buy several and ship them back, then came back to reality and realised this could not be done. I had come to my senses and was just leaving the bazaar when a voice in good English invited me into his shop.

"This is an antique carpet," he explained.

It had a beautifully fine design and colours that I had not seen elsewhere.

"It was made by a nomadic tribe living far away in the mountains and is a rare piece." He continued. "There are none other like it in the bazaar."

It was small enough for me to carry, so I could not resist bargaining for it, hoping that in some way he would reduce it to a ridiculously cheap price.

"I am a student and have little money left." I told him, but having come down to half the asking price he would go no lower.

I could not take my eyes away from this gem of a carpet, I could tell that it was very special, but if I spent all my money on it I would have nothing to get me back home. I was there for an age, torn between the sensible thing to do and what I had set my heart on, and my heart won.

I had this treasure of a carpet that I rolled up and put in the bottom of my rucksack and would always be a reminder of my journey, but how was I going to get back to England? I had very little money left and no way of earning any, what was I going to live on and how could I pay for any transport?

Shiraz was not far from the sea and I thought that if I could get to Bushehr, there might be a ship, but the agents in Shiraz told me this was not possible. I was tired from my travels and did not relish the thought of travelling all that way back overland, but in my financial state there was no alternative. The heat, deprivation and a poor diet had caught up with me in Shiraz and I spent much of my time when not exploring the city sleeping. I blessed my hosts for feeding me and giving me such a pleasant place to stay, but after some days I felt strong enough to move on again. I had enjoyed my bit of paradise, but I had to face reality and that was to get back home again.

I went to say good-bye to the Dean of the Medical School who was a little surprised to see me leaving so soon. It was as though he had read my thoughts and was expecting me to come and ask him if I could continue my medical studies there. He asked me how I was going to travel and I told him about the way I had used to come this far. However he would not let me go on the road unprepared and rang up a reliable transport company that agreed to take me.

A large Chevrolet truck pulled up and squeezed me between the driver and assistant, setting off westwards on the main road to the coast. It was swelteringly hot and the road surface was nothing to talk about, but we passed through the most spectacular scenery. Climbing out of the valley of Shiraz we gained another two to three thousand feet over the height that we had been, then lost it all too quickly in the space of about ten miles. The road had been cut into the rock face as we zigzagged down, for what seemed to a never-ending bottom. Looking out there were parallel mountain ranges cutting across flat valleys, arranged like a series of gigantic teeth in a huge prehistoric mouth.

It was an eternity before we got to the bottom as the lorry with its heavy load burnt its break linings to ensure we did not go down at too fast a speed. It was a dangerous road so in one way I was glad when we got there, but knew that the heat would be even greater at the bottom and there would be no views over the mountains. The flat plain shimmered with the heat, and date palms replaced the cypress that had been so abundant in the mountains.

We picked up two passengers, one I called "Happy" because of the perpetual sullen expression he carried on his face, and the other I named "The chicken man." He shuffled his poor birds from place to place, which no sooner had made themselves comfortable in one corner than he had to disturb them again and move them to another.

We turned off the main road to Bushehr, heading north-west along a road that was not marked on my map. It travelled through mountainous valleys with vertical walls of rocks on either side. As soon as we had got through one range of mountains there was another, to twist and turn our way through until finally coming out onto the flatness of the desert. Now dark we more rapidly completed our journey to Abadan. This was oil country with the orange glow from the refinery and huge pipes stretching across the desert in all directions.

We had spent much of the night travelling so it was a short sleep amongst the boxes and stalls before the early morning market. With the first light the noise was so phenomenal there was no more chance to sleep so I began the long walk through Abadan to the river and the border with Iraq. After clearing the Iranian immigration, Happy, the Chicken-man and I were at the mercy of an unscrupulous ferry boat that took the last bit of my money and dropped us on the other bank at the village of Seeba. The formalities to enter Iraq were quite rudimentary and despite me having no more money, this did not seem to concern them, they stamped my passport and I was in.

Somebody had offered me a lift to Basra, but I waited there practically the whole day before it materialised. Still it was a pleasant place to wait, the junction of a small canal with the main Shatt-al-Arab waterway, sheltered by date palms. It reminded me of Juba and the White Nile where I had waited several days for a lift into Uganda. To keep my interest I saw my first lungfishes that seemed just as happy on the muddy banks as in the water. Using their fins like legs they wriggled into holes in the mud and were even able to climb trees.

Along the waterway there were many canals and rivulets, crossed by a multitude of bridges and filled with gaily-coloured boats. The people lived in mud houses and there was an abundance of date palms, such a contrast to the scene of oilrigs and barren desert on the other side. Basra had little to offer and although built on one of the oldest centres of civilization had nothing of antiquity to interest me.

My grandfather hadn't known that I would be travelling this way or else he would have told me before that one of his brothers had been killed here in World War I. There had been much fighting and Britain's interest in this part of the world had started from this time. A monarchy was established in 1921 under British protection and independence achieved in 1932, but because of German interest during World War II, Britain re-occupied Iraq in 1941. A revolution ended the monarchy in 1958 and a series of military coups made British presence unwelcome. British and American money had developed the oil industry, but its subsequent nationalisation began the strife with the country that has continued to this day.

Basra has one of the oldest mosques in the Islamic world (first constructed in AD 665) and it was the call to prayer from its minaret that woke me the following day. With such an early start I thought I stood a good chance of getting a lift to Baghdad, but there was a confusion of roads and I soon found myself heading in the wrong direction. The real road was in fact just a line of concrete posts marking the way across the desert. As I tried to sort myself out I was given a short lift by some friendly types who wanted to help me. They knew the owner of a bus company who agreed to take me on his bus, an incredibly uncomfortable experience as we bounced our way across the unmade surface. Every so often there was a police check and they spent an inordinate amount of time on my passport. At one place I had to have a long discussion with a senior officer over the phone before we were allowed to proceed, but the bus took these delays with more patience than I did.

We passed the great ziggurat of Ur, then came close to the refreshing site of the Euphrates that had been the lifeblood of this ancient city, before it changed its course. It was hard to imagine that this was where the first civilizations had started, there seemed many more suitable places, but the heat, the river water and sand, which can be surprisingly fertile when irrigated, must have been the conditions required to begin the agricultural revolution.

The bus bumped on through the night until we reached Hilla where I was obliged to camp near the police station. This served me well next day though as they stopped a bus and told them to drop me off at Babylon. With such stories of wealth and power in my imagination I expected to find the remains of a great city, but nothing could be more disappointing. Mounds of bricks and broken down walls could have belonged to buildings at any period of history. A glazed tile gateway and a temple had been reconstructed with such precision that they looked like modern buildings. Here and on the road to Baghdad, through the heart of ancient Mesopotamia, there was little to indicate how great this area had been in ancient times.

Baghdad was a large modern city with all the problems of traffic congestion and pollution that are found in any other city. It was not an Istanbul or a Damascus, there was little of its past to indicate the city of *Tales from the Thousand and One Nights*. Only the treasures in the Iraq museum and the Abbasid palace, brought back something of the glory of this great city, while the pleasantest views were of the Tigris, as it flowed through the centre. It was made even more depressing by the site of tanks at street corners and troops everywhere, Saddam Hussein had recently come to power and he was going to keep it this way.

Baghdad was meant to be an important staging post for me as I was expecting letters from home. Each day I would go to the British Consulate, but still there no letters. In those days of waiting I tried hard to find some interesting places in the city, but even the bazaar, vividly described by explorers and travellers, was a shadow of its former self. The more I waited the more money I used up until I reached a situation where I had to find a way of subsidising my finances. On the grapevine I had heard that Baghdad gave the best price for a pint of blood, but hesitated as there were risks in doing this. Fortunately it was before the time of HIV and hepatitis B was not the problem that it later became so I went to the hospital and assuring myself that the equipment was sterile, earned £5 of blood money. It had been a big quandary; I was quite opposed to a system that paid for blood, yet I had absolutely no money left and no way of earning it. I just hoped that my blood was put to good use and perhaps saved someone's life.

It was on these daily trips to the Consulate that I met a couple similarly waiting for mail, who were planning to drive by Land Rover across the desert to Jordan. This was going to be a difficult part of the journey and I had been trying for some time to find a way across. They offered to take me, so I readily accepted.

We set off in the late afternoon, soon reaching the Euphrates with its blue waters and green palm groves, and stopped for a while at Lake Habbamya to swim. It was blissfully cool and a pleasant place to stop, but travelling by night was really the only way to miss the intense heat of the day, so we set off again that evening to cross the unforgiving desert. Peggy was not feeling well so when we reached the unlikely town of Rutba, we decided to stop for the night. Even by early morning the temperature had climbed to almost 50°C but when we set off we were soon at the border and had to wait for the Customs officer to wake up, so did not get far that day. The road then joined the oil pipeline with the few stopping places having the unlikely names of H-3, H-4 etc. We made it as far as H-4 where Peggy was violently sick, so we stopped there for yet another night. Some sleep and a respite from the heat had the desired effect and next days progress was good, reaching some semblance of pleasant scenery at Mafraq. Here I left my generous hosts, and what had become good friends, in those last few days of travel together.

I was now back in civilization and soon a bus appeared offering to take me on to Amman, the capital of Jordan. This was a welcome contrast to Baghdad, with a mountainous position and remains of its ancient past. Most notable were all the Roman remains especially the amphitheatre, which was still used for live performances. Jordan seemed proud of its Roman past and had not obliterated the ruins with mosques and skyscrapers, as had other Islamic countries. Many of the city buildings were faced with an attractive pale stone that gave it a distinctive appearance.

In 1963 it was before the six-day war and much of the Holy Land was in Jordan, so I decided to see it while I was in this part of the world. Everywhere I went, if only a few miles along the road there was a story that I could remember from the Bible. This was a time of life when religion was important to me and although I had come to doubt some of the more improbable claims of Christianity, to actually visit the places of those childhood stories was a moving experience.

After the long desert crossing, distances seemed so short and within no time I was in Jerusalem. The entire old city was in Jordan and the armistice line separated it from New Jerusalem, which was in Israel. This was wired and mined and there was only one crossing place, a one way passage, for once you had gone into Israel no Arab country would allow you back. The stalls that lined the streets and the donkeys that wandered through the narrow passages added a sense of antiquity to the old city, which died when Israel took it over. I was glad that I had been able to absorb the atmosphere of how it must have been for thousands of years.

It was a humbling experience to walk along the Via Dolorosa, to the Holy Sepulchre where the tomb of Jesus is reputed to be and visit the many other churches, all indicating some important event. Most prominent is the Dome of the Rock where Abraham intended to sacrifice his son. It was the central feature of the Jewish Temple of Solomon and is now roofed over by one of the holiest mosques of Islam. The Garden of Gethsemane where Christ was betrayed and the Mount of Olives from where the best view of the old city can be had are all just outside the walls of the city.

There was much to discover in this the most ancient of cities, and even as I tried to search for the hospital of St John of Jerusalem, I traced it back to the place where I was staying. I wondered why on entering the front door the steps had descended some way to the ground floor, but I then realised this was the original street level when it was first constructed.

Two of the people staying there with me suggested that one night we find the tunnel of Citron, so armed with torches we left by St Stephen's Gate and after some difficulty found the entrance. Stepping into the cold water which came up to our thighs we followed an amazing tunnel through the rock, round bends and past crevices for over half an hour. Although a tortuous way the level never changed and after about 500 metres of passage we came out in the Pool of Siloam. The tunnel was an escape route constructed over 3000 years ago.

There was so much in the Promised Land that I decided to retrace my steps to Jericho and the Dead Sea, back along the road to Amman. Jericho is perhaps the oldest city in the world with five different cities, each on top of the other. I could see why it had been such a favoured site as there were date palms, citrus fruit, grapes, papayas, Bougainvillaea and many other exotic plants. Overlooking Jericho is the so-called Mount of Temptation, where Christ was tempted by the devil for 40 days and 40 nights. In reality it is the steep edge of the Rift Valley escarpment, but as in all the holy sites it is looked after by a monastery. The old monks looked like they were the last of a series of genial souls who had guarded this place for centuries.

The lowest part of the Rift Valley and the lowest place on earth is the Dead Sea, 1,350 feet below sea level. It looks like ordinary seawater until you get into it and find yourself floating high on the surface, but when you tried to swim you got nowhere.

Returning to Jerusalem there was unexpected activity that night. Normally all was quiet and the border tense, but every so often there is suspicion of attack and one side decides to fire on the other. Shooting continued for much of the night for no real purpose except to provide something for the tensed up soldiers to do. I hoped nobody would take a shot at me when I came to cross through no-mans land in a few days time.

Despite the West Bank still being part of Jordan, it was full of refugees from the original division of Palestine. A generous, friendly people they were ever in hope that their land would be given back to them again, when what was to take place was for the West Bank to become part of Israel as well. I came across many refugees on the road to Hebron, where Abraham and Sarah, Isaac and Rebecca, Jacob and Leah, as well as Joseph and his family are buried. A holy place for Jews, Christians and Moslems, a mosque now covers the site. The mosque is like a fortress and the city itself a series of covered ways and passages, some so dark that even in the bright sun lights are needed to find your way. I had come through Bethlehem on the way here and stopped on the return, to spend the night, invited to stay with a family I had met on my way to Hebron. They were amazingly kind and generous when in reality they blamed the British for the creation of Israel and for continuing to support it.

The road between Bethlehem and Jerusalem was particularly attractive so I set out to walk back. I had gone some distance when I was stopped by gun waving soldiers. They came out of the bushes, rushing towards me in a menacing way.

They must have been shouting "Halt" or something to that effect in Arabic, so I stood still and let them come up to me. They seemed much more nervous than me, despite the guns they were carrying. They were about to arrest me when a UN vehicle came along and rescued me from my predicament. My beard was now fully grown and the UN soldiers explained that I looked like an Israeli, perhaps I was a spy? We were very close to the border and they presumed I had crossed over illegally.

Even taking a walk along the road was fraught with problems in this part of the world!

I was sad to leave the eternal city, as my good friend in Morocco many years before had called it. There are few places that give you that intensity of feeling, and this was how I felt about it. It was upsetting to see it divided with barbed wire and all the accompaniments of war as I made my way through the Mandelbaum Gate. I felt so exposed walking across no-mans land with guns pointing at me from both sides, but the actual formalities were very simple. My name was ticked off a list on one side and then again on the other and I was across. It was a one way journey though, I could never go back that way to continue my journey through Syria and the other Arab countries as I had originally intended, I had entered a cul-de-sac and must leave either by plane or by ship.

New Jerusalem was as much a contrast to the old city as it could be. There was no atmosphere of the past with in its place a modern city, much like any other. There were not even the children that always used to follow me around like a cloud of gnats, hurling stones as though this was the way to greet strangers. In Jordan foreigners were easily distinguishable, as in my case by wearing shorts and sporting a large bushy beard, but in Israel beards seemed to be everywhere and the dress code even more relaxed than what I was wearing.

Around the city there were still parts of the bible story, Mount Zion where King David was buried, and the tomb of Herod, who was only important because it was during his reign that Christ was crucified. There was the crypt of the Virgin, the place where the Last Supper was celebrated, and Ein Kerem where John the Baptist was born. But I did not stay long and made my way to the coast to the twin cities of Jaffa and Tel Aviv, which was the capital of the country at that time. I missed the mountains with their vineyards, cypress trees and pine forests, to be replaced by the flat irrigated fields of the plain. This was the coast and an unattractive one at that, where much of the population lived and all that was old and interesting had been swamped by modernity.

Jaffa had been an ancient Canaanite port, later occupied by King David. It was to Jaffa that much of the timbers and valuables arrived on their way to build the temple of Solomon in Jerusalem. Alexander the Great came to Jaffa, as did the Romans, and the Crusaders. Captured by Saladin in 1187 it was recaptured by King Richard I on one of his crusades. After World War I Tel Aviv rose in importance next to the old city, to totally absorb it in an industrial conurbation.

My main reason for coming to the coast was to reach the northern port of Haifa, because it was from here that a Greek ship called regularly on its way to Greece and Italy and on which I hoped to make my way home. Haifa also was a much nicer place than Tel Aviv with pleasant Mount Carmel just behind, where the Carmelites had built their mother church and more recently the Baha'i had their principal sanctuary. Set in beautiful gardens, looking down to the blue Mediterranean, the domed building signified a unity of faiths, an idea that seemed to be the answer to this troubled part of the world.

If I was going to be leaving the country then I wanted to see as much of it as I could before I left so set off inland to Nazareth. Although this was where Jesus spent much of his youth there is little known about this time and few churches to mark places of significance. Nazareth was a quaint and pleasant town, but because of its Christian population seemed out of place in this Jewish dominated country. Christians seemed to fit in better in Jordan and even better still when the whole area was Palestine. I was told on many occasions that when Israel was created most Christians found it better to move across the border than stay in a Jewish country.

I continued on to the Sea of Galilee, with a breathtaking view of Tiberias. Around the other side of the lake was Tabgha, where the miracle of the bread and fishes took place, and Capernaum where there was the synagogue built by the Roman centurion, to thank Jesus for healing his servant. While walking I met up with a group of Brits who were spending their summer working in a Kibbutz, and they invited me to stay with them for the night. It was an interesting experience to see what it was like, not realising that I would soon be working in one myself.

North of the lake is attractive hilly country around Safad, then returning to the coast again I came to Acre. The old town was lovely with its Crusader castle, narrow bazaars, covered squares and picturesque mosques. The crypt of St John d'Acre was one of the loveliest I had seen. From here it was a short journey back to Haifa and the ship that was due to leave the following day.

I had been in a quandary because my money was all but exhausted so I had sent for some more, but until it came I could not buy a ticket for the ship. Every day I would go to the bank where a friendly lady would search through all the mail to see if it had arrived. The day the ship was due to leave I went early in the morning but the money had still not come. There were very few places left on the ship so I went back later and pleaded with them to look again. I was in luck, the money had just arrived, so triumphantly I rushed down to the ship again. However when I got there the last remaining places had been taken. My disappointment was complete, I was longing to get home and just to stay in one place, especially expensive Israel, would use up all my money. So I bought a ticket for next week's ship and wondered how I could live for a week without spending any money?

Perhaps it was fortuitous that this had happened, because the night I had spent in a Kibbutz had so impressed me, it became something I wanted to do. It was a social experiment I was interested to experience and Israel was the only place I could do this. It would complete my visit to the country if I could only find one that would take me in. Not only would this be a unique experience but the only thing I could do without spending any money. Normally you have to offer to work for at least two weeks before a Kibbutz would take you, so I was not particularly hopeful when I went to the nearest one at Ramat Yohana. I explained that I would be taking the boat the following week and the many difficulties I had been through and to my delight they kindly took me in.

The Kibbutz principle is perhaps the purest form of communism, with everybody working for the common good and sharing everything. You go in with nothing and come out with nothing, there is no accumulation of wealth and all eating and living conditions are communal. When I arrived I was in time for supper and the way it was organised demonstrated how the system works. The dining room was set out with tables arranged in a circle and the first people who come in sat at the first table and when this was full they then started on the next table and so on round until each table was filled. Nobody sat next to special friends or bagged a table for the people they wanted to sit next to them. As a consequence you might meet some interesting character that just happened to be sitting next to you and soon I got to know most people in the Kibbutz. Several had come from Europe with horrendous stories of their wartime experiences, many of whom had survived concentration camps. They passionately believed in Israel and felt that this was the way to create the ideal country.

Most of the work was agricultural with the production of fruit and vegetables a major money earner for the community. As a consequence there was an abundance of nutritious food, which I was much in need of. I had lost quite a lot of weight and knew I had a long voyage ahead, so perhaps it was better that this delay had happened. I was looking forward to learning more about the Kibbutz system, but was worried that I might not be strong enough to contribute equally in the work.

The first job they gave me was with the chickens, counting them, weighing them, sorting them into different cages, cleaning out chicken houses, I saw enough chickens to last me a life time. Fortunately after a few days I went out in the fields and picked tomatoes. Agriculture was on a very large scale so you could be gainfully occupied doing the same job for several days.

I stayed in a wooden cabin, shared with several others. We started work at 4 or 5 in the morning so by breakfast we were in need of a hearty meal, but in compensation we finished by early afternoon. There was a swimming pool where I spent some of my time off or else walked round the grounds, which were quite extensive. The boundary was well marked and at one place there was a memorial to 21 of the occupants who had died defending their Kibbutz in the early days of Israel's creation. All children were looked after communally, living in large huts, separate for boys and girls and only visiting their parents at weekends. Military training was part of their education so Israel always has a ready supply of people to take up arms to defend the country.

It had been a good experience and a lesson in communal living that was a valuable one for me. I had got on well and was rather reluctant to leave as they also seemed to be to loose me, for instead of just wishing me good-bye they gave me a huge bag of fruit that would see me through my voyage.

As I waited for the boat I met several people I had come across in my travels then to my surprise Pat and Maureen, from my medical school. By now we were 7 in number and with my sack of fruit, I could contribute to the common food pile, so we had a little co-operative of our own. We claimed as much space on the deck as we could for our party and then settled in to an enjoyable voyage. Slowly the ship moved out of Haifa, its many lights bidding us farewell. I was going home at last, but on leaving there is always sadness and this time it was going away from Ramat Yohana, an impressive and brave ideal that had worked.

Our first sight on waking the next morning was the coastline of Cyprus, quite close and even at 0530, brightly lit by the sun. By the time everyone else had stirred themselves from their place on the deck we were in Famagusta, the main port on the eastern side of the island, situated on a flat spit of land. A massive wall protected the city from the sea, and behind it lay innumerable churches. This was the old city which when we went ashore we found to be quite empty, everyone living in the new town built to one side.

It was a brief stop and we then followed the uninteresting coast of rock and scrub with little habitation, round to Limasol. In contrast this looked more interesting with its backdrop of mountains, but there was no time for us to go ashore and after a brief stop we were on our way again. The coastline here was more spectacular, becoming ever more precipitous as the mountains dropped almost sheer into the sea. Gradually Cyprus disappeared into the distance and many thoughts came to me, especially of Bridget who I seemed to be able to see in the waves.

The same pattern was repeated the next day, waking up to the sight of land but this time it was the most southerly part of Turkey, Lycia, before we came to Rodhos, in Greece, where we anchored in the bay. One could imagine where the colossus had once stood and later on how the city was fortified with its massive walls, which still surrounded the city. Inside are the quaint streets, while on a promontory stand three windmills that have long since stopped turning. All was quiet and peaceful, the sea a beautiful deep blue and with a few fish playing round the stern of the ship.

From Rhodes we threaded our way past the Turkish mainland and around numerous Greek islands, their rugged shores preserving their independence. White villages dotted the mountainsides and on their slopes were groves of olive trees. They seemed never ending, with land on either side of the ship, until finally the sun set and they were lost until the next morning. This was our last evening together, for the next morning we would go our different ways. Our consortium had added more wanderers, sharing all our food and bringing enjoyment and friendship that I for one had gone without for a long time.

It was still dark when the first rays of the dawn, in a deep red colour, showed themselves between the sinister dark cliffs of the Greek mainland. Before us lay the lights of Piraeus with its conglomeration of ships and quays. As we moored in the cool morning air there was already much activity on the wharf, trundling cranes and busy shipping agents. It took us some time to disembark as we made our way to the subway and on to Omonia in the centre of Athens. Here we felt the full realization of the break-up of our happy party, our group had made the voyage enjoyable, but now I was on my own again. The day in Athens was a brief glimpse of the Acropolis, the Roman Agora, and many other wonderful places, a land that I had to come back to and explore in detail some time in the future.

I returned to the ship, to a certain extent regretting that I had booked my passage all the way through to Venice as I could have travelled back with some of the group. But as it was, it was a spectacular trip, and in later years I was to make the journey overland in much greater detail than I would have done on this occasion. After all my objective now was to get back as soon as I could and this was the quickest way of getting to northern Italy.

Disappearing Piraeus and behind it Athens, crowned by the Acropolis, was a fine sight as we made our way westward. After following along the coast we entered what appeared to be a fjord with land on all sides. On we steamed across the calm sea, with lovely wooded mountains on either side, until our way in front appeared to be completely blocked off by a ridge of land. It was not until we came closer that a way through became apparent, the narrow entrance of the Corinth Canal. It seemed much too narrow to allow us to pass through, the sides climbing vertically and appearing to almost touch above us. Slowly we made our way, the end always visible, but seemingly never coming to it. Our voices echoed back to us from the smoothly hewn sides, while high above could be made out tiny figures looking at us from the bridge above. Then as suddenly as we had entered, we were out the other side, into what seemed like a large lake, with tree-covered hills and pleasant dwellings. Gradually the sides of the lake became steeper as they closed in on us again and we passed through the narrow exit near Patras, as the sun set.

I was up early to catch sight of the last piece of Greece off our starboard side, after which it was open sea. The sun was much cooler here than the intense heat of Iraq and I relished the sight of all the water around us as I thought about the desert crossing. On our port side, more like a mirage than reality was a thin white streak and a few blue cliffs of what must have been Brindisi. But we passed this by and sailed up the middle of the Adriatic, not stopping anywhere until we reached Venice the following morning.

Venice must be one of the most beautiful of cities to approach by sea, as its fine buildings appear to rise out of the very surface of the water. Entering the lagoon the ship sailed up the main waterway and moored right in front of the city, as so many ships must have done in the past. We disembarked almost onto St Mark's Square, one of the most famous ports in the whole of the Mediterranean. But this was the end of my voyage, from now on I was back on the mainland of Europe and my way lay across the Alps to the next piece of sea, the English Channel.

It was to be as rapid a journey as I could make it, as I was now virtually broke and my stomach was telling me, as it had on those few days from Athens, that it was hungry. It was late summer though and Europe was awash with free fruit, grapes in Italy and apples in France, so I was able to live on very little. The first night I reached Brescia and by the following day I had not only crossed the Alps, but the whole of Switzerland as well. In France I was lucky to be given a lift by some Italians to the other side of Paris, as I had bad memories of trying to hitchhike in France. Then another night camping out in a field and eventually to Calais where my last remaining money was just enough to buy the ferry ticket. Strangely, also on the ferry was an Israeli who had been on the Greek ship with me. I was to return temporarily to my time in Israel and the long journey I made to get there, a reappraisal of my whole trip before it was to come to an end. I was back in England and to the flat in Balham, it was hard to believe that I had been all that way and back again.

There was something even more important though and this was to go to Devon and see Bridget. During those long waits by the roadside and while I was on the ship I had more than enough time to think about our relationship. For a moment I wondered whether it had been too long or had been the wrong thing to do as there was a little shyness between us. We had not seen each other for three months, perhaps she had found the separation too long and had different thoughts from when I left her? I had not received all her letters, maybe she had said something important in one of the ones I did not receive? She had been with a group of volunteers from many different countries, like-minded souls, had she met somebody else? It was surprising how many thoughts went through my head in this brief period.

No, it was just a temporary uncertainty brought on by the long time we were apart. Our hesitancy did not last long, it was like a repeat of our first meeting, but this time with the knowledge of the outcome. It was wonderful to get to know each other again.

The separation had been a testing time for both of us, but as I was soon to realise, more difficult for Bridget than it had been for me. She had not had the fulfilment of travel and had returned before me. We had both missed each, from now on we would always do everything together.

CHAPTER TWO

The Making of a Doctor

The second year of medical training was the make or break year when the medical school took the opportunity to weed out those that were not likely to succeed. For Bridget and I we were torn in two, wanting to be with each other for most of the time, but knowing that we had to study if we were going to get through the exams as individuals. The final exam of our pre-clinical period loomed ever closer and the intensity of our studies increased, until the final day arrived.

The exams were harder than expected, Anatomy went well and to my surprise I also got through Biochemistry, but it was Physiology where I came unstuck. In my haste in reading the exam paper I answered a question on the Hypophysis (Pituitary) instead of the Hypothalamus (a part of the brain). I could see the whole of my life and the struggle that I had to get into Medical School come to nothing. It was Bridget though who felt it more strongly than me because if I was stood down this would have separated us. I would have dropped down to the year below, all our timings would have been different and if I failed a second time I would have been out. Similar feelings were felt by many of the staff who had watched our love affair unfold, recalling romantic memories of their lost youth. So I had a special viva with the external examiner, who was quite oblivious to the concerns that surrounded me.

The first question was as expected,

"Where is the Hypothalamus and what is it for?"

In fact I now knew so much about the Hypothalamus that I answered everything the examiner could throw at me. After that we ranged through a number of subjects that found answers from some deep down store of knowledge that even I didn't know I had. Suitably satisfied I was let through.

By now my mind was made up, I could see the way ahead for both of us and so I proposed to Bridget. We bought a ring at a Hatton Garden jewellers with a student reduction and announced our engagement.

The clinical years were so much more interesting, here was what we really wanted to do and from now on I never looked back. At last all that preparation could be applied to the real person and one had a place in improving the health of your patients. However we had to work more in earnest, even than before, and any holidays were spent in studying. In fact things were beginning to get so tight we wondered how we would be able to get sufficient time off to get married. We had known each other almost two years before we got engaged and neither of us felt that a long engagement was a good idea. Elective Periods had just been introduced, this therefore seemed to be the time, get married and then go abroad for our honeymoon and continue straight into our elective in the same country.

It was one of those glorious days in March, when the sun shone from a clear blue sky onto the garden of the Marine Hotel in Instow, that we were married. We then left straight away for Morocco where arrangements had been made for us to work in a hospital. However we had not been long into our honeymoon when we had a close shave with disaster. We had crossed the Atlas Mountains to the desert on the other side, but the melting snows had filled the rivers and the normally dry streambeds were now rushing torrents. There had been several of these floods that we had successfully negotiated and we thought we were through all the difficulties until we got to a place where the road finished in a fast flowing river. We stopped and stared at the flood, hardly able to believe our misfortune. A lorry attempted to cross, got stuck and had to be dragged back again, so what hope was there for our tiny little Fiat 500? We studied the map, there was no way round, so anticipating that these kind of rivers can fall as quickly as they rise, we found a place to camp and spent the night waiting in anticipation.

At first light we went down to the river and tried to convince ourselves that the level had gone down. Vehicles were still waiting to cross and there was an ever-present band of helpers willing to push you through. We decided we could wait no longer, there was a strong chap on our side who convinced us we could make it with his help, so with Bridget driving we set off, the two of us pushing.

Bridget was doing an excellent job, with her foot full down on the accelerator she managed to keep water out of the submerged exhaust. All went well until the last bit where the ford was deepest and the current the strongest. The car suddenly shot forward and I lost my grip. It was floating and threatened to be carried downstream, with Bridget inside it. But quick as a flash our helper threw himself on the car, the tyres gripped and the car quickly reached the other side.

We wondered how we ever made it as we bucketed out the water. I don't think Bridget quite realised how serious the situation was as everything happened so quickly. I had almost lost my precious wife before we had started life together. We gave the lad all the loose money we had and made as much distance away from that fearful river as we could.

Somehow, we should have anticipated that when we got to the hospital in Marrakech no one would know about us. The Embassy in London had made all the arrangements and probably informed the Ministry of Health, but this was as far as information had travelled. There were a few phone calls and we were told to go to the main hospital for the city, situated in the old town. Here the Medical Superintendent assumed that two interns had been posted to him so he put us on the medical rota with the other doctors. As we had some medical training he considered us as good as qualified, giving us charge of any cases with virtually no supervision.

We were put on call for 24 hour periods or else for a whole week-end stretch, dealing with everything, whether it was surgical, medical, obstetric or any thing else. The most demanding was Casualty, or "Urgence" as it was called, which was kept busy day and night with many serious cases referred from outlying dispensaries, apart from any accidents that were brought in directly. As students we always had someone to ask, but here we had seriously ill patients on our hands, their fate entirely up to us. We realised the limits of our knowledge and experience, which was only aggravated by our lack of fluency in the language. If these problems were not enough there was also the system of French medical practice, which was quite different from what we were used to. We felt that not only was the situation impossible but decidedly dangerous and went to the Médecine-Chef to ask for his help. He was a product of retreated French colonialism, whose only concern was that he had someone doing the job and was not sympathetic to our predicament. The ethics of the situation did not worry him. We felt trapped, we were obliged to do our elective period, but were refused help, so reluctantly did the best we could, feeling that if we left, many of the patients would probably have gone without any treatment at all.

It was a rough neighbourhood and one of our first cases was the chap who came into Casualty, with as the nurse on duty described it, "An axe in his head".

We went to look, thinking of the cartoon sketch of someone walking around with a chopper in his head, which was almost exactly what it was. The axe had been removed, but there was a deep gash and when we x-rayed it there was a depressed fracture, with large fragments of bone pushed into the brain. Our medical training taught us that it should be operated on immediately, but when we called the surgeon on duty, he reprimanded us for disturbing his sleep, telling us to suture the wound and he would deal with it in the morning!

There were also two Swiss students, who at least had the advantage of language, and possibly the way medicine was practised. As it was Easter all the existing interns decided to take a holiday, so for one whole week the principal hospital of Marrakech, with its 500 beds, was run by four medical students.

Then even the Swiss students left as they had come to the end of their electives so for the three days of Easter we were the only ones on duty. We were called every minute of Saturday and never went to bed that night, Sunday we got about 4 hours sleep and Monday was the same. As well as pneumonias, which seemed to be two-a-penny, there were numerous fractures, a suspected case of smallpox, a status-asthmaticus, a very severe jaundice, two overdoses (one arriving dead), several dysenteries, two heart failures and four comas, apart from a mass of minor complaints. Two of the comas were due to cerebral haemorrhage, one old lady having been in a coma for four days before the relatives brought her in, and then expected us to cure her. The third was a child with an overwhelming gut infection that we could do something for, while the last we diagnosed as a ruptured cerebral aneurysm, for whom probably nothing could be done, but because he was European, was rushed to the hospital in Casablanca.

Our saddest case was a middle-aged woman who came in with heart failure, but she did not respond to treatment and we suspected an underlying condition with which we needed help. So we took some blood for the lab to test and in the meantime rang every doctor we knew of in town, but none would come in. The lab could only test blood urea and glucose in an emergency and then it took 6 hours, anything else having to wait until normal working hours, when the results would probably take a week. When we got the results, we treated as they indicated we should, but the patient continued to go downhill and eventually died. A few minutes after her death the lab rang us again and said they had made a mistake, instead of a high blood glucose level she had in fact a low one! We were appalled that such a basic mistake could be made and infuriated that no doctor could make an effort to come in and give us some support. We had spent hours fighting for this woman's life and with help and experience we knew we could have saved her.

Such was our first experience of medicine in a developing country, but a method of practice that we hoped we would never have to work in again. We learnt a lot in a very short time and especially that we needed to be experienced in as many fields as possible before we went abroad again.

There were many unique conditions that we would never see in hospital in England, such as typhoid, which was endemic in Morocco and meningitis which was often the diagnosis when a child came in with fever. More common than we would have expected were scorpion stings, four coming in one evening. These could be fatal, either from the poison itself or the treatment administered by a local healer. Little children were given the most potent brews for even minor complaints, often damaging their kidneys, adding to the already high incidence of renal disease in the country.

We had practical experience in reducing fractures and dislocations as exceptionally we could always get anaesthetic help. Instead of having doctors as anaesthetists some of the experienced nurses had been trained in anaesthetics and did a very good job. They would always come when called and had a sense of responsibility quite different from the doctors.

We had not yet done any obstetrics in our medical course, so some of the things we saw were a rough introduction to this subject. The midwifery department was large and on the whole very good, but they would receive some appalling cases. Women in the mountain villages would remain in labour for days before they started to worry about obtaining any help, so after a further few days of travel by donkey, it would be a week of obstructed labour before they finally reached hospital. By then the baby was dead and in an advanced state of decay. One young woman arrived with an infected uterus, which when removed revealed a fistula that had formed between the vagina and bladder. Another had a ruptured uterus and the baby could be bobbed up and down in the abdominal cavity. These were horrors that we would never see back at the Royal Free, but were sadly all too common problems in developing countries.

"Urgence" was only our second job as every morning we were obliged to assist with the operating lists. This was not our choice, but since they had no one else, we felt obliged to help. We found ourselves doing half the operation as we were the only assistants, so our surgical technique improved rather rapidly. The surgery left much to be desired and we learnt as much about how not to operate as the proper way to do things. In return for our surgical duties in the morning we could do as we wished in the afternoon, so went to medical outpatients or had a deserved break to see Marrakech.

The last week of our stay we revolted against always having to assist with the surgery and did a week of ward rounds with the medical consultant. At last we were doing what we should have done all the time, learning with guidance and a little teaching. The medical wards were some of the most efficient and well cared for wards we saw, not the barbaric medicine practised in the other departments. There were many interesting cases that we would not see in England, rheumatic carditis, TB and syphilis with all its manifestations.

Bridget was getting depressed with our job at the hospital as most of the translating and therefore the responsibility of what to do fell upon her. In comparison with her ability in the language my French was very poor, so latterly I made her stay in bed while I dealt with the night calls as best I could. Much of the diagnosis could be done from observation, as often there was no history, rather like veterinary practice. This is often the case in developing country medicine, where the patient goes to the hospital much as they would go to a witchdoctor. When you ask them

"What is wrong with you", instead of telling you that they have a pain or cough or some other complaint, their response is rather,

"This is why I have come to you, for you to tell me what is wrong with me."

Some doctors even take on the role of a witchdoctor and use it to effect, based on the diagnosis they have come to, but it would be many years before I was to learn how to do this properly. In other cases the patient would just say that they felt unwell and no amount of asking questions would enlist any useful information, so one had to come to a conclusion based on any physical signs and your knowledge of conditions in the country. I was beginning to learn how to do this, so it was good experience for when I was to later work in developing countries.

We knew that somehow we had to keep at the work, demanding though it was on our mental and medical abilities, as we did not have enough money to keep us going until our flight back. We lived in the interns' hostel where the one compensation was the quality of the food. The cook was a middle aged Moroccan woman who had for much of her life worked in a French household so had been taught the niceties of cooking as is characteristic of this nation. If there was something wrong with the meal then she would be yelled at by one of the interns with the oft repeated, "Mamma Hadooch", at which she would come out of the kitchen with a long-suffering look. She was a big woman though and if she felt the call was unjustified she would draw herself up to her full height and give the commanding voice an appropriate reply. Her forte was crème caramel, which she would serve as dessert at frequent intervals, as she knew there would never be any complaints. Never have I tasted such exquisite crème caramels since those of Mamma Hadooch.

We were also determined to see out our time as a positive contribution to our medical training, that our medical school had allowed us to take. We did not want to return with a defeatist attitude and possibly make it difficult for any subsequent medical students to try what we had done. As well as our obligation to our medical school we also felt a commitment to the poor people who came to the hospital, as limited though our knowledge and abilities were, we were at least doing something for them. Every day there would be an endless queue and if you did not get seen one day, then you had to wait there all night or else come back the next. So the more medical staff there were the greater the chance of the sick being seen before their condition became too bad to be treated.

So much had happened since I first came to this country as a wandering youth and stayed with a missionary doctor in Tangiers. He was still there, pleased to learn that I was on my way to becoming a doctor as well. We recounted our experiences in the hospital in Marrakech, which came as no surprise to him. He felt that the mission hospital was providing an alternative and better form of health care. Quite possibly this was a truth in Morocco, but later on I was to come across missionary practice that left much to be desired. I have always been convinced that the health of the nation is a government's responsibility and improving the service offered by the government of the country a preferable strategy than an alternative system with religious connotations.

It had been a tough introduction to the practice of medicine abroad and a strain on our early married life, but we had survived and returned to England with a mixture of relief and achievement. Bridget and I had worked well as a team in Morocco and had supported each other through difficult times. Now we were coming to the end of our course and the spectre of examinations was upon us once again, so with the same teamwork we had used during our elective we now helped each other towards the finals.

The first test was the exams of the Royal Colleges of Physicians and Surgeons, not essential, but a good practice run and a means of qualifying early so that you could get a job and start earning some money. A few months later we were back in the exam halls again, to start the long gruelling series of exams that constitute the final MBBS. We had been married ten months, and almost as a relief from the strain of exams, Bridget conceived her first child.

Medical exams are as gruelling as the course of training; an attempt to see if you have absorbed the vast amount of knowledge required to become a doctor. But as well as the days and days of written exams, there are the clinicals, in which you had to examine patients under exam conditions. Some of the patients appeared time and time again for the exams, occasionally offering a helping hand if you had forgotten to do something. The examiners countered this by thinking up new questions so it became a kind of game. It could have been fun, if it was not so important, and to our relief we both got through.

Bridget was now heavily pregnant and had gone through all the exams in this condition. When it came to the Obstetrics exam there were many ribald comments from our colleagues suggesting that she would pass this exam with flying colours. In fact she was a top-scoring student and would have been offered a job in our teaching hospital, but this was not what she wanted to do.

We had the qualifications, but no personality in this new guise, were we to be let loose on the world as qualified doctors, to help, advise and cure the sick? Even worse, if we should make a mistake, this could possibly result in the person's death, was this really where we were? So I started my first hospital job to try and remedy this situation, a time perhaps when you learn more about being a doctor than all your studying ever did.

I remembered when I was still a laboratory technician at the Maida Vale Hospital and on learning that I had been accepted by the Royal Free the friendly pathologist had said that getting qualified was not the difficult part, but the house jobs after. This all seemed so far away at the time and I had thought nothing could be harder than getting qualified, but now her words were to come back and remind me. The transition from qualified student to practising doctor is a huge stride; I was now having to face this at first hand.

I started with a surgical job and on the very first day I didn't get to bed until five the next morning, to be up again at 8 am. We were operating all night on emergencies and then there were the routine patients I had to get ready for the list the next day. The number of patients carried on at this phenomenal rate so I had to learn quickly how to cope. It was as though I had been trained as a doctor, but never told how to be one. The house jobs are where you really learn how to function, and for most junior doctors it is a pretty devastating experience.

Gradually though I learnt my trade, and after assisting at operations I was soon doing them myself. This to me was my reward, practical surgery could be a great skill, and the pleasure of performing a neat operation from which the patient recovered, with no ill effects, filled me with immense satisfaction. There was also the dramatic occasion when one of our surgical patients had a cardiac arrest while recovering on the ward. Fortunately I was close by and able to perform cardiac massage. It took some time, but the patient's heart started again, and a few days later she walked out of hospital, thinking she had just had a faint.

On my half days and weekends off I would go home to London, or Bridget would come down and stay with me in the doctors mess. It was no way to strengthen our marriage though and we decided that we must find married accommodation for my next house job, no matter where it was in the country. Eventually Bridget's time came, which could not have been more convenient as I was home for the weekend. She went in to hospital at 4am on Sunday morning having been in early labour for most of the night and at 2.15 that afternoon was delivered of a 6lb 11onz girl, who yelled even before all her head was out. Little Lucy filled a gap in our lives and brought us very close together. The strain of my first house job and the living apart had not been good for us, but the arrival of Lucy rejuvenated our marriage and gave it more purpose.

My job at Chelmsford was coming to an end so we scoured the journals looking for a medical job that had married accommodation, a rather difficult combination at that time. Eventually a vacancy came up at Sedgefield General Hospital, and on going for interview I was offered the post. It was a good job, busy at times, but here I had much more responsibility. I would see the Consultant about once a week, otherwise we managed the patients ourselves. Everyone was friendly, with a great sense of humour, the hospital being more like a village community. The great character was the ward sister who knew her medicine as well as any doctor and was a reliable source of information. She had seen a succession of doctors come through her ward and was always willing to give them a helping hand. There was one occasion where an overseas-trained doctor was trying to do a lumber puncture, but kept on failing. He had made several attempts and each time missed the spinal canal, so the sister who was becoming increasingly concerned about her patient, reached under the sterile drapes and grabbing his arm guided him straight in.

Our three bedroom, centrally heated flat in the hospital grounds was luxury for us and a great boon that we could live together again. Lucy was growing up fast and with so much superb countryside around us we took every opportunity on my days off to explore it. We had the York Moors not far away on one side, the Dales on the other, while on longer trips we could reach the Lake District. There was so much to see we went out in all weathers, even when it was snowing. One day we were returning through the Pennines when it began to snow very hard. We had no alternative but to go on and try and get over the pass as the snow was already thick behind us. Our little car did marvellously up the slippery hills, and we were across, but as we started downwards we suddenly came to an abrupt halt. In the dim light we had not seen a huge drift across the road and we were now stuck in the middle of it. We forced the doors open and pitifully began to dig with our bare hands, but soon realised the hopelessness of the task. Suddenly the awful realisation struck us of being stranded there in the freezing cold, with a young baby, probably all night. We had read stories of people being in similar situations and their bodies being found the next day, we wondered if this was going to happen to us? Instead of working in the tropics, we would perish in the snow.

We huddled together in the car and tried to make the most of what warm clothing we had, preparing ourselves for the ordeal. We had only been there half an hour though when gloomily through the driving snow we could see some lights making their way slowly towards us. They came closer and looked like they were going to crash into us when we realised it was a snowplough. They cheerfully dug us out and we were on our way again, thankful we had not had to go through the ordeal we had expected.

Bridget was now weaning Lucy and beginning to think about doing her house jobs. The hospital was delighted with the thought of having another doctor on their doorstep, without all the process of advertising and interviewing a string of less than satisfactory candidates, so readily offered her a job on the surgical wards. It was an ideal arrangement for Bridget to do her registration, but a considerable strain on both of us, as we had to arrange our on-call when the other had time off. This meant in fact that we were never off duty for when one of us was not working we were looking after Lucy, and she was a demanding child.

My medicine job came to an end and we had found a local girl to look after Lucy during the day times, so I decided to do another house job, while Bridget went straight on to take my place on the medical wards. I was now registered and Bridget would be in six months time, after which we could have set off for the tropics, as was our ambition. But the time in Morocco had shown me that I needed to be as prepared as possible for all the kind of cases that I might have to tackle and to have more practice with obstetrics was probably the most important. Fortunately they had just completed the first phase of the North Tees General Hospital, a new hospital that would eventually replace Sedgefield and several other small hospitals in the vicinity. The first phase was the maternity wing, so I applied for the job and became the first hospital doctor to ever work there. It was no distance from Sedgefield so I could spend my off-duty there, but had to sleep at the North Tees when on duty.

Not only was I starting in a new discipline, but in a new hospital, there was the whole process of creating a new enterprise. The unit was a mixture of consultant wards and what had been cottage hospitals, now all in the same building, which brought together many different personalities; midwives who had been their own bosses, alongside bright, recently qualified staff and the usual rivalries between GP's and Consultants. The stage was set for teething troubles.

I was now a senior house officer, which meant that I was expected to be able to do everything, only calling the consultant when there were major problems. This is a quick way to learn, but also a big responsibility as often the consultant could not come that quickly and things happen rapidly in obstetrics. Mostly I would call him when there seemed no alternative than to do an emergency Caesarean, but soon I was doing all of these as well. I had been assisting my consultant, gradually doing more of the operation myself, when one night he collapsed in the middle of the procedure, leaving me to do the rest. The mother and baby did well, so the next time I did the whole operation with the consultant assisting me, and after that did them all on my own. When I went abroad I was to find that this was the commonest emergency operation I would have to do, so I was thankful of my time at the North Tees, when I learnt how to do it properly.

We had decided to work through, not having any holiday, so when Bridget finished one house job she went straight on to the other. Registration is a necessity for you to practice, so while we had the facility of married accommodation and someone to look after Lucy, Bridget got this out of the way. We would both come in tired and exhausted after a busy day in our respective hospitals, so it was a relief when this period finally came to an end.

* * * * *

The old Royal Salop Infirmary was a grand palladium style building in the middle of Shrewsbury and the casualty department, where I did my last job before going abroad, was on the ground floor. All sorts of cases used to make their way to us as well as some very severe accidents from the major roads nearby. Early on there was a motorcyclist brought in who had been trying to do "the ton" (100 mph) along the motorway, but with his head down had crashed into the back of a lorry. I knew he would need emergency surgery so called the duty surgical consultant, but because he also had broken legs as well as his head and internal injuries the surgeon called the orthopaedic consultant. They both had a polite argument as to who should take him because they knew that he was likely to finish up as a long-term patient and block a bed for months. All the time I was left keeping the patient alive with blood transfusions and maintaining his airway, it was a problem to know what to do with such cases.

I learnt much from the job, especially how to deal with the many fractures that came in. For Bridget she was getting ready for the impending birth of our next child Sophy, born in the early hours of 26th of September 1969. The following month I finished at Shrewsbury as the time for our going overseas was now not so far away.

While still a medical student there had been a new scheme by the Ministry of Overseas Development to encourage doctors to work abroad. In return for a commitment to work in a developing country they agreed to pay for my course in Tropical Medicine and give me a small annual allowance. When the time came for them to decide where to send us we were given three choices, Sabah (Malaysia), Fiji and Solomon Islands. At our meeting I also asked them,

"What about Guyana?" as I had always wanted to go to South America, but not being able to speak Spanish or Portuguese, realised Guyana was the only country where I could work on that continent. The reply was not promising,

"The last person we sent there we never heard from again, so we are reluctant to send anybody else." I had images of this poor soul trekking through the jungle to his fate at the hands of some yet undiscovered tribe, but in reality the reason was probably far more mundane. Still it was not to be South America so we read all we could about each place and decided on the most interesting and remote.

CHAPTER THREE

Solomon Islands arrival

Guadalcanal was shrouded in cloud and steady rain fell as we disembarked from the plane. Where were the palm trees and the blue sea, everything just seemed to be a drab homogenous green? There was no time to dwell on these thoughts for long though as both the Physician and Surgeon Specialist were at the airport to welcome us. I could never imagine a Consultant coming to meet his junior arriving at London Airport, but we soon learnt that no new doctor had come to the islands for two years, so our arrival was something of an event.

I was to become the obstetrician as my six months post-graduate training made me more qualified than any of the others, but this was hardly sufficient for the task at hand. As well as doing the obstetrics, the anaesthetist had just left, so the surgeon asked me if I would "gas" for him. I had done anaesthetics as a student, totally disliked the subject, and learnt up just enough to get through the exams, but this was the kind of thing I expected would happen, so I reluctantly agreed. I was given a few brief instructions on how to work the EMO machine, which I had never seen before, and away I went on my first patient. Fortunately he went to sleep without much trouble, gave a few twitches to annoy the surgeon when he made the incision, and most importantly woke up afterwards, no worse for his experience. So I was now the anaesthetist and obstetrician for Central Hospital.

On New Year's eve we had been invited to a party and I was all dressed up in my black trousers and bow tie for the occasion, when the phone went. It was Tony Cross, the surgeon, he was very apologetic, but could I come and do the anaesthetic for an emergency case. I arrived at the hospital thinking that it was probably a New Year reveller that had become injured when I saw a girl of about 10 or 11 lying on the trolley. Tony pulled back the sheet to reveal the remains of one of her legs. The foot was not there and a ragged stump needed urgent attention to stem the bleeding. I then learnt that the girl was splashing around in a river mouth and a shark had come right into the shallow water and bitten off her foot.

There were two more shark-attacks on children at the same river mouth in succeeding months, but apart from these this was an uncommon event. Guadalcanal had a bad reputation in the past due possibly to the number of corpses in the sea during the heavy fighting that took place during World War II. The sharks had become conditioned to thinking that a human form floating on the surface was an easy meal and attacked people when they swam. However it was some years since that time and the sharks alive then must have all died off, so why had these attacks taken place?

One explanation was that sharks are irritated by sea lice, which cannot survive in fresh water, such as found at river mouths. So the shark may have purposely gone into the estuary to rid itself of these parasites. But an agitated shark seeing something splashing round in the water might have been spurred on to attack. Having done this once and got a meal from it the same shark probably came back to attack again. What was so surprising though was that this was just a few feet of water, not out in the open sea.

The only other shark attack I heard about was of a man spear fishing. The shark took the man right into its mouth, but he struggled, searching for the eye into which he thrust his fingers. This made the shark let go with the result that the man was left with a necklace of tooth mark scars to proudly show off to his friends. On the other islands shark attacks were unknown and people swam in the sea without any fear of them.

Compared to my obstetric job in England, work here was much better organized with the highly capable midwives doing the whole delivery from beginning to end and only calling for assistance when they anticipated trouble. They repaired their own cuts and there was none of the nonsense of being called up in the middle of the night to stitch up a recently delivered mother. This was the only way the heavy workload could be handled and I was full of admiration for the skill of the nurses.

When they called me I knew it was for something serious, the main problem being an obstructed labour. But as with anaesthetics where the simplicity of the EMO machine made this procedure so much easier and safer, so with obstetrics there was a far better method of dealing with these problems than the trauma inflicted by forceps. Spurned by my medical school and mentioned as some quirky tool invented in Scandinavia the vacuum extractor was the ideal instrument for complicated deliveries. The main advantage was that it assisted delivery as a normal process rather than applying force that could damage both the mother and baby. Where this failed then a Caesarean section had to be done. If this was the case then I did the operation and Tony became my anaesthetist.

However this was not what I had come to the islands for, to be tied to Central Hospital, always on call and just doing obstetrics and anaesthetics, I wanted to work in the district and manage the full gamut of medical problems. Eventually after four months in Honiara, the posting came through; we were to go to Gizo, the district headquarters of the Western Solomons.

We had planned to travel there by ship, taking all our crates of luggage with us so I had booked our passages on a government boat, but when I phoned up to confirm I was told that a more senior officer had decided to go by ship at the last moment so there was now no room for us all. This was my first rude shock of the colonial system that still reigned in this last outpost of empire.

As if in compensation the flight from Honiara to Gizo must be one of the most beautiful in the world as you pass over a succession of spectacular islands, the volcanic peaks of Gatukai, Rendova and Kolombangara and the sheer maze of islets and reef that fill the Marovo lagoon. Gizo, our destination, was set on a promontory at one end of one of the smaller islands, its fine harbour being the reason it had been chosen as the district headquarters in 1889, the first district post to be created. But this was the problem there was no place for an airport. Originally one had to land at the wartime airfield of Munda and travel to Gizo by ship, but recently a new airfield had been constructed. We had not been told where this was though and as the plane came down to land, as it seemed on the sea, it was not until the last minute that we realised the airfield was on another island. Looking more like an aircraft carrier Nusa Tupe had been flattened and the reef infilled to make just enough room for the Islander to land on.

From the airfield we boarded a small boat that came out to meet the plane, which after the calm of the flight seemed to rock around unnervingly on the swell. On our way over we made our first contact with two people we were to get to know very well in the months ahead, one was a Chinese lady who had travelled on the plane with us and the other the airline agent. A fat, uncouth man, his broad Australian accent being punctuated with a series of swear words, which were so much part of his speech that one might have thought that they were essential to understand the meaning. Every other word was "Bullshit," said so frequently that I even wondered whether it was the name for some new animal that I was not aware of. We didn't see him again for a few days and thought no more of it, but Bridget being a Catholic went to mass that Sunday and who should be standing in front of the altar but the abrasive airline agent! Not only was he the agent for the planes and much of the shipping, but was the priest as well. This unlikely character was responsible for both the spiritual and financial needs of much of Gizo! Despite his manner he had considerable abilities, especially as a linguist and it was said that when he went on a voyage he would get talking to someone from a place he was not familiar with and by the end of the voyage had learnt the rudiments of their language.

Gizo was about as different from Honiara as it could have been. We were part of a small European community, but of a much larger Solomon Island one, here there was no division. Everyone got on with each other and made a happy community. It was like living in a large village with its scandals and intrigues, gatherings and public events, we knew we would be happy here.

The hospital and the few government offices clung onto the small piece of level ground around the harbour. A road ran along the coast to Chinese stores and a boat yard at one end, and round the point to the remains of some houses and an ill-sited over-sea latrine, at the other. This stood on the reef as a proud monument to a bad experiment in sanitation. At the crossroads where a road led to the Catholic Church was a marble obelisk to a Captain Fergusson who died in 1875. This always seemed so out of place, especially as he was killed on Bougainville, the biggest of the geographical Solomon Islands and hundreds of miles to the north. I later learnt that he was a well-liked captain of his ship the *Ribble*, so his body was brought back to Gizo to be buried in a place where there were probably no buildings at that time. The chief of Shortlands, called Gorai had been so incensed by his murder that he took a raiding party to Bougainville to avenge the death. This was how justice was meted out in those days.

Gorai was one of a handful of supreme chiefs who had obtained power from recruiting. As a condition for providing men to work in the cane fields of Queensland he had been rewarded with guns. This upset the power balance and allowed him to dominate all the islands from Bougainville to Roviana, where another formidable chief, Ingava held sway. Gorai was perhaps the role model for the cannibal chief so popular with *Punch* magazine at that time because when a recruiter went to visit him they found him dressed in a top hat, belt, sword and white spats on his otherwise naked body.

Behind the town was a short steep hill where the houses were so well arranged that each had a magnificent view, one of the most beautiful I have seen anywhere in the world. There was a complete panorama, in the southwest the active volcano of Simbo, then following round to the east, successively you could see Rendova, Rarumana, WanaWana and in the distance, the peaks of New Georgia. In the foreground were the small islands off Gizo, with behind them Kolombangara, and on a clear day parts of Choiseul.

The harbour could accommodate large ships, but once they had negotiated the passage through the reef they were dwarfed by the five and a half thousand-foot peak of Kolombangara. An extinct volcano of almost perfect proportions, it rose straight out of the sea to make a backdrop to the scene. Our house was on the harbour side, so Kolombangara often seemed as though it was growing out of our garden. Shades of light at different times of the day changed its appearance, sometimes it was a foreboding giant, other times it was a delicate pink cloud, but always it was a wonderful site.

The road continued along the ridge to finally end on the highest point, with a commanding view in all directions. In this superb situation Ernie Palmer had built his house.

Ernie first came to the Solomons as a recruiter for the Russell Island plantations. He owned a boat called the *Ancient Gizo* in which he sailed round the islands looking for potential recruits. On his arrival at a village he would fire a blunderbuss to attract peoples' attention and anybody wanting to join would come on board, where he signed them up for two years and paid the parents £7. Soon after though he would recover most of his cash when he opened up his small shop, where the money he had given them was rapidly spent on knives, pots and foodstuffs. After Ernie gave up his life of wandering the islands he married Inge and settled in Guadalcanal, where he ran a plantation at Bara. They were dislodged by the war, so moved to Gizo, which from the name of his boat was perhaps where he always wanted to live.

The Palmers had a large family, some went to Australia while three boys remained in Gizo. To find a living they tried many schemes to make money and when we arrived the latest was pearl culture. Most of the operation took place near Rob Roy island, off the eastern end of Choiseul, where the conditions were ideal for the growth of Gold Lip. A small hemisphere of plastic was carefully inserted into the shell and in time this would become overlain with lustrous mother-of pearl. Although they were successful in this difficult process, the business was not commercially viable and was finally wound-up. Most of the work involved diving and chief amongst the divers was Ernie's oldest son Phil. He made a compressor from an old car engine with which all the tanks, including mine, were filled.

The Japanese occupied Gizo in October 1942 using its fine harbour for their war efforts. Once this was discovered by the Americans it was heavily bombed, destroying all the buildings, except for the Government store and the District Officer's house. Several ships were sunk making it a superb place for diving, which is its main attraction today.

The best coral reefs were on the little islands just off Gizo, Mbanga Island or Fisher-man's Island, and Kasolo or Kennedy Island. This took its adopted name from the late US President, who's PT 109 was rammed by the Japanese destroyer *Amagiri*, just off Gizo, and it was to this small island that John F Kennedy swam. His boat was cut in half, two of his crew killed and two badly injured so he and Ensign Thom managed to drag the wounded on bits of debris to the island. They spent two days and a night there before swimming to Olasana Island where they found some islanders who could take a message to Rendova to have them rescued. Kennedy scratched his message on a coconut and it is said that he kept this coconut on his desk in the White House when he was President.

Sadly much of the lower town of Gizo was devastated by a Tsunami in 2007, probably originating from an undersea volcano. The hospital was destroyed along with many houses and the Gilbertese village of Titiana swept away. It has been rebuilt but will never be quite as it was.

When we arrived there were just two doctors working in the hospital, a Fijian and myself, but after a few months the authority came through for Bridget to work part-time on a local salary. We were responsible for the small base hospital and a population of 35,000, scattered over many islands. There were mission hospitals and clinics, with only one other doctor amongst them, so the bulk of the work, especially visiting all the islands, came under the charge of Gizo.

There was a long association between Fiji and Solomon Islands, having been combined in the Western Pacific High Commission by the British during the colonial period. The higher training institutes, including a University and Medical School were in Fiji so the brighter Solomon Islanders were sent to Suva for their education. Prior to sufficient being trained, several of the services, particularly the medical, was manned by Fijian doctors, so there were quite a number of Fijians living in Solomon Islands, bringing aspects of their culture with them. With Fiji's independence in 1970 the Western Pacific High Commission ceased to exist, but memories of those days still remain and several Fijians stayed on in the Solomons.

There was also a more sinister connection with Fiji that lived on in the memory of the older islanders. In the days of the blackbirders, Solomon Islanders were taken to work the sugar cane fields not only of Queensland but also those in Fiji, so going to Fiji could have ominous connotations.

Measles, normally a disease of children, had devastated all ages when accidentally introduced to Fiji in 1874. Because it affected adults as well as children at the same time, there were no parents to look after the children during their period of illness, so there was a huge mortality. By 1919 there were only 83,000 Fijians remaining, from a former estimated population in excess of 200,000.

The Fijian population never properly recovered and is now outnumbered by the descendants of the indentured Indian labourers brought in to work the sugar cane fields, when black birding was outlawed. However all the land is owned by the Fijians in the traditional system of communal land ownership, controlled by chiefs through whom the British continued to rule. Yet the Indians, who regard themselves as Fijians and in their entrepreneurial skills, have become wealthy, are not able to share the country of which they belong. This has been a continued source of friction. Attempts have been made to form a governments representing all people, with some means of sharing out the land, but this has been strongly resisted by those of ethnic Fijian origin.

The doctor I worked with, Tim Bavandra, later returned to Fiji and became its Prime Minister for a brief period as he tried to tread the balance between the majority Indian population and the land owning Fijian. He was deposed by the nationalist movement that returned the islands to ethnic Fijian control, ushering in a dark period in its history of democracy.

When our GP in Shropshire learnt that we were going to the Solomons he asked us to look out for a student colleague of his. It soon transpired that the person we were looking for had run the medical services of Gizo for the past 5 years. He had been a misfit in his previous job and finishing up in Gizo felt he had found the perfect place to lead a life of leisure, letting the world drift by and the District to run down. He was known locally as Dr 4 X (after the well-known brand of Australian beer that was the main imported drink in the islands). When he went on tour, which was a rare event, the ship was filled with crates of beer, which were liberally dispensed as he went round the islands. When they reached a clinic the Medical Assistant was invited on board for a drink and was asked,

"Is everything alright?" Not wishing to dislodge the doctor from his happy state the reply was normally in the affirmative so few patients got seen.

As a result the hospital got a bad name and people, even from nearby islands, were going elsewhere for treatment, so the District Commissioner (DC) felt obliged to interfere and had Dr 4 X transferred. Our job therefore was to rebuild the medical service, especially in the more outlying parts of the district. (We never did tell our Shropshire GP what had happened to his old classmate).

My first visit was to the small island of Simbo, a magical place with active volcano and good looking people, it could easily have been the mythical Bali Hai of South Pacific fame. The medical assistant had not seen a doctor for over a year, despite it being only a short distance from Gizo, quietly getting on with looking after his people, delivering babies and maintaining the routine vaccinations. His clinic was two palm thatched buildings that had seen better days, while for sterilising his instruments and keeping his fridge going he depended on a supply of kerosene.

The island rose steeply from the sea to a sharp volcanic point, but the active crater was lower down, coloured bright yellow by sulphurous encrustations, issuing out steam and an acrid sulphurous smell. However in this seemingly inhospitable place lived one of the most remarkable of birds, the Megapode (*Megapodius freycinet*). The name means large egg, and for its size this is a very appropriate description. Looking rather like a large Moorhen, the Megapode's egg is twice the size of a chicken's. This is laid in the sandy soils surrounding the active craters so that the constant heat incubates it. For the people this is an ideal arrangement for if they find an egg they can take it to one of the hot springs and boil it, food and cooking facilities supplied completely free of charge, what more could one wish for on a paradise island!

The people are tall and thin with intensely black skin, and would make any fashion model envious of their proportions. A friendly and welcoming people they wanted to take me to one of their other surprises on this fascinating island. Paddling round the outside there was no indication of anything more special than a forest covered interior, when we came to a small river and started to paddle towards the centre of the island. The way was tortuous and I had no idea of what we were going to, when rounding the last bend we entered a brightly coloured lagoon. The water was a mixture of reds and yellows and there was a trace of the rotten egg smell that had been so pungent higher up on the peak, so I realised that this too must be volcanic. We paddled over to one side of the lake and indicating that I should put my hand into the water, I discovered it to be quite warm. Not only did these people have food and steam cooking, but also here was an abundant supply of hot water for washing.

A particularly unusual feature of this volcanic paradise was an under sea geyser. At periodic intervals the surface of the sea would become disturbed and then a column of steam would blow up through the surf, to some 20 feet into the air. This must be one of the few places in the world where such a phenomenon is found.

Simbo is actually a series of volcanic peaks which erupted one after another. At the north end is the rounded, worn down peak of the first eruption, complete with crater lake, reputedly inhabited by a crocodile. Straight above the clinic is the second peak rising to a prominent hill with patent vent. This is said to go down through the ground and come out on the edge of the sea, because one time somebody fell down it. After wandering for four days in the darkness the unfortunate man found his way out through this passage. However during the time he was underground the devils got to work on him so that by the time he came out, he was so disturbed he survived only long enough to tell his tale.

Devils and sudden death were not so long ago an ever-present feature of Simbo, for it had the less envious reputation of being a major base for headhunting. The raiders particularly favoured attacking Gizo and the surrounding islands, so by the time the British came looking for a district base they found Gizo uninhabited. An early European trader called Andrew Cheyne, visiting Simbo in 1840 noted that 93 heads were taken in just one raid.

The skull has a particular significance, not only as a symbol of manly prowess in raids on unfortunate neighbours, but also as the part of the body of a noble ancestor to be preserved. These skulls are kept in *tabuna* or skull houses and one near the village of Masuru has become a tourist attraction. As well as all the skulls are the remains of shell amulets and the mysterious *beku* idol with its long arms, extended ear lobes and deep eye sockets from which the mother-of-pearl eye inserts have long since fallen out. Perhaps it was because so many heads finished up in Simbo that the island became regarded as the home of the all the spirits (*ove*), by people from as far away as Gatukai, at the extreme eastern end of New Georgia.

There was so much of interest in this remarkably small island that I could have stayed there for weeks. If this was just the first island to be visited, what other fascinations were there in store on the others?

CHAPTER FOUR

Paradise and cannibals

The main island group of the Western Solomons is New Georgia, given its very English name by John Shortland when he made his visit there in 1788. It is made up of three volcanic islands, Vangunu, Gatukai and the main mass of New Georgia. These are linked together by the Marovo lagoon, said to be the longest in the world.

The story was the same here with the clinics, they had not been visited for a long time, there were a lot of problems and several trips were required until all was running smoothly again. On this occasion we travelled by government boat and as it was a week's tour the whole family came. The cabin was small and the cooking facilities simple so if the weather was bad the ship bobbed around like a cork with things thrown all over the cabin, but when it was fine it was blissful.

Strategically situated at the end of New Georgia is Sege, but to reach it one has to go right out to sea and round a long ribbon of land. Towards its end it breaks up into islets, but these are joined together by sand banks, so it is not until you reach Hele bar that you are able to enter the lagoon and welcome calm water. Sege saw considerable action during World War II as it was the base of Donald Kennedy, a former District Officer, before becoming a coast watcher. With his group of trained Solomon Islanders he carried out a lone war against the Japanese, attacking patrols and sinking barges, until the Americans took it over as a forward base for their assault on Munda.

Kennedy's right-hand-man was Bill Bennett who showed himself to be a ferocious fighter, leading many commando style raids. After the war Bill became the voice of the Solomon Islands Broadcasting Service (SIBS), which was a vital service, giving news and services messages. The radio was a very powerful means of communication as the phone was practically non-existent in rural areas. If I intended to make a medical tour I would send a service message and be quite sure that people would be expecting me when I visited.

The trip through the Marovo lagoon was like entering a wonderland. It is formed from a fringing reef some distance off the coast of New Georgia and Vangunu, at its southern end. This is a rugged volcanic island with immense jagged peaks. Black lava from a not so ancient eruption covered its sides and where it could grow, vivid green vegetation wound its way down ridges to the sea. Within the lagoon are so many islands you can't count them and where there aren't islands are stretches of partly submerged reefs, making a patchwork of differing shades of blue.

As Vangunu is rounded two pretty sister islands come into view, Telina and Lilihina. Further round is the mission station of Batuna with its wooden buildings and tall bell towers, looking like some Bavarian village on a palm strewn shore. From here one gets the first views of Gatukai, a beautifully shaped volcanic island with large areas of green grass on its slopes, giving the impression of fields left by some long lost civilization. In reality they are the attempts by the most rudimentary of vegetation to cover the lava flows of the last eruption. The one place of habitation is on the outside of the lagoon, most easily reached by going through Bili passage, a maze of cliffs and water, from which you eventually emerge onto the outside.

We received reports from all our clinics on the general state of health of the area and the Medical Assistant at Bili always used to make the same report, writing, "Bili passage is clean". This was mixed in with comments on patients, so when I first read it I understood that this poor patient called Bili(ly) had been given enemas until he was well and truly cleaned out!

A forbidding island set off to one side of Bili Passage is a taboo place to all except when a burial takes place. Here are stored the bones of generations, giving every impression that the island must be haunted. On the other side, waves crash against the rugged cliffs of Gatukai, the last of the chain of volcanic islands. At its southernmost point is the small village of Biti, unique in the islands because of its stone carving. There is an abundance of volcanic rock that is relatively easy to carve and so the people fashion all sorts of objects out of it, particularly stone bowls. Before the advent of the metal pot these were highly sought after, as the art of pottery had been forgotten and wooden bowls could not be put on the fire.

The northern part of the Marovo lagoon is controlled by the island of Vakambo, small in size but heavily populated. As one goes further north-west the outer island barrier closes in on the mainland and the bottom becomes so shallow that even a canoe has difficulty in getting through. One then comes to a part of the coastline where an intriguing experiment in social cohesion took place.

The Solomon Islands are one of the most intensely missionized areas in the world, with rival churches vying for converts, staking out their claim on an area of coastline. Generally the whole village or string of villages would be converted, probably because the chief accepted the faith. This part of the coast, from its base in Munda, came under the province of the Methodists. Local pastors and lay-preachers had been trained to work amongst the people, extending the range and influence of the church. One of these was Silas Eto who became a preacher in 1923, but so gifted was he with his preaching that he attracted a personal following. He became over-awed with the importance of the task and broke away to form his own church, called the Christian Fellowship Church (CFC). As its name implies it set-about creating an equal society where all worked for the common good, more like an Israeli Kibbutz or Communist Commune. Areas of jungle were cleared and houses built all of the same size and in regimented lines, so unlike the haphazard village plan found in the rest of the island. The central meeting place and where their own version of church service took place was a huge leaf and wood building, which must rank as one of the largest ever built in these materials.

Silas Eto had taken the title of "Holy Mamma" which in fact means Holy Father to his flock. A most engaging character he had a presence that immediately instilled respect and something of a religious aura. His handmaidens were the angels, who followed him wherever he went, and question is not asked as to what their real function was. To complete the effect the main village is called Paradise, with Bethlehem and suitable biblical names for the other villages.

I first went to Paradise on a clear open day, with as we left Gizo the sea as calm as a lake. The mass of Kolombangara was to the north and a long string of palm covered islands lay ahead. These were joined by coral reefs, made visible by breakers crashing on their outer side so that there appeared to be no way through. Ahead the shore of New Georgia was a homogenous green with no sign of habitation until we came to the entrance to a long inlet that could not be seen until we were almost upon it. It was a difficult channel to negotiate, there were huge heads of coral growing up from its otherwise deep waters, but once inside, it opened up into a large and calm stretch of water. From the wharf I walked up a steep track, beautifully lined with a flowering hibiscus hedge, watched by inquisitive black faces, nobody said anything. At the top of the path was the largest stilt building I had ever seen and radiating from it in neat rows were all the houses. Each had its own well-kept path lined with a hedge; it was the picture of organization.

There had been an immediate and spontaneous response to the creation of the CFC, with many people from all over New Georgia and Rendova embracing the faith. It answered a need for an indigenous Solomon Island organization, without the interference of external missionaries, but believing in Christianity that these islands had so strongly adopted. It is a total faith with everyone working for the good of the church, the church paying all taxes, providing schools and a clinic, paying the staff from the profits of their joint labours. As a result the church owns large areas of customary land that it cultivates to a high standard, from which most of its revenue is generated. What is also interesting is that many government officers are members of the CFC church, so it does not see itself opposed to the administration, rather the opposite with its unexpected motto of "The Church and Government are one".

The second visit I made to Paradise was by special invitation. Bridget and I were to accompany the District Commissioner Tommy Edgar and his wife Florence to attend the tenth anniversary celebrations of its creation. We set off before dawn and although the journey was smooth it was more overcast than before. Following the same route as I had travelled on the previous occasion we arrived off the entrance to the passage to be greeted by an amazing sight. As we approached two huge war canoes with 30 paddlers in each, shot out of the entrance and closed in on our boat with amazing speed. An even larger canoe, containing a complete band in full tune followed them. Forming a procession they guided us into the channel, through its tortuous entrance, and into the large harbour inside. Perfectly in rhythm, each paddle stroke was marked by striking the shaft against the side of the canoe, making a drumming sound, as sixty paddles all hit the water at the same time. The speed was immense and even the ship at full power could not keep up with them. One could feel the terror that must have been generated as these war canoes, barely 50 years previously, went on head hunting raids to villages on other islands. So sudden and frightening must these attacks have been that there would be little chance of escape. I wondered how this show of force could now be incorporated into a church that preached peace?

As we approached the wharf we could see a mass of white, with lines going up the hillside. When we drew close we realised it was rank upon rank of people extending from the bottom right up along the paths, the hedges of which had been cut right down for this occasion.

One felt like royalty as we stepped ashore and with the band playing, were presented to the Holy Mamma, his entourage, and important representatives from all the villages. Such was their planning that they had cleared a whole new area of land to provide sufficient food for this multitude. As we relaxed in readiness for the celebrations we were plied with orange juice and fresh fruit as a testament to this achievement.

When all was ready we were shown into the vast leaf building that normally functioned as a school during the week, church on Sunday and meeting house at any other time. We passed through the rows, upon rows of people all perfectly silent and dressed in white, to our seats on one side. The Holy Mamma then entered and proceeded to a specially built dais on the other. He was strangely dressed in a white full-length wrap around sarong, pure white bodice made of a silky material and covered by a piece of net like a cardinal's cassock. In his thick black curly hair he wore a wooden crown with "Holy Spirit" written across it. One felt a tremendous presence and a collective total obedience, so unusual in these islands. A short prayer was offered, followed by speeches from the invited guests, all punctuated by a unique salutation. On the command "Salvation" everyone made a one-fingered salute (signifying all was one), which was revoked by the counter command of "Hands down". At the end of the speech, the saying was "New life", to which the response was a unified "Alleluia" accompanied by a series of long and short claps all in perfect unison. This all completed I had time to look round and take in the decoration and uniform of the people. Everyone had a tricolour ribbon sash, while draped around were flags of a heraldic nightmare. These were a combination of the Stars and Stripes and some pageantry symbol peculiarly set in the centre. The Royal College of Heraldry would have had a fit.

After the formalities everyone relaxed and behaved in the more easy-going way that I was used to in the Solomons. They took great delight in giving us rides in the war canoes, racing each other with great gusto, but always making sure that the canoe containing the Holy Mamma won its event. The tremendous power was impressive, the simultaneous paddling making the canoe lunge forward at great speed. I was struck again by the incongruence of this benevolent Christian Church and the perpetuation of war canoes that had always been so symbolic of raiding parties and cannibalism. On the prow of one of the canoes was written "Christian genius", which offered something of an explanation. To me it signified the preservation of an ancient art, for only here was the skill of building these magnificent craft still preserved, but in complete contradiction to its original purpose.

Our send off was equally impressive, bands playing, crowds waving and guided out to sea by that lingering marvellous sight of the two war canoes.

* * * * *

On the southern shore at the western end of New Georgia is Roviana, infamous in pre-Protectorate days as one of the main centres of headhunting. The Roviana people would come paddling across the water in their war canoes and surprise the villagers, killing all the men, stringing their heads on the high prows of their canoes, and carry off the women. The women then became wives of their captors and in this way there was an unexpected transfer of peoples around the islands. Several of these captured women were pointed out to me as I travelled round the Western Solomons, it was hard to believe that these head-hunting raids had taken place such a comparatively short time ago.

Headhunting was different from cannibalism, as the objective was not to take captives to eat, but purely for the collection of heads. After the heads were cut off the bodies were left where they were. This was a glorified form of stamp collecting, but had a particular purpose. The head was regarded as the repository of the *manna* (the soul or spirit of the person) so it was believed that the more skulls collected the more *manna* accrued. This horrifying idea probably started in Borneo, where according to Coates (1970) there was no headhunting before 1430, so some time after this date, probably in the sixteenth century, the idea spread along the island chain and eventually came to the Solomons.

Ingava, the supreme chief of Roviana accumulated a huge number of heads from raiding all the surrounding islands, utilising the services of recruiters in exchange for providing recruits for the sugarcane fields of Queensland. He would get the ship to tow his war canoes to the target village from where he would mount his attack meaning that he could extend his area of influence considerably. So large and devastating had this become that *HMS Royalist* was sent to shell his village and in the process destroy his huge pile of heads. Unfortunately this punitive raid had the opposite effect persuading Ingava to go even further in his headhunting raids, so depleting most of the south-western shore of Santa Isabel of its population.

Cannibalism was also practised, but was not as extensive as early missionaries described, and did not consist of boiling people whole in immense pots as cartoons of the day depicted. The main reason was to obtain superiority over your enemy and to eat them was the complete dominance of the foe. Babies were particularly favoured because they represented new life, so by eating them renewed vigour could be transferred to the warrior to give them prowess in battle. This particularly was the practice in the Western Solomons, but in other islands cannibalism was a way of subsidizing the diet. Captives would be kept as food for a feast and in Pidgin they were called "long pig". I met a planter who had been invited to a feast many years ago and when he asked what type of meat he was eating was told it was long pig!

There are many tales of cannibalism by early missionaries and the first Resident Commissioner Charles Woodford, in his book *A Naturalist Among the Headhunters*, describes some of the them. One of his stories tells of a village in Marovo Lagoon where a chief named Parovo wanted to kill and eat a white man, so was always on the lookout for an opportunity. At the beginning of 1888 he set off with a headhunting party to attack Guadalcanal 200 miles away as he had heard that there were Europeans there. He never found his quarry so attacked a village instead but his reception was stronger than anticipated, his raiders being driven off without getting any heads and loosing some men in the process. They started back home but bad weather drove them on to Murray Island where they had no food. Parovo died, so they cooked and ate him instead.

It was these practices that were so vividly described by the early missionaries, often with considerable embellishment, that helped to persuade a reluctant Britain to declare a Protectorate over the islands. What finally tipped the balance into protecting the people though was against the greater depletion of the islands by the "blackbirders".

In Australia, Queensland was being opened up with sugar cane plantations that required a large labour force, but since the transportation of convicts had stopped and the wandering Aborigine was not a good worker, the plantation owners looked to the islands of New Guinea, Solomons and Vanuatu (then New Hebrides) for labour. A type of slave trade developed and the blackbirders, as they were called, would attack a village and take away the men, or more commonly would strike up an arrangement with the chief to provide men. They would give him knives and guns, in exchange for recruits, which the chief saw as an opportunity to wage war on his neighbours, so encouraging more headhunting and the carnage became even greater.

When blackbirding was finally outlawed the stolen islanders were returned to any island that the ship was going to. But the chance of them being landed on the island from which they came was small, so once they were put ashore these unfortunate people were promptly killed.

A greater scourge than both headhunting and blackbirding was the introduction of diseases that the people had never met before. These caused the death of a large number of people resulting in considerable depopulation. In 1916 a third of the population of Makira were reported to have died from chest infections and diarrhoeal disease in the previous two or three years, and by 1920 there were three deaths for every birth. This was very similar in many of the other islands.

On 6th October 1893 the British Government proclaimed a Protectorate over Guadalcanal, Gela, Makira, Malaita, New Georgia and Savo. Santa Cruz, the Reef Islands, Taumako, Utupua, Vanikolo, Tikopia and Anuta were added in 1898, and in 1899, following the Samoan Tripartite Convention with Germany, Santa Isabel, Choiseul, the Shortlands and Ontong Java were exchanged for Samoa. Bougainville and Buka, which are geographically Solomon Islands and have a very similar people to those in Western Solomons, became part of the Territory of Papua New Guinea.

The first Resident Commissioner was Charles Woodford, appointed in 1896. He was a naturalist, making a first visit to the almost unknown Solomons in 1886, to study the plants and animals. He returned the following year and made three other visits, living at Aola on Guadalcanal and Roviana on New Georgia, from where he visited many of the islands and learnt some of the local languages. With such a knowledge of the islands he was a natural choice and as it turned out an excellent one to bring government to the islands. He was liked by the local people as well as the missionaries and planters, making visits on his small steamer the *Belama*. (*Belama* means seagull and was the name given to a succession of government ships right up to independence). His administration was by respect rather than a great show of force as he only had a few islanders trained as policemen and was, in effect, himself the government. He made his base in Tulagi, an island off Big Gela, a good choice as it had a very good harbour and was central to all the islands. This remained the capital until World War II when it was destroyed in the fighting.

The period of Protectorate was surprisingly peaceful and in those early days there is only one incident that marred this record. In 1927 District Officer Bell and Cadet Lillies with a group of island policemen set off for Sinerango on Malaita to sort out a dispute that had arisen over the payment of taxes. Paying taxes was not understood as the people did not see any direct benefit, the resources going to support a distant administration. This tax was particularly onerous as it was a tax on dogs, and to add insult to injury the amount was the same as that on humans. As the people said when they heard this "Me allsame dog?"

The chiefs of the area decided to consult the spirits and after the required ritual the omens were bad. On the requisite day a large group of people had collected and started to peacefully pay their taxes, but when it came to the turn of Basiana, the custom chief, he strode forward and killed Bell with a single blow of his club, calling to the people to join him in his bloody task. Cadet Lillies, the clerk and twelve policemen were killed, but the rest of the police managed to escape to tell the story to a shocked administration. As so often happened in these colonial days the retaliation was out of all proportion to the incident. A warship came from Australia to shell the villages and an army of armed planters and traders invaded Sinerango country to find all those responsible. Many were imprisoned, dying there of disease, while the ringleaders were hung. It was a sad event in the otherwise peaceful Solomons, but both sides seemed to realise this was not the way to solve problems and such an incident did not occur again.

CHAPTER FIVE

The Commander of Rendova Harbour

The period of Protectorate brought peace and an end to the killing, but by now the islands were depleted of their populations and where once many villages surrounded their shorelines, now large areas went unoccupied. These became the property of missionaries or early planters who negotiated with the chiefs large tracts of fertile land to farm. To the northern end of Rendova, came one of the most unlikely of expatriates.

The "Commander" as he was commonly called, had been in the British navy during World War II and decided to turn his hand to farming when the end of the war left these men of action with nothing to do. As he openly admitted the only thing he knew about was how to command men, so he took any advice he was given on farming his stretch of land.

Most people grew coconuts, but he realised that the fertile volcanic soils had far greater potential and he built up a pedigree herd of cattle that were highly sought after as breeding stock in other parts of the Solomons. He also had great success with cocoa, persevering where others had failed, as he enjoyed telling the story.

An expert came on a visit and suggested that cocoa would be a suitable crop to grow in the islands, recommending a particular variety of tree. Many people took his advice, replacing the ubiquitous coconut with the new kind of tree, but it was a dismal failure. The expert then made another visit and said that he had made a mistake the first time, recommending a different variety as being more suitable. By this time nobody would listen to him, but the Commander, not knowing anything about growing cocoa was prepared to try again. He imported the new tree, it was a great success, and because he had re-planted straight away stole a march on everybody else, commanding a good price for his high-grade crop.

The Commander ran his plantation with naval efficiency, instilling punctuality and obedience into his workers. Such was his independence that he used his own time, which was neither GMT or Solomon Islands time. A large clock hung over the plantation buildings and this was the time that determined the routine of daily work.

However he was no tyrant and earned the respect of the workers from the care he took of them. He gave them proper housing and provided the community with a school, church and clinic. He made sure that every child had milk and provided each family with a bottle of kerosene a week for their hurricane lamps, while at Christmas he gave them a cow to have a feast. Used to the conditions of proper service he introduced the concept of paid holidays and pensions for his workers, which were not found anywhere else in the plantation industry.

His domain was very much a little bit of the old country with his imported marmalade for breakfast, raspberry jam on scones for tea and records of Gracie Fields singing war time favourites. He even transferred some of his Britishness to the Solomon Islanders, when on pay-day evening all the children would line up outside his house and sing songs he had taught them, such as *London Bridge is falling down* and *Where are you going to, my pretty maid?*

This was his world and he particularly resented uninvited yachts sailing into his harbour or worse still government officials making an unexpected call. Visitors had to make a formal request to enter Rendova Harbour. He respected Tommy, the DC, because he had a distinguished war service, but other members of the administration were not so welcome. One day a young District Officer sailed into the harbour unannounced so the Commander fired a shot across the bows and prevented him from coming ashore.

He had a large work force with a small clinic so we were keen to visit and assess the health care of his workers, so wrote a polite letter requesting permission to land. Fortunately Bridget was the daughter of a Royal Marine Colonel and knew how to drink her pink gins, so the formidable Commander dropped his ferocious pretence and made us most welcome. He had built a wonderful open-plan house that was always cool from the breeze that blew through it and strategically placed to capture views over the water. In reality he was a lonely person but his formal attitude had been his undoing. To talk to him was like going back to the days when Alfred Russel Wallace was collecting in the Indonesian Islands not so far away, when etiquette and the correct procedures had to be observed.

He had decided he needed a wife and making contact with his relations back in England had arranged for a suitable lady to come and visit him. The lady arrived and with Victorian formality all the correct protocol was observed, but England had moved on further than this and his intended could not cope with a return to times past. After some time she went back to England, the Commander to remain forever a bachelor.

He didn't talk about his wartime service which had been most commendable, earning him the DSC for his part in the battle of Sirte. As a First Lieutenant on the destroyer *Zulu* a Malta convoy was successfully defended against a much more powerful attacking Italian fleet. In a subsequent action the *Zulu* was sunk and Scott-Elliot became a prisoner of war. However on his way to POW camp he escaped by lifting the floorboards in the carriage in which he was travelling, dropping through onto the lines below as the train passed over him. He made his way to the Swiss border, walking over the Alps, and as his Obituary in the *Daily Telegraph* mentions, paused for some skiing on the way. It was not long after this that he was given command of the

Amethyst, instrumental in the sinking of several U-boats, for which he was awarded a bar to his DSC. From the cold waters of Scotland, ancestral home of the Commander, the *Amethyst* was posted to the Pacific Fleet, where he saw the lush islands of the Solomons and decided to go there when he finally left the navy. He arrived on April Fool's Day 1954, to remain there for the next 25 years.

The Commander continued to rule his little piece of Rendova until independence, when a combination of local political pressure and a decline in the economy decided him to sell up and leave the islands to seek his fortune elsewhere. I still retain the picture of this small, portly but very upright gentleman, with shorts that stretched from his midriff to the knee, and carrying a wickerwork case from Fortnum & Mason, striding along the main street of Gizo, on his way to do battle with one of the Chinese stores.

CHAPTER SIX

Peoples from another land

The reputation of headhunting and cannibalism had kept the islands largely unvisited by traders but the greatest power in this part of the world, China, had always had an influence. There is a history of Chinese trading with the islands of Malaysia and Indonesia for thousands of years. Many natural products, such as spices and bêche-de-mer (sea cucumbers) were wanted by the Chinese which they exchanged for porcelain, material and utensils. In time large Chinese jars became family heirlooms and were passed on through the family at marriage. The Chinese probably did not come into the Western Pacific at this time, but more recently found their way there as part of the colonial intrusion.

The earliest record of Chinese coming to the Solomons is 1910 when they arrived as boat-builders and skilled labour for the shipping company Burns Philp, who began to serve the islands. Others followed, setting up as traders.

Most of the Chinese in the Solomons originated from Hong Kong setting up stores to retail a wide range of goods, while others traded in trochus shells (used for making buttons) and copra. Gizo had several of these Chinese stores lined along both sides of the main road. At the end, near a small inlet a Chinese shipwright directed construction of large wooden hulled ships. These were the main craft that travelled between the islands.

The Chinese kept to themselves, setting up their own school in Honiara, where there was more of a Chinatown, and only marrying amongst themselves. It was rare that there would be another Chinese of the right age and sex to find a partner in Solomon Islands so they would send back to their relatives in Hong Kong to find an appropriate match.

I mentioned earlier the Chinese lady who had been on the plane when we first came to Gizo, who everybody knew as Fan (Wong Gok). She had come as a bride from Hong Kong on an arranged marriage. She knew nothing about her husband except for a photograph that had been sent. Similarly she had sent her picture and on this slim recommendation the marriage had been arranged. The flight to the Solomons was expensive, so it was a one way ticket; there was no turning back.

When Fan arrived she took one look at her husband-to-be and yelled at him,

"You lied".

He shouted back to her, "You didn't tell the truth either".

He was very much older than she realised, as he had sent a photograph of himself as a young man. Similarly Fan was not the most fine featured of Chinese women and had her photograph doctored to make her appear more attractive. Still the agreement had been made, Fan knew her place in society and she was to help run the store and maintain a home, so they got married. Even more remarkably they had a son called Billy, that Fan doted on. She loved children and was always trying to entice our two girls into the store, showering them with presents and wanting to have them to stay.

* * * * *

With so many island territories scattered over the Pacific Britain attempted to administer them as one unit, creating the Western Pacific High Commission in 1877. This included the Solomon Islands, New

Hebrides, the Gilbert and Ellis Islands and Fiji, where the High Commission was based. Not only were the peoples very different, with Micronesians in the Gilbert Islands, Polynesians in the Ellis and Melanesians in the Solomon Islands and New Hebrides, but there were also considerable differences in the topography of the islands. The Gilbert and Ellis Islands are small, low-level coral atolls, whereas the majority of the Solomons and New Hebrides are large and mountainous. On independence the Gilbert Islands became Kiribati and the people known as ni-Kiribati, while the Ellis Islands became Tuvalu.

The Gilbertese in particular had multiplied to such an extent that they were facing problems of overpopulation, so in one of those events in history that follow wars or the imposition of colonial rule, groups of Gilbertese were moved from their home island to three sites in the Solomons. These were a part of Honiara, known as White River, the island of Wagina at the south-eastern end of Choiseul and Gizo Island.

The Gilbertese in Gizo had been settled on the southern part of the island at Titiana and to go there was like entering a completely different world. The people had light brown skins, slanting eyes, straight black hair and a tendency to obesity. The girls would start off slim and attractive but once married and with children they would rapidly put on weight.

Their houses were differently constructed, using mainly coconut palm thatch and built on the ground rather than on stilts. There was no greenery around the houses and everything was bright from the glare of the white sand that surrounded them. But they had more of a community life, focused on the large meetinghouse or *Maniaba,* that was often used for celebrations, which would include much dancing and singing. To the Gilbertese dancing and singing are the basis around which life revolves, they are taught as young children and continue to perform until they are old and cannot move around any more. This is quite different to the Melanesian way so to have these contrasting cultures on the one island only added to the interest of living in Gizo.

A young child making its first performance was the height of any celebrations and if that child was a European they delighted in it even more than their own. Lucy and Sophy had not had the opportunity to do ballet dancing as young girls so when we made our second tour to Gizo I asked if they and two of their friends could be taught to dance. The chief dance-master took it upon himself to personally train them and when the allotted day came they were adorned with flowers, coronets made from coloured straws and grass skirts. There was some nervousness but when the four of them appeared on the floor of the Maniaba everyone went mad with excitement. Sophy in particular, because she was the youngest and able to swing her hips as good as the best of them, was a popular performer whenever there was a dance.

Sadly the strength of the community was brought home to me following a tragic accident in which I was inadvertently involved. The little road down to Titiana culminated in a steep hill into the village. Two girls on the same bicycle, one riding pillion, were freewheeling down the hill when they lost control. Careering down at great speed they crashed at the bottom and the girl riding pillion was thrown off, hitting her head. She was brought to the hospital unconscious with unequal pupils, a sign that she had sustained an internal brain haemorrhage. I phoned up Tony in Honiara and asked if I could fly her down for urgent surgery, but he felt that the bleed was probably deep inside the brain and regrettably nothing could be done for her. (We always had to carefully consider any emergency flight as it came out of the medical budget and the cost of a flight was equivalent to vaccinating a lot of children).

I couldn't just stand there though and see this young woman, still in her late teens, die before my eyes, so I set about making a hole in her skull to see if I could find any blood clot. Brain surgery was not something we did in our small hospital so we did not have the right instruments, but after searching every cupboard a trephine was eventually found and we proceeded with the operation. By now not only the immediate family and friends but practically the whole of the

Gilbertese community had gathered outside the hospital and were waiting in respectful silence. The hole was made, the patient seemed to get a little lighter, but sadly there was no obvious bleeding point. I tried one more time with another hole, but it was the same, so sadly I had to give up. The relatives took the dying girl back to their village, followed by all the others that had gathered there. Normally such a happy people the entire community went into mourning for days after this tragedy.

An even bigger tragedy was to challenge these people in 2007, when a large Tsunami devastated their village. Living close to the sea they were at the mercy of the sea as it came sweeping across the land. Many of the houses were totally destroyed, but fortunately there was no loss of life.

Some years later I had the opportunity to visit Kiribati, which the Gilbert Islands are now called. As in the Solomons the Maniaba was their spiritual strength, with dancing and singing welding them together. I was delighted to find them no different from those I knew in Solomon Islands, they were immediately friendly and wanted to ask about their distant relatives. Some I knew by name, but mostly it was a curiosity at how their people had managed to survive in islands so different from their own. Melanesia was still regarded as a place where cannibals lived, so they were pleasantly surprised to find that their people had not all been eaten.

Their houses were just a roof and floor, without any walls, which keeps it cool, but means there is no privacy. All goods and chattels lay around, open to anyone to take, but nobody steals as everyone knows what anybody is doing; the ultimate in communal living.

The main staple is taro, with its large spade shaped leaf, but the part eaten is the bulbous root. It is grown in natural or man made pits in the coral, which are often breeding places for day-biting mosquitoes, so cultivating the plants, normally done by women, can be an unpleasant job.

The type of canoe is very characteristic to Kiribati and they are some of the finest in any of the islands. They are very narrow, pointed at both ends and have a single solid outrigger. The hull is planked, stitched together with vines, colourfully painted and always looks clean and elegant. The single sail is triangular, without a boom or any means to turn it round to the other side. This means that the canoe is sailed first one way and when tacking, is reversed and sailed the other way round, so what was at first the bow now becomes the stern. Capable of very high speeds, when they wish to come ashore they sail full speed at the beach and the momentum carries them some way up onto the sand.

South Tarawa is the main centre of population and witnessed one of the bloodiest conflicts during World War II. Fortified by the Japanese this single action cost 3,200 American casualties (889 killed). Somebody forgot to find out when the tides were so when the armada of landing craft arrived at low tide there was a long stretch of sandy beach to cross with devastating results. The great guns still remain defending the corners of the island, and the Japanese blockhouse, solid and sporting its war wounds, stands as a reminder of that grim struggle.

Kiribati is one of the most extensive countries in the world, but with only 811 square kilometres of land scattered over this vast area. It extends from the main island group of the Gilberts to the Line and Phoenix Islands, thousands of miles across the ocean. The people have always been great travellers and there is evidence of regular contact between Banaba in the Gilbert group and Ontong Java in the Solomons, including trade and chieftainly marriage. It was probably through this means that the calophyllum tree (an exploited hardwood tree) came to Banaba.

In earlier history the people had a myth which is remarkably similar to one that led to the downfall of the Incas of Peru. Their culture was founded by a white god "Matang", who came from across the seas. When the Europeans first came to the islands, they were therefore welcomed as a return of the gods and appropriately called Imatangs. The results were not as devastating as in South America, but even so it indicated a change in the culture of these happy people.

The link between Kiribati and the rest of Micronesia was provided by Air Nauru, the airline of one of the richest nations in the world. Like Faust, they had sold the soul of their island, and the devil was a mining company. The company had mercilessly extracted bauxite until there was little left of the island's interior. The people live round the outside sharing in the communal wealth, which they spend on cars that can only be driven round and round, or load up trolleys from the supermarket with mountains of food. As a consequence they are some of the most obese of people and have the highest rate of diabetes in the world. The reason why diabetes should be so serious a problem on this small island is probably more subtle though.

Formerly the people took long canoe journeys and it would have been an advantage when rations on the voyage became short to easily break down body tissue to maintain sufficient energy. There was probably a genetic selection for those with a higher blood glucose level, which would not have been a problem in conditions of semi-starvation and the slimmer person, but once these restraints were removed then this became a distinct disadvantage.

Nauru can also claim another medical curiosity, being where one of the few-recorded epidemics of leprosy occurred. Leprosy is normally a chronic disease affecting some unfortunate individuals, while others are not susceptible to developing the disease, even when they meet the organism. However communities on isolated islands share a common absence of previous contact with infection. When leprosy was accidentally introduced an epidemic raged between 1921 and 1925 when 30 percent of the population developed the disease. But as with many epidemics it burnt itself out so there is very little sign of the disease today.

CHAPTER SEVEN

Choiseul

The long island of Choiseul lies north of New Georgia and the main group of western islands, to begin a parallel line of islands that continues to Santa Isabel and Malaita. It was given its French name by Bougainville in 1768 when he passed through the channel between it and the island that bears his name. Choiseul was the French foreign minister of Louis XV between 1758 and 1770 and was probably Bougainville's sponsor. Despite this foreign name and now pronounced without quite the same verve of its namesake it is how it is still known today.

The people are an intense black colour with fine features, which makes them all the more good looking. They are friendly and good-natured and had a society that would be considered desirable in many parts of the world. Now largely missionized I was told that in the past parts of Choiseul had quite a free society with a very loose arrangement between the sexes.

It was quite acceptable for the young men to go creeping during the night in search of any available woman. If she fancied her suitor then she would make him welcome. As long as he was out of the house by the morning no questions were asked, but if the young couple wanted to get married then they allowed themselves to be caught together the next morning and it was accepted that they were having a relationship. If children were conceived by a single girl then paternity was of no consideration, the children automatically belonged to the woman. In this way parents were glad to have daughters because any grandchildren would be theirs and the more children the greater the wealth.

There was gossip about two brothers who were both married, one had several children while the other had none. This situation went on for some time, then quite unexpectedly the wife of the childless couple became pregnant. After the first child she then had a second and gradually the story leaked out. Because children are considered so valuable the barren man had asked his brother to sleep with his wife until she became pregnant. There was no jealousy or upset caused by this act, the value of the offspring was considered much more important.

I never learnt any of the Choiseul language, but Roviana was one of the first languages to be translated by early missionaries and became the lingua-franca in the West before Pidgin took a hold. One can always tell the importance of something by the number of words in the language, like the number of words for rice in the languages of Asia. There are different words for recently harvested rice, rice that has been de-husked, boiled rice, fried rice, sticky rice etc., while in English we only have the one word, rice. In Roviana the importance of sex can be determined from the many different names for the sexual parts, especially the female vagina. The word for that of a young girl is quite different from that of an adult, and like the Kama Sutra there are colourfully descriptive terms to indicate the different sizes of the female opening. Being a people closely allied with the sea they describe it with the same name that they use for a clamshell. They have different words for each species of clam, extending from the very small, right up to the giant clam!

Many of the Roviana and Choiseul girls, with their dark skins and fine features are very beautiful and one can see why early traders and wandering Europeans came under their spell. Sex is openly discussed from childhood so they become knowledgeable of all aspects of the subject, as part of the growing-up process. But it is not just the facts of life, all the techniques of lovemaking are passed on making them some of the most sensual women anywhere.

Throughout the islands there was a high birth rate and after delivery we attempted to promote family planning. However it was not well received as the husband was generally uncooperative. To him children were wealth and the more children he had, the better. This resulted in some very large families and all we could do then was to offer sterilisation. This operation became one of our commonest surgical procedures, but on Choiseul they appeared to have found the answer even to this problem. When a woman had completed her basket, as they colourfully described having enough children, they would eat the small white flowers of the *Vendeke* tree. I was told that this worked without fail and that once a sizeable quantity of these flowers had been eaten the woman would not conceive again. Several women I asked testified to its effectiveness, but unfortunately I was not able to prove this categorically and could not get any pharmaceutical company to investigate the potential of this remedy. This was a pity, as it would have saved many an operation.

We made an arrangement with the catholic mission station at Moli to spend our local leave there, so we travelled up by ship. They had a small hospital, but no doctor so we ran it for the period of our stay in return for board and lodging. On hearing that two doctors were based on the island people started to come from far and wide. However, we were not always needed as happened in one interesting incident.

A woman came to deliver her twelfth child and I could not understand why she was labouring so slowly. I could find nothing wrong with her and with this number of previous deliveries it should have been a quick birth. After some time I left the delivery room for a short brake and to my surprise found she had delivered by the time I got back. I was mystified as to why there had been the delay, until the midwife explained to me that the woman did not want to deliver in front of a man, even if he was a doctor. She had been able to suppress her contractions until I left!

After this experience I left Bridget to look after the hospital so that I could pursue a problem that I had noticed on a previous visit. There seemed to be a large number of people with elephantiasis, a disease produced by a nematode worm that blocks the lymphatics, causing the disfiguring and disabling swelling of the legs and dependent parts of the body, such as the scrotum in men and the breast in women. This is the final stage of the disease called filariasis. There are many other problems associated with it so I decided to do some surveys to find out the extent of the infection. Little did I realise that what I thought would be just a one-off survey was to be the beginning of a research programme that was to involve me for over seven years and a reason why I returned again and again to the islands.

Blood slides needed to be taken at night as the parasite had developed a clever adaptation, with its larval form coinciding with the feeding habit of the mosquito, the transmitter of infection. I had bought a second-hand outboard motor and borrowed a dinghy, so every night I went to a different village taking slides from as many people as I could. The next morning I would read the slides with my microscope and then go off to another village to explain to the people the purpose of the study. I would also learn the passage through the reef so that when I returned later that night I could find the way to the village in the dark. There was never any difficulty with the villagers who knew about this awful disease and clambered round me to make sure they had their blood taken. This was an event and developed into something of a festive occasion.

All went well until one particular threatening night, when the clouds covered the moon and an ominous wind began to stir the sea. The passage was a difficult one, going straight in to a certain point, then I had to make a right angle turn, go parallel to the coast for about 50 metres and turn again sharply into the shore. I carried out this manoeuvre as I had practised, except that I started it a few metres too soon so instead of following up the passage I turned right onto the reef. There was a bang and the motor stopped.

We paddled the rest of the way in and quickly did the survey as the sea was getting more and more threatening. When we had finished and started back, to my surprise the motor worked, but I must have damaged the gears as it would only go in reverse! So we travelled stern first all the way back to Moli. One of the catholic brothers had wanted to come with me, but going backwards through what were now quite large waves evoked many muttered prayers and much signing of the cross.

The worst areas for filariasis were north Choiseul and the Shortland Islands, but to my surprise I found nobody infected in this other island group although there were just as many cases of elephantiasis. I was intrigued by this finding and realised that it might be of considerable significance. There was a malaria eradication programme in operation which had started several years earlier in the Shortland islands than Choiseul so it seemed that this might be the reason. The same mosquito transmitted malaria as filariasis so perhaps reducing the mosquito could control both diseases at the same time? This meant that if I conducted ongoing surveys in Choiseul I would be able to see if the disease would die out due to control of the vector by the malaria programme. So every year I returned and repeated the survey and sure enough the infection completely died out after a number of years. This had not been shown anywhere else so was a valuable discovery.

I published the results and spent many years trying to convince people that filariasis transmitted by a malarial mosquito, was a disease that could be eradicated. Later working with Chinese colleagues in Hubei Province in Mainland China, we showed that if the same threshold of control was achieved with drug therapy, the disease would similarly die out. Sadly it was not until I had almost retired from my medical work that these findings were finally recognised and the World Health Organization declared filariasis a disease that could be eliminated. I was pleased to think that the Solomons had been an example to the rest of the world and that other countries might, through international effort, become free of this awful disease.

* * * * *

Choiseul became an island that I visited more frequently than any other, but it was always a long journey as I had to get a ship to near the most northerly end and then find another way of getting round to the other side. There was one old village in the middle of this part of the island called Baukolo, so I wondered if following the ancient tracks it was a feasible way of crossing the island from one side to the other. There were also many interesting stories about Baukolo so my curiosity was raised.

I set off from Pangoe with an old man who knew the way and a boy to carry some of the luggage. As we climbed up to the middle of the island my guide and carrier became ever slower but we eventually got to Baukolo, which turned out to be uninhabited. It was the original village site from which the people had come down to the coast and was therefore of significance to them, but it was now too inaccessible so nobody actually lived there. Eventually the boy gave up exhausted and lying down asked to be left there to die. So I took his bag and helped him along, but by now it was getting late and there was no chance of us reaching the other side by nightfall. The old man made a leaf shelter and we shared out what little food we had, sleeping badly because of the damp and cold. Next morning we soon reached the dividing ridge of hills and progress down the other side was rapid. Clearly this was not a feasible route that I could use to regularly cross the island, but going to Baukolo showed me how different languages had spread in this part of the world.

As you travel round the coast of Choiseul you come across one linguistic group on one side, their neighbours along the coast are of another group, but when you get round to the other side of the island you come across the same language again. The island was probably first inhabited in the interior, or certainly the people moved there to avoid headhunting raids, but once this had stopped and trade and missionary goods lured them down to the coast, they migrated to the nearest shoreline.

This explains how there can be more than one language on a single island and the languages of one island can be quite different from another close by. Choiseul has 7 main languages, its eastern neighbour Santa Isabel 8 and the New Georgia group, south of it, 9. Malaita and Makira both have 10, while Guadalcanal has 3 languages. It is estimated that some 60 distinct languages are spoken in the Solomons with many dialects. These dialects can almost be like separate languages, so out of this problem of inter-island communication grew the universal use of Pidgin, first spoken in the cane-fields of Queensland by indentured labourers and subsequently brought back to the islands.

Pidgin is a simplified form of English with virtually no grammar or standardised spelling, but has now grown into a language in its own right. Originally just a spoken language attempts have been made to write it down and bring some conformity to its spelling. The Pidgin of the Solomons has different words from that of Papua New Guinea and Vanuatu, which naturally has several French words included, but the basic language is the same. This can have advantage for visitors as well as the indigenous population as I was to find on a visit to Vanuatu. I had been invited to a party by a French couple where the majority were speaking the language of their hosts. My French was not good enough to carry on a reasonable conversation but I soon discovered that I could converse quite successfully in Pidgin.

The main languages of the Solomons are Austronesian, although there are remnants of older Papuan languages in parts of Western Solomons and on islands such as the Russells and Savo. Austronesian languages are all part of a large group which include Malay, Indonesian and Polynesian, but the Melanesian form is probably the most ancient. The people of Makira speak of the earliest immigrants as the people of *Tawa*, but there is no J or V in their language so that Tawa could mean Java. In the same way there is an original root *Kala*, not very different from the word *Tawa*, that has given rise to three names for islands of the Solomons, Mala (now commonly known as Malaita), Gela or Ngella and Gera, which is the old name for a large part of Guadalcanal.

Perhaps there are closer links with the people of Indonesia than realised. (See Annex 2)

* * * * *

Between Papara and Sasamunga on Choiseul is a volcanic lake joined by a subterranean passage to the sea. When the sea rushes in fish enter the lake and then have difficulty in finding their way out again. The people make good use of this by erecting fishing nets over the entrance of the passage to catch fish trying to make their way back to the sea. On one occasion a girl called Martha was visiting the nets and dived down to collect trapped fish. Unfortunately for her there was a crocodile with the same idea and she literally dived straight into the crocodile's mouth. The crocodile having tried to swallow her headfirst was incapable of closing its mouth on her solid skull so she fought like mad to free herself. Gradually by supreme effort and with what must have been considerable pain she pushed her head out of the beast's mouth and escaped to the surface. Rushing to the hospital at Sasamunga they stitched back her scalp and she survived. Martha then became one of the staff in the hospital and the scars of her awful encounter are still clearly visible to this day.

Between Sasa Point and Voza is another natural phenomenon that was to be the saving grace of some Choiseul fishermen in the days of the headhunting raids. Occasionally war canoes would come to Choiseul from Vella Lavella or Roviana and on this occasion some fishermen in a canoe saw the headhunters closing in on them fast. However to the amazement of the attackers the canoe suddenly disappeared. It just seemed to have gone from the surface and they could not see it anywhere.

As you travel along the coast it is only when you come very close that you are able to see where the fishermen hid until the danger had passed. There is a very narrow passage that a canoe can pass with difficulty, carefully judging the wave. This leads into a spectacular series of caves and caverns formed in the soft limestone rock. The passage finally goes into what was a large cave, but the roof has fallen in leaving a vertically sided hole draped with ferns and exotic plants. A wonderful place to visit now, it must have been a superb hiding place when the war canoes came.

The south-eastern end of Choiseul ends in a fjord like coastline before breaking up into numerous islands. The largest of these is Wagina which was used to re-settle Gilbertese people from the former Gilbert Islands (now Kiribati). The indented coastline is made from old volcanic craters eroded by the sea and then flooded to form some most attractive inlets. Between Wagina and the main island is Rob Roy Island, probably named by some wandering Scotsman. The passage between it and Choiseul is a long and impressive waterway that allows the island to be rounded in calm water by canoe.

It was in this southern end of the island that I finally found some Kisa (or Kesa in the Katava language). Choiseul had its own system of money, made from giant clamshells, the most valuable piece of which was called Kisa. This was cut out of the thickest part of the shell and hollowed out to form a tube. The owner, normally of chiefly rank wore this on the upper arm. A less valuable form (ziku, poata) is made like a bracelet and worn by women also on the upper arm. This is still made today.

With searching there are still a few old remains and I came across an urn near Polo with a drawing on its side, showing a very large individual with a much smaller one at his side. The main individual had lots of Kisa on his upper arm so presumably was a powerful man, showing his dominance over the rather diminutive figures he held below him.

Choiseul seemed to have many interesting features as I was told a remarkable story by a friend of mine Jon Green, who had been a Peace Corps volunteer in the malaria programme. It was on a canoe journey round the north of Choiseul and I will recount it exactly as Jon told it to me many years later.

"In the last six months of my time in the Solomons I took a month-long trip around Choiseul, it would have been around March 1975. I had Julias Kera and Steven Walle with me and we picked up Isaac Quoloni and one more of the malaria staff near the southern tip of the island. After several days of travel we rounded the northern point of Choiseul and got soaked in the waves and a rainstorm, but finally stopped on an island near Nykiki, if I remember correctly. No one was there, but about five new government structures had been built, and so we moved into one of them for the night and had dinner.

The next morning was one of those fogged-in, cold days with about a half foot ground swell and an oily sea. We headed southeast, about a kilometre or two offshore. I was in the prow in a very pained condition from bad sunburn from the day before. I had just learned that sunscreen did not work well in the Solomons and was peeling my face off in parts as the spray from the saltwater touched me from time to time.

The men started yelling, but I was peeling one of the more painful parts of my face and did not look round. Suddenly the canoe lifted about a foot and dropped, and there was silence. In about 10 seconds the men started yelling again, so I looked this time. Coming at the canoe from the seaward side towards land was a Loch Ness sort of head. Everything happened so fast, but my brain went into the measurement mode, and in the next 20 seconds I could see the skin was the colour of a diver's wetsuit and very smooth. The head of the thing was taller than the 22 foot canoe, if the canoe had been stood on its end, straight up. The eyes were brown (oddly enough the same colour as mine) and on the front of the head and not to the sides. They were round. It was travelling through the water at about 3 or 4 knots and just looked like a disembodied snake's head straight up out of the water, but there was no snake under the water, just something much bigger to hold all that head up so high. Well, the thing's head dove under the canoe without stopping and the canoe lifted and dropped about a foot, and then there was silence. I did not have a camera, and it was probably too foggy anyway. We were all in mild shock, but the canoe never stopped moving.

The last I saw was two of the creatures heading toward a river somewhere near Zavare. Evidently the canoe course had perfectly intersected with the course of each creature, as the first one was ahead of the second, and it was the first one that had lifted the canoe the first time. I thought to turn and follow them, but they had been gracious enough to duck under instead of going through us, and by the time I had wrestled with the pros and cons of a course adjustment, they had disappeared into the fog."

In all my time in the islands I never heard any other account of such monsters being seen, but Jon is a very reliable witness and I am sure there was no mistake. It is intriguing that the description of the monsters is so similar to that reputed to have been seen in Loch Ness, perhaps Nessie does survive in the oceans of the world!

* * * * *

I continued to visit Choiseul once a year to do my surveys, concentrating on the areas around Voza and Ogo. Pioneer studies on filariasis had been undertaken during the war by the American forces medical teams, mainly on Guadalcanal. However the more serious problem was that of malaria from which the Americans suffered badly but even more so the Japanese, who are thought to have lost more soldiers to this parasite than they did to American bullets. Malaria has always been a serious disease in Solomon Islands and in the 1960's the World Health Organization started a Malaria Eradication Programme. This was phased, starting with islands in the Western Solomons, and then continued into others, allowing one area to be compared with another, which was very fortunate for my research.

Success with the control of malaria was very effective to start with and it looked like the disease could be finally eradicated from the islands, but the continuing high level of infection in the central islands of Gela, Malaita and Guadalcanal meant that the islands which had become free were continually being reinfected. First insecticide resistance and then drug resistance, were the final death knoll to the traditional methods of control, so new methods had to be looked for.

I had long since left the islands finishing up in the London School of Hygiene and Tropical Medicine when there was a Ministerial visit from Solomon Islands. Accompanying the Minister was the Under Secretary for Health, Nathan Kere who at a quiet moment in the visit took me to one side and asked,

"Roger I want to study for a PhD, can you help me?" I was very pleased with the idea but knew it would be a long hard road.

"Can you get WHO to sponsor you as you will need financial support?"

It took some time to organise but eventually approval came through and I became Nathan's supervisor, delighted with the thought of being able to return to the Solomons and see his research. Nathan, himself from Choiseul, was one of the new breed of Solomon Island doctors trained to a high level in the University of the South Pacific Medical School in Fiji. He then did a higher degree in New Zealand and was rapidly promoted to the most senior position in the Medical Service.

The project was to use insecticide treated mosquito nets, a method used experimentally but not tried in the islands or on such a large scale. He set up trials on several of the islands and showed them to be very effective, Nathan becoming the second Solomon Islander to get a PhD and the first in Medicine. He was able to get the Government to change the malaria control strategy, with the Solomons becoming one of the first countries in the world to adopt this new method of malaria control. Sadly Nathan was such a useful person that he became pressurised to become a politician, which he did not want to do. Preferring to continue working as a doctor the only way he could get himself out of the pressures put on him was to leave the Ministry and take up private practice. This was a tragic loss of such a highly trained and capable person, but seeing how the political scene continued to deteriorate, Nathan might well have made the right decision.

Subsequently he probably did more for the islands than if he had stayed in government service by becoming President of the Solomon Island Rotary Club. In this influential position he was able to get businesses from Australia and New Zealand to sponsor subsidised mosquito nets to islanders, so that most of the islands were covered. The success of the programme became a model for other countries to follow.

CHAPTER EIGHT

Bali-ha'i

The Shortland Islands are the furthest west of the country that is now known as Solomon Islands, but not of the geographical group which includes the largest of all the islands, Bougainville. This is now part of Papua New Guinea and although separated by a narrow straight there is no official connection between the two countries. The people of the Shortlands are ethnically identical and feel closer to their northern neighbours than they do to other Solomon Islanders. Canoe traffic across the narrow strait is therefore frequent, a journey I was to make myself in the future.

While there are traditional names for each of the islands the whole group continue to be called the Shortlands. Lieutenant John Shortland while on his exploratory visit of the Solomon Islands group in 1788 went ashore and planted a Union Jack, claiming the islands for Britain. This was the easy way to have islands named after you.

The Shortlands saw some of the fiercest fighting in the war as the Japanese had built an airfield on the small island of Balalai, manned with squadrons of zero fighters. From the airfield one could wander into the jungle on either side and find aircraft entwined with creepers, but otherwise in surprisingly good condition. Even more impressive was to dive in the shallow waters and glide down on to the top of one of these aircraft, seemingly so small and insignificant compared to the terror that they once unleashed.

The main island of Shortland is Alu, which is comparatively flat and inhabited by quite the largest and blackest people of any in the islands. They would have been formidable opponents in any headhunting raid and with their islands removed by some considerable distance from others in the Western Solomons meant that they were left well alone. Not only large in physical size they also build some of the biggest houses, which they line up in neat rows on either side of an open space in the middle of the village. The most attractive part of the island is in the south, around Nila where the Catholic mission has established a station.

In comparison to Alu, the second largest island, Fauro is mountainous with almost the identical plan form, but on a much smaller scale to Sulawesi in Indonesia. Long arms of land spiral out from the centre like an octopus, shaped in this peculiar way by a series of volcanic eruptions. This is one of the most beautiful islands out of all of the Solomons and one I loved to go to. The visitor is made particularly welcome, as it is the custom for the chief to offer you accommodation in his own house. A favourite delicacy is *pisu*, balls of fine tapioca flour cooked in coconut cream, and whenever I visited these always seemed to be on the menu.

Near Tomna is an intriguing cave containing the Fauro Kuhi. This is a regular stylised shape consisting of a diamond within a curve and crossed by two lines with angled ends, perfectly symmetrical in shape. It looks like someone has drawn it with a piece of chalk, but if you try and rub it off, scrape it, or even chip it out, it will not go away. It is right through the rock, like a sugar stick from Blackpool, but how such a perfectly regular design in an otherwise plain-featured surface came to be formed remains a mystery. If it had been found in France or Spain it would have been associated with a religious event and soon become a place of pilgrimage, but here on Fauro it remains just a mystery.

The other island in the Shortland group is Mono, a more isolated and impenetrable island. There is only one village, Falamae on the south coast. I took a walk with John Marihasi the medical assistant, who was a living dictionary on herbal medicines. He also knew all about the war as this tiny island had been an allied base and the scene of much fighting. After about an hour's walk to the east, we crossed a stream which John told me had been where the people lived during the war. Apparently there had been much concern that the local people, especially the women, would be exploited by the troops so all the villagers had been moved to this new place. This had become a place of mystery for the troops and one they tried to find any excuse to visit. I asked him what this place was called and to my surprise he said Bali-ha'i, which means "The place over there, or on the other side". I knew Michener had been on Guadalcanal and possibly came to Mono, so it seems that it was from here that he took the name for his mystical and ideal island in his *Tales of the South Pacific*. It was remarkable that this place on Mono island, so poorly known by most people, had given a name as an enchanted place of beauty and mystery, so famous around the world.

The setting for Bali-ha'i was probably the island of Oba in Vanuatu, the group of islands south of the Solomons. The American forces were based on the larger island of Espiritu Santo or Santo as it is more commonly known prior to their major offensive into the islands further north. While waiting for things to happen and history to be made an idle Michener might well have started the jottings for his famous book. Most of the stories were apparently told to him by John Wells, the son of Mat Wells, who had been a pioneer planter on Santo.

In the story Bali-ha'i is a volcanic island full of beautiful women, home to Bloody Mary and out of bounds to the troops. It could however be reached by small boat, so was unlikely to be that far away, which would fit in with the base on Santo. Oba is a steep volcanic island, about the right distance from the Santo base and contained several mission stations. When I visited it I was told that during the wartime young women had been sent over to the island in the care of the mission to protect them from the troops.

In the story Bloody Mary is Tonkinese, the corrupted name given to people from the northern part of Vietnam, around Hanoi or Dong Kinh as it was originally known. The Tonkinese came as indentured labourers to work in plantations in the then New Hebrides before the war and although there are none left in the islands now there were probably quite a few at that time. Lolowai, one of the main villages on Oba has a beautiful circular harbour formed from a partially sunken crater. Just inland is another crater, but this time containing a fresh water lake which seemed to be the ideal setting for the scene of Bali-ha'i portrayed in the stage show and film. The actual island used in the film was Pulau Tioman, off the east coast of peninsula Malaysia. On its southern end it has the most spectacular mountain peak, which provided a suitable background without having to travel all the way to the Solomons or Vanuatu to portray it.

Michener was a naval historian serving in the Pacific from 1944 to 1946, and was said to have written his *Tales of the South Pacific* in the Mendana Hotel in Honiara. Another candidate for Bali-ha'i is therefore the island of Savo which is easily seen from there. Sharing many characteristics with the volcanic island of Simbo it could easily have been idealised into an entrancing place.

This was not the only secret that the small island of Mono had to keep. Further beyond Bali-ha'i was an ancient village site where pottery had been found by archaeologists. There was no local knowledge of the village and even less how to make pottery, so this ancient art had died out and pottery is no longer made in the islands.

Off Fauro are some of the most unspoilt of places. There is the strangely named "Cyprian Bridge" island, which I imagined had some geographical feature that characterised it, when in fact it was named after Admiral Sir Cyprian Bridge. However the local people called it picnic island in their own language and I soon found out why. It was a veritable paradise of bird and animal life, home to turtles, megapodes, coconut crabs and fish, it was like a food larder to the islanders. Fortunately it was uninhabited and infrequently visited, so had time to recover from this human onslaught. It is one of the most exotic places I have ever been to and I was pleased that its remoteness meant that it stood a chance of remaining this way.

CHAPTER NINE

Malaita

We had been a year in the Western Solomons and would happily have stayed there, but with such a small pool of doctors one could be moved around to fill a vacancy or avert a crisis, and so it was that we went to Malaita.

Malaita lies opposite Guadalcanal, in a chain of islands in line with Choiseul and Santa Isabel. It is by far the most densely populated island and has a reputation for a ferocious and traditional people. Quite different from the Western Solomon islanders, the people are noticeably brown in colour, with light curly hair that can even go blond in parts.

The island should strictly be called Mala as Malaita just refers to about twelve miles of coast on the Northwest corner of the island. Malaita means "original Mala," indicating that it was to this area that the original migrants arrived. This was also where the Spaniards came in 1565 and learning that this part of the island was known as Malaita called the whole island by this name.

Soon after we arrived there was a royal visit and it was to this northern part of the island, Malu that the *Britannia* brought its important guest. It was the second time the Duke of Edinburgh had been to the Solomons, but on this occasion he made a more extensive visit, combining it with his role as President of the World Wildlife Fund. To the Solomon Islanders he was a "big man" and they could easily identify him with a very powerful tribal chief. They were however a little confused over the formalities of treating a dignitary from the West. To make quite sure that they had got it right they built a large seat, decorated it with palm fronds and flowers, then wrote a prominent notice above the back of the seat with the single word "Throne". Prince Phillip took it all in his stride and sat on his throne to watch the festivities that had been prepared for him, making one of his famous remarks, to the amusement of the Europeans that had also come to see him.

Malaita was a harder place to work, there was a lot of illness and much resistance to Western medicine, although the hospital was bigger and had twice as many doctors as we did in the West. I had become particularly interested in the district work, supporting the rural health service, so instead of working so much in the hospital I became the District Medical Officer.

Most of the islands of the Solomon group are virtually uninhabited in the middle, all the people living on the coast and only going into the central parts of the island to farm their land or hunt. Guadalcanal and Malaita are the exceptions, with inland peoples who only come down to the coast to exchange goods and market produce with the coastal people. Formerly they resisted any incursions into their territory and the markets that took place were strictly controlled by customary practice so that no fighting developed. Malaita was the only place that a British administrator was killed in the course of his duty and even when I was there one had to be careful that customary practices were not transgressed. Most of these consisted of male and female taboos. There were certain places that only men could go and others restricted to women, a completely different practice to other islands where harmony between the sexes was the rule.

To visit the saltwater people one took a boat and travelled round the coast, but on Malaita, where a large proportion of the population lived inland a different method of touring was required, so called "bush walking." A way was cut through the jungle to follow traditional routes into the interior. With such dense jungle one only rarely had a view, or for that matter could look up and see the sun, so it was impossible to navigate by normal means. It always amazed me how my guides ever found their way.

We normally started off by following up a river and then reaching the head of the stream would climb up steeply to cross into the next valley. With its hilly, indented surface and high rainfall the steep surfaces were very slippery, while in the troughs the mud collected into deep sloppy puddles.

My first experience of touring in this way was to go by boat round to the other side, visiting clinics on the way, and then walk across Malaita from Manawai to Hauhui, visiting the one clinic in the centre of the island. I soon realised that this kind of walking was quite different from anything I had ever done before. We started off by climbing up a very steep hill so that by the time we had got to the top I assumed we would follow ridges until we got to our destination. But not a bit of it, we descended the other side at a perilous incline, sliding all over the place in the mud. Eventually reaching the bottom, we crossed an attractive river and then repeated the whole process again. The third time up, higher than the previous two, we eventually came to our first signs of habitation, two houses occupied by a couple of women smoking pipes of home grown tobacco.

We now followed along a ridge to the next village and I thought the route would be easier, but when we got to the village my guide left me in the trust of two Are Are bushmen, having carefully explained to them that they were to follow the ridge all the way to the clinic. These two were interesting, they had travelled with us for some while, one carrying my rucksack containing my clothes and medical supplies. All they had were a pair of shorts and a small basket slung round their necks, as well as the utilitarian bush knife with which they cleared away overhanging branches and new growth on the path. They had been travelling for several days so I was curious to know what they carried in their small basket as they seemed to have no spare clothes or other possessions. One of the contents soon became obvious when they took out a small tube containing lime that they poked with a short stick into the corners of their mouths to mix with the beetle nut that they chewed. Beetle nut is a mild stimulant and chewed incessantly by the bush people so that their teeth become permanently stained. The other content of the small bag came to me as a complete surprise and was only revealed, when despite the instructions given to them I soon found us descending the hillside again at a phenomenal rate. We eventually reached the bottom, where there was a river, and to my astonishment out came a bar of soap from the tiny bag and they started washing themselves. Normally bush people would just wash themselves with water in the nearest stream, soap not being used, but this must have been their one luxury that they now proceeded to indulge in it.

I could see little point in joining them as I knew that I would be covered in sweat and spattered with mud as we climbed up the other side, which when we came to it, was exactly what happened, taking us almost two hours. It would have been so much easier to have followed round the ridge, even if it had been further, but whether their sense of navigation was a straight line, despite the difficulty of sliding down the slippery slope and the gruelling climb up the other side, or they really just wanted to have a wash in the river, was not revealed to me. I was now completely exhausted. We had reached Rioahia where the clinic was situated, so I found a place to collapse and nurse my aching feet and knees.

No doctor had been here for some while, but despite this the medical assistant gave me a rather cool reception, as though I had invaded his domain, which for the moment remained a mystery to me. The reason however, soon became clear.

As well as being the government medical person he also practised local customary medicine, including what might be called witch-doctoring, and somehow combined this with being the local lay preacher. How he could rationalise these conflicting interests was amazing, a mixture of compromise and choosing the best remedy for the individual situation, but the combined effect was to give him inordinate power and I had now come into his world to challenge him. We spent some time discussing his patients and the strictly medical needs of his community and he realised that I could help him with these while being careful not to interfere with his other practices. He was up in these mountains on his own, the only help for miles around and I could tell that he was genuine in his service to the people, so if there were practices that were somewhat unorthodox, but were effective, then who was I to try and stop them.

I was worried about the next day's journey, the walk had been far harder than anything I could possibly have imagined and to make matters worse an old cartilage injury in my left knee was beginning to remind me of its presence. The people had given me a place to sleep for the night and fed me with sweet potatoes both for supper and breakfast, so I left hopeful that all would be all right. There was only initial stiffness when we started, but on going down hill the pain in my knees began and the more we went down the worse it became. My new guides were very sympathetic and did not mind going slowly, joking that the reason for my slowness was that I was married and my energies were used elsewhere. They cut me sticks with which I levered myself down the steep slopes like an old man. I was in agony, I just wanted to sit down and die, but I knew there was no other way out, so I struggled on.

After what seemed an interminable and agonising time we eventually descended the last hill to the lower stretches of the Wareha River. Now on the flat I could throw away my sticks only to realise that my palms were raw and bleeding for such was the pain in my legs that I had not noticed the chaffing of my hands. But to my joy, now the way was on the level I made rapid progress as we followed the river to its mouth. Seeing the sea crashing on the beach as the sun went down was one of the most memorable of sights, I felt like I had crossed a continent, rather than just an island, and had not seen the sea for months.

While I had been struggling across the island I had concluded that I was not the bush-walking type, but finding my stride again on the flat gave me new impetus so I decided to try again after I had rested my injured limbs. So within a few weeks I was off again, crossing Malaita from a different place to take in villages that had not been visited for some length of time.

I think if it had rained on my first walk, I probably would never have tried bush-walking again, because when I subsequently met this delight I realised how much more difficult everything became. At the lowest level the rivers flooded, stranding you or making crossings hazardous, then on the flat the ground became a muddy quagmire as you sank up to your knees in a black ooze. But of course as you tried to climb the inevitable hill, or especially come down, one slipped and fell all over the place, grabbing on to trees and bushes to save yourself. There was no chance of keeping yourself dry, the rain was so intense you were soaked in a few seconds and the so-called paths became rivers as you sploshed your way onwards.

One of my most memorable walks was when I crossed Malaita at its widest part. Despite having good guides we got lost, a hazard I was to accept occurred at least once in every walk. By the time my guides had cut a new path and we eventually joined up with the one we were meant to follow, much time had been lost. Then of course it started to rain, and rain, and rain. We plunged on and asking when we would reach the village I was given the reply,

"Close up". This is a lesson you soon learn that "close-up" can mean anything from half an hour to half a day.

There is a story of a rather corpulent District Officer who secretly detested bush-walking, but had plucked up all his courage and embarked on a comparatively easy walk. He had taken all that he could possibly need on his trek so had a long line of porters as well as his guide. They progressed very slowly and all the time he kept asking how far it was to the next village to be given the proverbial reply of "Close-up" each time. Eventually his patience was exhausted and after having his umpteenth "close-up," with still no sign of getting to his destination he ordered that they stop and make camp for the night. Temporary camps such as this are always uncomfortable and everyone always depends on the next village to be fed, so his guide and porters were hungry as well. The next day they set-off again, and within twenty minutes they were in the village, it really had been "close-up".

So with this story in my mind I continued on with our "close-ups". Soon it got dark and I was restricted to using my torch to walk by. This revealed an interesting biological diversion by lighting up a luminous fungus. I tried to work out what evolutionary advantage this would give it as no spore-transporter would have carried a source of light like me, but anyway this temporarily took my mind off the wet, dark, slippery predicament I was in. We slithered down a muddy bank to a river and I was hoping against hope that we were near our destination, but the inevitable came. There was still just enough light to make out the tops of the hills, and of course that black skyline, high above us was where we had to go. I was wet, muddy, sweaty, tired and hungry, and mirage thoughts came to my mind of a dry house, warm shower, a bed, clean sheets and a fabulous meal. For every two steps forward I slipped back one, but then eventually we got to our village, but was this really what they meant, the village consisted of only one house!

The house had two parts joined by a covered way. A man and his wife lived in one end and their three grown up daughters lived in the other. These girls (in their late teens) were completely naked, not even a loin cloth or string of beads hid their pubic hair, but this nakedness was so natural to them that they were not abashed by our presence, not even that of a white man.

The custom is that when they are unmarried the girls must go completely naked, except for a red cane belt around their waist which hides nothing. When they marry they exchange their red cane belt for a black cord one, from which is suspended a small loincloth, as sported by their mother. Of course we could not sleep in the girls' room and there was not much room in the other so I opted to sleep under the covered way. Fortunately I had a sheet of plastic to put on the sodden earth and my sleeping bag was reasonably dry, so I shared this piece of ground with three pigs, who helped to keep me warm in the cold mountain night. So much for my thoughts of a few hours ago!

Another journey from Sinerango to Buma was amongst the people who had murdered Bell and Lillies. Known as West Kwaio it is the area most set in its custom ways. Villages as such do not exist, the people living in single family units of one or two houses or even just on their own. An agreed meeting-house is maintained where people congregate when there are matters to discuss or there is a visitor, such as on this occasion. The reason for this was because of the intricate customary practices that involved all of life's actions. If any of these were broken then one could face the custom court, be fined or punished in a more severe way. However so involved were these customs that it was almost impossible not to break any of them, so by living in isolation meant that minor infringements would not be noticed. They were amazing in their resilience and individuality, but then all coming together when called by the conch shell, such as by my visit.

Women have a particularly hard time of these customary practices, for as explained to me the Kwaio man is the boss, next comes his land, then his pigs and in third place his wife. She becomes his property, and he must pay for her with customary money and pigs. She is his beast of burden, both in growing food and in bearing children for the rest of her life. Because it takes the man some time to accrue sufficient wealth to afford the bride price he will probably be in his thirties or even forties by the time he has obtained sufficient money, while his wife will still be in her teens. There is no question of fornication or adultery in this traditional society, it does not occur. If it does the solution is very straightforward, both are put to death. This is why the unmarried girls can go around naked with complete impunity, on show with nothing to hide from a prospective husband, but once married she must then hide the pubic area from view. This is the only part of the body considered taboo; breasts are entirely for functional purposes, buttocks of no concern and thighs or knees not even considered to be covered.

An unfortunate custom and the only one I strongly opposed on my tours was the practice the woman had to observe when giving birth. In their inferior position women are segregated from the start, some parts of the village and certain paths are out of bounds. Only in their homes can they be with their husbands and sons. A menstruating or pregnant woman is considered unclean so they are not allowed anywhere near the village. The woman must go to a specially built hut (the mbisi hut), situated some distance away, and remain there until her period is finished. When the woman is pregnant she must continue to work in the fields as hard as ever, then in the final month go far away into the jungle and build a shelter, taking sufficient food to sustain her until her baby is born. She must then stay there for 30 days after delivery, following which she is considered cleansed.

The woman cannot return to the village before this time no matter what difficulties she might have and neither can anyone who has gone to help her. The problems of this arrangement are obvious, what if the mother cannot deliver due to an obstruction, or she continues to bleed, how can she be aseptic in handling the babies cord, and what if she has problems feeding her baby? Then of course if she needs help, she cannot use any path because this will be contaminated and her helpers likewise. Many are the women who have gone into the jungle to have their baby and never come back, or else come back without a child so you didn't know whether it died naturally or was smothered because it was the wrong sex!

When I reached Buma hospital I was told of such a story. A message had been received that a woman was in obstructed labour so one of the nuns went up into the jungle to help her. Realising that she would have to be brought down, nobody was willing to help for fear of being contaminated, so the nun had to get helpers from the mission to come up. They could not use the usual paths so new ones had to be cut, and when they needed a canoe none was available because it would then become unclean!

I was now becoming ingrained into the problems of the people of the interior and of the required bush walking to get to them. The number of people in the bush was not that great, but the intervals between visits by doctors were anything between 5 and 20 years in some places. Certainly some of the children had never seen a white man before and ran screaming in terror when I came into the village. However, when I went down to the river to wash, they would then hide behind the rocks, peeping out to see if I was really white all over.

On one of my journeys I found a case of yaws when this disease was thought to have been eradicated. Fortunately it can easily be treated with depot Penicillin. Leprosy is a disease of the interior so often goes undiagnosed, while tropical ulcers which can be so debilitating, are left to fester and eat away the underlying tissue until they cause a huge loss of tissue and skin. The only treatment then is surgery, but the people will rarely come down to the coast for help.

The villagers always fed me, it was the tradition to treat visitors in this way, and I got quite used to existing on a diet of sweet potatoes. There would always be someone to carry my bag, making it easier for me to cope with the very difficult terrain, as well as slow down my guide, as they could walk at an incredible rate. It was quite natural for the bush people to walk through this difficult terrain as we would stroll along a road and despite the number of times I did these walks I never could match them.

CHAPTER TEN

The power of custom

Custom men hold considerable sway over the people in their community, maintaining the tradition of the tribe. Ingrained in the ways of their ancestors they practice the customary beliefs and impose a strict law on the people. As such they are highly respected, more with fear than admiration. When one went into a village you took particular pains not to confront them and negotiation was always a difficult affair. They were seen as the guardians of the spirits so if you upset them you were upsetting the spirits and a taboo would be placed upon you. Some were considered so powerful that even outside their traditional areas they could cast the evil eye.

On one occasion we had two custom men sick in hospital in Malaita, so knowing the problems that could ensue if they were in the main ward we put them in a small two-bedded room. They had not been there long when one of our cleaning ladies, who was not from the traditional area, in fact came from another island altogether, was doing her cleaning duties and backed into the small ward where these two men were lying. She hadn't realised they were there, but in the middle of her sweeping she looked up and suddenly recognised them for what they were. They said nothing but showed their displeasure at being approached so closely by a woman, a matter of customary significance. She realised straight away what had happened and shot out of the ward terrified.

Up to now she had been a very normal person, we knew her well because she had two little girls who played with our children, but this event was to send her completely crazy. She became severely disturbed and we had to admit her to hospital as a mental patient. We filled her up with all the medicines we had, but nothing would calm her down and we were seriously considering sending her to the specialist mental hospital in Honiara to be confined. However hearing of her plight her priest came to visit her in hospital because she was a very devout Christian, and offered to exorcise the evil spirits.

Having completely failed with western medicine we were prepared to try anything, so readily agreed to this suggestion. I think the priest had learnt some of the ways of the custom men and used a little more than the laid down exorcism ritual of the Anglican Church, for after several treatments our patient was miraculously cured. For every force there is an opposing force and the priest was able to use the same power and fear engendered by the custom men to counteract the spell that they had placed on her.

This brought home to me the limitations of Western medicine for some conditions, especially for psychiatric disturbances. Mental illness was more common than what I had expected and from now on we used the help of local healers more often.

I used to dread psychiatric cases, feeling so helpless with our treatment, so once when we received a call of a problem case in one of the villages, I was reluctant to ask the captain to call in and take her on board. The rowing boat went ashore to bring her back and while I watched I could see this figure standing stiffly at the bow as the boat tossed its way back to the ship. The woman had been through a religious experience that had quite changed her, thinking she was the new Christ she stood at the bow of the ship with her arms stretched out from her side as though she was crucified on the cross. She kept up this position all the way back to Auki, several days journey, refusing all food and never sleeping, but fortunately when we arrived in the hospital she responded well to treatment.

She suffered from schizophrenia and this was the commonest condition we had to treat. Once stabilised on treatment the patient returned to her village where she was well looked after by her relatives. The support of the community was considerable and most of the minor mental illness did not require any treatment because this was so strong. It was only when things got out of hand and the relatives could not cope that the person ever came as far as hospital.

The evil eye was a very powerful force and unexpected deaths or severe illness were often blamed on it and because the belief was so strong people would often go to a custom man for treatment of their illness before going to the clinic. This delay resulted in a worsening of the condition when they eventually came to see us. In the same way if we failed to treat somebody then this could drive the people to go to a custom doctor before trying Western medicine again. This was a continual battle we had to fight and gradually an acceptance was built up as to the value of the health care we could offer.

Dr Lambert who spent over 20 years in various islands of the Pacific in the early part of the 20th century and wrote about his experiences in *Doctor in Paradise* mentioned that he became so aware of the power of suggestion that he would sometimes use it himself to cure people who were suffering from illness due to this cause. He also mentioned that cases had been recorded of people being told they would die, and despite no signs of any illness, would progress rapidly to death. I had not read about this when a fit young man came into hospital saying that the evil eye had been put upon him and he was going to die. I examined him carefully and could find absolutely nothing wrong. In fact he looked so fine a figure of manhood that I was reluctant to admit him and did so on condition that I would discharge him the following morning if nothing should have happened.

Next day I found the bed empty and presumed he had discharged himself, but the nurses told me that true to his word he had died during the night. His relatives had taken the body away so there was no chance of doing a post-mortem and I was never able to determine if there had been a physical cause for his death. This was a powerful force that could not be explained.

The forces of evil that the people so feared generally did not have any influence on Europeans. Once when I had to sack a member of staff I noticed that some pieces of a local necklace I had been given were missing and on asking my house-girl she said they had been taken to work magic on me in retribution. Either the magic was not powerful enough or the justice of my action was stronger than the evil force sent against me, as there was no effect.

However, on another occasion I had asked someone to take me to an old village site, called Bau, in New Georgia. I had heard that there were some interesting stone remains there. They warned me that it was a taboo place and if I went with them I must keep close to them and observe all the conditions they specified. As we approached they said I must tie a frond from a palm tree round my neck like a necklace. This seemed ridiculous to me and I refused, saying I could not see how this would have any effect.

When we arrived at the place I looked around at the stone artefacts, wandering into the jungle to examine the full extent of the ruins. Meanwhile my companions went off hunting. Before they went they told me not to go far or else the evil forces would take hold of me and make me confused so that I would become lost. By now I was experienced with being in the jungle and had become good at following trails and retracing my way, so did not worry about what they said. However, after about half an hour of looking around, try as I may I just could not find my way back to the meeting place. I knew I had not gone far and attempted many routes to get myself back, but all to no avail. I felt quite confused and disorientated and unexpectedly began shouting to my friends to come and find me. It took time because they had gone some distance, but when they did finally come they led me back to the agreed meeting place in less than five minutes. I was amazed and could not understand what had happened to me, but they rebuked me for not following their instructions and wearing the palm frond to protect me. So I let them tie one round my neck and after that I was able to walk about with impunity and no fear of getting lost again!

CHAPTER ELEVEN

Violent retribution

The independence and ferocity of the Malaita people is not far below the surface and never more so than when a land dispute occurs. People from Malaita are now spread all over Solomon Islands, owning land or marrying into land ownership as land is in so short supply back in the home island. However if the reverse takes place with another islander marrying a Malaita girl and claiming land ownership in Malaita, then conflict can take place. This was the case with one family just south of Auki as it resulted in the death of the unfortunate immigrant, and as with all police cases the doctor on duty was obliged to perform the post-mortem.

Apparently there was resentment by the local people at the man farming some land, which he understood his wife had right to. One night he had a visitor, his wife was in the house and heard them arguing, when all of a sudden there was a bang and when she went outside she found her husband dead.

The police started looking for a man with a gun, but brought the body to the hospital for me to do the post-mortem. There was a ragged hole in his back just below the rib cage and on first examination it looked as though a shotgun had been fired at close range. However when I opened the body there were two clear stab wounds, one of which had gone through the left kidney and the other up through the lung to pierce the heart. I then realised that the wound had been inflicted probably by a bayonet (a treasured possession from the last war) which has a serrated part near the hilt. Also knowing that the two men had been arguing, so facing each other when the stabbing took place, the assailant must have pulled the victim towards him and driven the knife up underneath the rib cage, in the manner that special service soldiers are taught to use. The murderer might well have been an older person who had learnt this technique fighting in the last war, or had at least learnt it from somebody experienced in this method of killing. I concluded that a professional killer, sent to settle the dispute in the old manner, had committed the murder. A firecracker had been set off to tell people that the deed had been done, so explaining the bang.

Professional murderers were known as *ramo* on Malaita and could be employed to settle a blood feud or do away with someone who had transgressed the custom. They were savage and fierce fighters, having obtained their reputation by their prowess in war and the number of people they had killed. The more people they killed without injury to themselves the more they were considered to embody the power of ancient ancestors. With such ancestral power, normally to just be confronted by a *ramo* was sufficient to settle an argument, but this man, coming from another island was not in the grip of customary power as the Malaitans are, and suffered the consequences.

I thought with this information it would not be too difficult for the police to find the culprit, but they never did. The wife heard the two men arguing and must have known who the attacker was, but she was too frightened to give any clues, knowing that the problem had been solved in the customary way. The power of custom was stronger than her marriage. A silence closed in on the island and the murder was never solved.

CHAPTER TWELVE

Crocodiles and TB

Bridget had found her niche when we moved to Malaita, treating the tuberculosis patients. They formed the single most important medical problem and two wards in the hospital had been set aside for them. She had noticed that a large number of cases came from the south from what is called Small Malaita so we took a dinghy and outboard motor down there by ship and based ourselves in the rest house so that we could investigate further.

Malaita narrows down to a long peninsular, then across a passage of water (Maramasike Passage) is matching Small Malaita. In the channel between large and small Malaita numerous creeks are formed and the mangroves hide from view the many villages. First thing in the morning when it was still cool and patches of mist clung to the water, it was calm and exhilarating to speed down the passage and turning up a narrow inlet, thread a way through the mangroves until it would open up to reveal a village. We would enquire about anyone with a cough and finish up examining half the village. In this way we discovered 6 new cases of TB.

The saddest was a young man barely in his twenties who made his own way to where we were staying. He had seen us examining people but was frightened of his parents, so in the evening he paddled his canoe to the rest house and explained what had happened to him. They had used customary treatment and did not believe in Western medicine, with the result that his TB had advanced to the spine and he was now bent over like an old man. We could cure his TB and reassured him about this, but sadly we would not be able to straighten his spine.

The most impenetrable area was on Small Malaita. Local missionaries had started a new clinic some way into the island, which involved following up a channel for some distance, through a tunnel of mangroves. As we threaded our way through the mangroves, hoping we had taken the right turning, lying like a log on the bank was a good sized crocodile. As we went further up the river there was another. This is one of the few places where crocodiles are to be found, protected by the people and fed with the occasional ritual sacrifice of a pig. The salt-water crocodile (*Crocodilus porosus*), the same as found in northern Australia, used to be common around the islands but with the advent of the gun has been virtually hunted to extinction. There are very few places it can still be found and this is the main one.

After we had gone as far as we could through the mangroves we then had to trek through the jungle. It was very dark and tall trees shaded out the bright sun. There was something a little frightening about the place. Then we heard a strange whooshing sound like the wing beats of some prehistoric flying monster. I looked up half expecting to see a Pterodactyl, but instead saw a pair of Blyth's hornbills (*Aceros plicatus*). These huge birds have a wing span greater than my outstretched arms and a massive bill with what looks like another on top, which gives them their common name. They are adept at feeding on fruit and small animals making them veritable masters of the jungle canopy.

On our way back to Auki we travelled through the Are Are lagoon, one of the most beautiful places in the whole of Malaita. Other lagoons are in the north, the Lau and Langa Langa and have large populations living on artificial islands. These islands are made by building up lumps of coral onto shallow reefs to form a platform on to which houses are built. There are two main theories as to why the people went to so much trouble to construct these artificial islands;

one was defence and the other malaria. As coastal peoples any base on the land would mean they could be attacked from inland, but isolating themselves offshore left the bush people to attack by canoe, which they never did. These islands were also surprisingly free from malaria, as the porous coral left no breeding place for the mosquito and were too far from the shore for this fragile insect to fly. It seemed strange with so much land available that people should crowd themselves onto these artificial islands, but so devastating was malaria, and so feared were the attacks by the bush people that this way of life must have seemed preferable.

The method of increasing the area of an islet, or creating a completely new artificial island is found in other parts of the Pacific, so probably was brought by the people when they first came to the islands. Certainly it would suggest that when they arrived mainland Malaita was too dangerous and the only place they could safely set up home was off the coast of the main island.

Although there can be no connection the use of building artificial islands or *crannogs* was practised in Scotland and Ireland in those troubled days when the law of the sword ruled the lands. Shallow parts of the loch were built up with stones until there was sufficient level ground on which to construct houses. It is intriguing how the same idea seemed to occur in different parts of the world.

The Langa Langa lagoon is also the mint for traditional money. This is made from bivalve shells, both red and white, the former being more valuable because the shells live in deeper water. They are cut into discs and a hole made with a simple drill so that they can be strung on a string. The discs are then rubbed smooth on a sharpening stone to make them all the same size. The principal use of this traditional money is for buying a bride who is then adorned with it during the marriage ceremony. It is also used to pay serious custom fines so is more valuable than conventional money, which cannot be used in these instances. Such traditional money is found in the Trobriand Islands as well as here on Malaita, as part of the Kula trading cycle. It can be found in other parts of Papua New Guinea as well. Interestingly an identical form of shell money has been discovered in Inca burials in South America, but there is no suggestion that these are in any way linked.

CHAPTER THIRTEEN

Mission request

As with elsewhere in the Solomons the missions were ever present and held considerable sway over the people. Many of these had hospitals or clinics that we visited on a regular basis. There were national policies for the treatment of some conditions, such as TB and leprosy, and these needed to be checked regularly to ensure that the patient was progressing satisfactorily. Normally the missions were glad to see us and were always generous in their hospitality, giving us a meal or accommodation for the night, a pleasant break from the cramped conditions on board ship. There was however the temptation to compete with the Government service as the mission was in the business of winning souls, so occasionally they would introduce a new treatment or surgical procedure to demonstrate that they had something better to offer. There were also doctrinal differences, the most divergent being the Seventh Day Adventists (SDA) who accepted the bible in its literal sense and opposed ideas of evolution.

We were careful to try and steer a middle course, encouraging good medical practice but keeping clear of religious differences. Our visits to Atoifi, the SDA mission hospital on the opposite side of Malaita though were always tense occasions. In charge of the mission was Len Larward, a strong-minded, but very well meaning person, who ruled his station with considerable authority. I had on several occasions had my differences with Len and we treated each other like two Northern Ireland politicians. I was therefore surprised to be rung up by Len one afternoon,

"Roger, we have a woman in obstructed labour and we need your help."

"Where is your doctor?" I asked, as they had a recent incumbent from Australia who had been causing us some problems over the treatments he had been giving.

"He had to go back home suddenly, as his father had died, and we don't have a replacement" Len replied.

"Send the woman round to us on your ship and I will operate on her here."

"I would have done that", said Len, "But her condition is too serious for her to be moved. Could you come to Atoifi and do the operation over here?"

What had happened was that instead of sending the woman in the early stages of labour, they had hung on hoping she would somehow overcome the obstruction so it was now too late to do this and her condition was serious. This was a difficult matter to be confronted with, for on the one hand I was annoyed that the delivery had been allowed to get out of hand, while on the other had a duty to help the mother, and if I failed, would provide the SDA with ammunition to criticise the Government Service. My problem though was how to get to Atoifi in time to save the woman and hopefully her baby as well? By ship it would have taken 12 hours, which would have been too long, even if I could have got a Government vessel at such short notice, and to walk across, would have taken much the same time if I did not stop for the night. (At that time there was no airfield at Atoifi).

There was a road round the northern part of the island, but then some distance of open sea, so I came up with the idea of driving to the end of the road and doing the rest by dinghy and outboard, hoping that the sea would stay calm enough for such a small boat. I enlisted the help of a VSO (Voluntary Service Overseas) working with our malaria programme, as I needed to use one of their dinghies and outboards.

We strapped the boat on the roof and sped off up the road, arriving there after three hours, just as it was getting dark. I knew it was going to be risky going through this much open sea in daylight, but at night it was much worse. Fortunately there was just a small chop so we arrived in Atoifi three hours later, wet, but in one piece. The operating theatre had been made ready so we wasted no time and I got on with the Caesarean straight away. To my delight not only was the mother all right but we were able to give her a live baby as well.

This incident did much to improve relations between Auki and Atoifi and Len became a much pleasanter person to work with. In his devotion to his work with the mission he was quite unforgiving though. He would turn his hand to anything and it was in attempting to improve the mission's agriculture work that tragedy caught up with him. He was ploughing a steep hillside when the tractor turned over and he was instantly killed. Atoifi was Len Larward and without him it was never the same place again.

CHAPTER FOURTEEN

A passage to Ontong Java

After the main Polynesian migrations to Tonga, Samoa and other island groups, there were back migrations, with people from Tuvalu coming to Ontong Java and Sikaiana, outlying atolls some distance from Malaita. These needed to be visited but because of their distance one of the bigger boats was sent from Honiara and Government officers from each of the departments would make a combined visit.

Alvaro de Mendana after sailing for about two months from Peru first came across Ontong Java on 23 January 1568, before going on to Santa Isabel and Guadalcanal. The unlikely name of Ontong Java was given by Tasman in 1643 when he chanced upon the atoll after his many travels further west. It is thought that Ontong comes from the Malay *untung*, meaning lucky or fortunate so a translation would be "Java Luck" or good fortune. Various derivations of the word *Java* have been given to other islands of the Solomons, as mentioned before.

Later Captain Hunter re-named the islands Lord Howe, but this name is rarely used, which is probably just as well as there are several Lord Howe islands and it would only cause confusion. The Polynesian name is Leuaniua, but strictly speaking this is the name only of the main island, so Ontong Java seems to have stuck as the most suitable name for the whole atoll.

There was no airfield and so a ship went from Malaita every few months to Sikaiana and Ontong Java via the small island of Dai. On this particular voyage I went in company with the district officer, a friend of mine, Dudley Cook.

Our trip spelt ill from the start. There had not been a ship for almost two months and when one came from Honiara the water tank was leaking. We were expected to make do but the ship was packed with passengers and the journey would take three days so it would have been dangerous to leave in this situation. The ever-resourceful Dudley rushed round and found a 500-gallon water tank, which was lashed to the hold, but now the ship was less stable so we hoped for good weather.

We reached Dai Island by the first evening, an amazing community that had much to teach other parts of the world. They knew exactly how many people there were on the island and how many it could support, so when the number exceeded this critical figure they held a meeting and people were asked to volunteer to move to the main island of Malaita with which they had ethnic links. In this way the population was always kept in balance and the limited resources never exploited.

Sailing overnight we reached Sikaiana, a very isolated atoll of pure Polynesian stock. The people lived entirely off the sea and the coconuts that grew on the island, their only source of money. The coconuts were harvested, split open and dried to produce copra, which was then exported. However there is no anchorage and the ship had to float off the reef while canoes full of copra were pushed across the reef and choosing the right wave, paddled onto the open sea. Capsize was frequent and when the sea was rough the ship could only sail past, the people having to wait for the next ship in several weeks time. Fortunately when we called it was sufficiently calm for us to land and for the copra to be loaded without mishap.

We left that night, and a day and another night later reached Ontong Java. This is a huge atoll, which by some calculations is reputed to be the largest in the world. One side cannot be seen from the other and when you sail from south to north, the south disappears completely before the other end comes into view. On this occasion we visited just the main island of Leuaniua.

After Sikaiana Dudley had been a bit sick and we just thought it was seasickness, but by the time we reached Ontong Java, even in the calm of the atoll, he was still vomiting. Severe pain then set in and there was rigidity of his abdominal muscles, so I realised he was in a serious condition. We were now at the farthest extremity of our journey, there was no place for a conventional aircraft to land and no helicopters were in the islands, even if they could have flown this far, so there was nothing for it but to turn the ship round and sail back to Auki as fast as we could. However this was an important trip for Dudley as he had to deliver election notices, as well as hold court. As a government officer I could deliver the notices, but not being a magistrate the criminal cases would have to wait for the next trip. I did a very quick clinic, delivered the election notices and within a couple of hours we were sailing as fast as we could directly back to Auki. I gave him something mild to relieve the pain, but every time the ship lurched he winced in agony. We only carried limited supplies on the ship and during the journey I used up everything I had, but still he was in pain. When we reached Auki he was jaundiced as well and I was beginning to fear the worst.

We flew him to Honiara where Tony felt his problem was too complicated for him to deal with, so Dudley was evacuated back to England. When they did come to operate they found he had perforated a gastric ulcer which had also eroded the gall bladder. Fortunately the omentum had wrapped itself round the perforation so preventing peritonitis, and saving his life.

This was not quite the end of the story though for while Dudley was recovering in hospital he fell in love with one of the nurses that had been looking after him. We were all pleased to see him back again, but when he told us this extra bit of news there was considerable excitement. Chris subsequently came out to the islands and they were married. The wedding was held in Honiara so the large group of us on

Malaita hired a ship for the occasion and our daughter Lucy was one of the bridesmaids. Weddings in the islands are always very special affairs and this one was no exception.

* * * * *

With such a hurried visit to Ontong Java, I needed to go back again. Normally a ship went there only once a month, so one either made a brief visit and came back with the same ship, or you would need to wait there for the month until the ship returned. This would have been too long but the elections were particularly convenient as intervals for the process were set by law so although it was expensive to send another ship after only a week, this had to be done. So I took the opportunity to travel up with the first ship, remain in the atoll for the week and return with the following one. We had admitted several cases of TB and I wanted to examine the whole population for any more suspect cases. To get around I took my dinghy and outboard up with me, strapped to the ship's deck.

This was perhaps one of the most idyllic trips I ever made as atolls have the allure of the Pacific ideal of long sandy beaches, coconut trees and clear blue sea and Ontong Java certainly had all of these in profusion. The coconut is the main produce and when I visited it was the time for collecting up the nuts so many of the islands were occupied. Everywhere I went I was welcomed by a green coconut to quench my thirst and the people gladly rested from their labours while I asked them about any chronic coughs and examined their chests. Both men and women wore nothing on their tops so there was no need to go through the palaver of getting people to undress.

Although wearing little clothes, viewed from a distance the women look as though they are clad with a pair of dark blue bloomers under their sarongs. On closer inspection these are seen to be tattoos from the waist downwards to just above the knees. The tattoos consist of a fine pattern, generally of a fish motive, joined head to tail circling the whole body, with a series of these lines done one above the other. No part is missed out including between the buttocks and into the pubic area. Tattooing is a painful enough process, but to have so much of the body covered and especially these delicate parts of the anatomy reveals the tenacity of these women.

Collecting the coconuts was seasonal work, and when they were not doing this the people returned to one of the main island centres on Pelau, Avaha or Leuaniua. The latter was the only island with a clinic and the medical assistant had a particularly responsible job because of the infrequency of visits and the lack of an airfield to evacuate any emergencies. There was a rule that all first-time pregnant women, or those that had a difficult birth before, had to go to hospital in Auki to await delivery. However ships get cancelled and babies came early, so I taught the medical assistant how to remove a retained placenta, as this was the most common emergency he was likely to face. I was all for supplying him with a vacuum extractor to manage the less-serious obstructions, but at this higher authority in Honiara drew the line.

It was interesting to live with a Polynesian community for a change and realise how in the same way that the Melanesian is entirely adapted to the jungle and the land, the Polynesian is with the sea. Every morning the canoes would go out early to fish, while the women prepared the food, wove fresh thatch from coconut fronds, or did the washing. Fish or seafood was eaten at every meal and if an illegal fishing boat with its more total way of catching fish entered their waters, it had a devastating effect on the whole community.

The bliss of their island life was however disturbed by an ever-present nuisance, the rat. There was an original rat (*Rattus exulans*) which travelled as a stowaway in their canoes and came all the way with migrating peoples from Southeast Asia. This however lived on the crops they grew and did not appear to affect the endemic wildlife. Unfortunately the European ships, as well as bringing explorers, exploiters, missionaries and colonialists, also brought the European rats (*Rattus rattus* and *Rattus norvegicus*).

On Ontong Java they could not store food without it getting nibbled and the rat seemed to be everywhere. I used to lie on my camp bed in the clinic, looking up at the beams, to see the rats scampering about without any fear of attack. Even if you hung your bag of food on a piece of string from the ceiling the rats still seemed to be able to get at it, and one night they ate through the foil of my electric razor, a most unlikely source of nourishment.

Rats are a problem on all the islands, but on the Polynesian islands they have no predators and so have multiplied to the detriment of the people and wildlife. On Guadalcanal and Choiseul are found two of the largest true rats in the world, rivalling those found in the southern part of China. The larger of the two nests underground and can grow to the size of a cat. It lives on forest nuts, fruit and edible insects and is preyed upon by the Pacific Ground Python (*Engyrus (Candoia) carinatus*).

CHAPTER FIFTEEN

Miracle children

The month of June 1972 was now upon us, a month I would never forget for the rest of my life. Following Dudley's wedding there had already been one tragedy and soon there was to be another.

His best man at the wedding, another district officer called David Adams, was out on tour off the coast of Malaita. He was a quiet and sincere man absolutely devoted to the people and his job. David was on his way to sort out a problem that had arisen in one of the villagers but he never arrived at his destination. What exactly happened nobody knows, somehow he fell off the boat and being a non-swimmer was drowned. It is thought that he might have hung a bucket over the side of the boat to collect some water and the sudden weight of the full bucket pulled him over the side. Search as they could the crew never found him and his body was never recovered.

Then quite unexpectedly we had a cyclone. The Solomon Islands are in the cyclone belt so cyclones are expected at the end of the year, but in June we had one of the worst that ever affected the islands. Being quite a long island chain normally only one part is badly affected, but this one followed the passage between the two main island chains, called the "Slot". It zigzagged from side to side down the Slot, causing devastation on every island. On Malaita we could see the glass louver panes in our house bending under the strain of the wind and were just about to open them for fear they would shatter with devastating effect when the wind began to drop. Our garden though was completely destroyed and the roof of the veranda torn off its posts.

At the time I was due to go to Honiara for a meeting so as soon as it abated I went across. The plane flew over the intermediate islands of Gela, which are right in the middle of the Slot and took the full force of the cyclone. Normally covered in tall jungle trees, the scene was incredible, it was as though a huge lawn mower had cut all the trees down like blades of grass, there was not one left standing. Fortunately the islanders make their houses of wood and leaf thatch so are not killed by falling masonry. The loss of life was remarkably small the only deaths being of fishermen out in their canoes, the most dangerous place to be when a cyclone comes.

This was just a few days before Bridget and the children left to go back to England. Bridget had received news that her Father had cancer and although not yet terminal she wanted to spend time with him before he started to go downhill. I travelled with them to Honiara to see them off. Bridget was very sad at leaving so I told Lucy to look after her Mummy and our new baby, which was expected in three months time. They travelled first to Hong Kong where Bridget stayed with her cousin and then they were to go on to England via India. Meanwhile I returned to Auki to complete the packing up of the house ready for my departure at the end of July.

I spent more time at the hospital than usual and there was one particularly sad case I can still remember. A young woman in obstructed labour was brought in to us in a shocked condition already bleeding badly. We gave her several pints of blood, which as we had no blood bank had to be taken fresh from relatives or our panel of volunteers. I did a laparotomy with a view to doing a Caesarean section, but once inside I was greeted with a large black mass instead of the smooth uterus. When I touched it there was a rush of blood and the baby immediately behind. It soon became apparent that she had a huge tear the length of the uterus and the only thing that had held it together and saved her life was the peritoneum. The baby was already dead and

01. Volcanoes of Western Solomons; Kolombangara cover, Rendova above.

02. On tour on Malaita,
Bridget with Sophy.

03. "Who now pikanini?" waiting for the doctor.

04. Married and unmarried woman in Kwaio, Malaita. Only when a woman is married does she wear a loincloth or skirt. The small hut on the left is where a woman has to stay when she is menstruating.

05. A Polynesian family cutting copra on Ontong Java. Both men and women are tattooed, but more so the women with most of the tattoo between the waist and the knees, and therefore hidden from view. Note the booby chick kept as a pet and source of food.

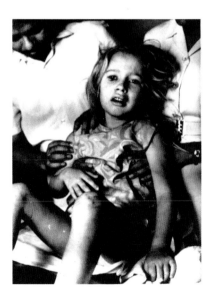

06. The picture that was seen around the world. Lucy receives treatment in hospital immediately after the aircrash. (With permission of Associated Press).

07. Lucy and Sophy after the accident with Heti Bea.

08. Royal visit to Gizo. War canoes getting ready to escort the launch back to the Britannia.

09. Choiseul dancers. Note the pan pipes and the large number of arm rings worn by the dancer in the front, indicating his chiefly status.

10 a & b. Chiefs'
skull place on Vella
Lavella.

11. Yam house in the Trobriand Islands,
Papua New Guinea.

12. Interior Guadalcanal,
Tetekanji.

13. Na Poli village in Tetekanji. Grass skirts were always worn by the women before being superseded by material.

14. On the summit of Makarakomburu (2447 m), highest point in Solomon Islands. The trees are gnarled and moss covered in the mountain forest.

15. Crossing a flooded river on Guadalcanal, John Tagabosoe on the right.

16. Tikopia.

17. Anointing the food bowl in Tikopia.

18. Custom queen contestant draped with strings of shell money.

the uterus beyond repair, so I had no alternative but to do a hysterectomy. I thought of the customary way of making the woman go into the jungle to deliver by herself. With proper antenatal care she could have been given a live baby and been able to have had several more, now she was lucky to be alive and would never be able to become pregnant again.

It was at another of these difficult obstetric problems I was worrying over when the news came through. I had got up that Thursday morning and listened to the BBC World News as I always did. The reception was poor, but I did hear fragments of something that sapped me of all my energy, I just sat there numb and motionless. There had been a plane crash the evening before, near Delhi Airport, the 14 June 1972. I could not properly hear which airline or where it had come from. The first announcement said there had been quite a few survivors, so it did not sound that bad, even if it had been the right plane. I went to work trying to push it out of my mind, re-assuring myself that there were lots of flights into Delhi that evening. Bridget had taken the detailed itinerary with her so I could not find the flight number but knew that 14 June was the day they were scheduled to fly from Hong Kong. I went to work and said nothing, but one of the doctors working with me, asked in his quiet way,

"Did you hear the news Roger, there was something about a plane crash",

"Yes" I said, "But I could not hear which airline it was"

He didn't say any more, not wanting to alarm me, but still it had the same effect, I started to worry even more.

By chance the travel agent that had made our bookings was in Auki on a visit, so I asked him if he had heard the news and whether it was their flight. He prevaricated,

"I can't remember which flight they were on but they might well have changed planes as they had open tickets. I will telex the airline office in Australia to find out."

By now I was becoming convinced that it was the plane that

Bridget and the children were on, and began to reason out all the implications. I tried to work but I couldn't, yet we had a woman who was labouring badly and I knew we had to decide whether to operate or not. I told my colleague that I would come back and review the patient later, but I wanted to go home and pack in case the worst should happen.

I had just straightened everything in the house and packed my suitcase when there was a knock on the door. It was Dudley and Chris. Dudley, in his very forthright manner and without hesitation told me that the plane had crashed,

"Bridget and Sophy were missing believed killed, but Lucy had been found alive."

The message had come from Hong Kong; Bridget's cousin had enquired direct from Delhi and then phoned the High Commissioner in Honiara. Chris flooded with tears while I just stood there in a trance. I knew that it had really happened, this was the final confirmation, the awful truth.

I left straight away and flew to Honiara to catch the first flight out to Australia and on to India. Special arrangements had been made for me to board the Air Nauru flight the following afternoon, which does not make a scheduled stop, but before boarding the Chief Secretary brought me a long telegram from India and said,

"Lucy had positively identified Sophy as a survivor, they both had broken legs. Sophy had a broken arm and was also unconscious."

I so wanted to be with them soon, but even by the fastest means possible it still took until Sunday (three days after the crash), before I finally reached Delhi. There I was to learn what had happened with the children and why there had been such uncertainty about Sophy.

When the children were brought to hospital in Delhi the wives of the British High Commission staff took it in turns to visit the hospital and be with them. The children had been put in different wards and the wives had worked out non-overlapping rotas for each child. Although Lucy was conscious she did not talk about her sister, so there was no suggestion that they might have been related, until by chance two of the wives were talking about their charges and realised from each others description that the girls looked like each other. So they took Lucy into the other ward, where she immediately recognised Sophy and the news was sent on to me.

On the flight from Sydney to Hong Kong I was sitting in the same row as people from New Zealand who had lost their daughter in the crash. They showed me the newspaper and the startling picture of Lucy that had been on the front page of newspapers round the world, and was headline news for several days. The expression of terror and distress on her face, overlying the beauty of innocent childhood only increased my sadness and longing to be with her. It was re-assuring to see her alive, but I worried about Sophy, especially as she was still unconscious.

The plane stopped briefly at Hong Kong where I met Bridget's cousin and heard about the happy days they had spent together. Coming into land at Bangkok it seemed that we might also have been fated as one of the engines stopped, making it a dangerous landing and with no chance that the plane would take off again. Fortunately there was another plane, with many spare seats, leaving a few hours later so eventually we reached Delhi in the early hours of Sunday morning.

I went to see the children straight away and was amazed at how well Lucy looked, apart from her leg in plaster. She did not have the slightest mark or scar to indicate that she had survived a plane crash in which everybody else, except Sophy and another little girl had been killed. Sophy however was still semi-conscious, with her left leg strung up on traction and her arm in plaster. She would wake up every now and then, give a pathetic whimper and fall asleep again. I had seen this state before in so many hopelessly brain-damaged people, I feared the worst.

Nobody had explained to the children what had happened and one of the first things Lucy asked me was "Where is Mummy?"

I had just arrived after an exhausting and stressful journey and did not feel I could break the news to them until I had been able to rest a little and gather my thoughts. I was so relieved to see the children, all my feelings went out to them, Bridget was dead, but at least something of my family remained, and this must be my total concern.

After breakfast and a short rest I went back to see the children again and explain to Lucy what had happened. I told her all about the crash and how so many people had been killed, but she and Sophy were all right. I told her that Mummy had died, but she was comforted when I told her that she had gone to heaven. Lucy was four and a half and took it very well, old enough to understand, but not too old to have a deeply ingrained memory of her mother. She cried for a few minutes and then got over her upset.

I tried to talk to Sophy but she resented being disturbed, her state of pathetic whimpering turning to one of aggression, thrashing around, crying and yelling. These outbursts affected me very much. There seemed to be no change for a while, and then one afternoon I went to visit just after a Buddhist monk had taken it upon himself to bless the children. I sat with Sophy, who seemed to be sleeping. She then woke up, looked around, gave me a smile and said something in Pidgin. I was overjoyed, because I knew that if she had remembered her Pidgin, then she could have no permanent damage. Sophy had spent much of her time with local children and was therefore much better in Pidgin than ordinary English and so was able to carry on from where she had left off before the accident.

From this time on she never looked back, she became happy and talked, and was again the little girl that I knew from before. She did however resent being strung up in traction. She fought it for a while, and then resigned herself to having to lie in this strange position, until she realised she could turn it to her own advantage. With her left arm in plaster and being forced to lie on her back, there was one thing she could do very well and that was hold a chocolate bar in her right hand and push it into her mouth. She never asked about her mother, but Lucy explained everything to her in small doses, so that she could take it in. She was only two and a half so I don't think she really realised, just as long as she had love and attention, she was happy.

When my father died in Zanzibar and I was at school in England I could never convince myself about his death because I had not been able to see his body. The same feeling was now happening to me with Bridget and I went to try and find her remains.

Temporary mortuaries had been made in two hospitals and the rows of bodies were stored in makeshift coffins, surrounded by ice. When the plane had crashed it had burst into flames so many of the victims were burnt and badly disfigured. It was not a pleasant sight, and even with my medical background and familiarity with death, the rows upon rows of charred bodies is still ingrained into my memory.

I went through all the corpses trying to find some recognisable feature, but not even the skin colour could be determined and sex only by dissection. In these circumstances I thought I would be able to identify Bridget by the fact that she had been pregnant. It seemed highly unlikely that there would be another woman of six months pregnancy on the flight, but even with this unique possibility I still could not find her remains. I went back two more times and worked with the doctor to search amongst the corpses but still we could not find anything. I never did identify her.

Eventually, after all the relatives had been round and those identifiable bodies had been taken away for private burial, all the unidentified remains were cremated together at the Ghat on the bank of the river Yamuna, in the traditional Hindu manner. Although Bridget was a Catholic, I somehow felt that she would have accepted being cremated in this way, in a country she so wanted to see and felt passionate about.

From the combined ashes of the victims two urns were filled, one was buried in the same grave as her father in Devon, the other went to Gizo, and to the islands she loved. The Bishop led a procession to the cemetery on Logha Island where the ashes were buried, a wonderfully peaceful place.

The crash site was near Basantpur village on the banks of a large irrigation canal, some 25 kilometres from Delhi. The tail section of the plane was intact; impressed upon the bank of the canal, while ahead of it lay a mass of twisted and charred metal that was not recognisable as the fuselage of an aircraft. Here and there were littered seats and the paraphernalia of an aeroplane, but some personal belongings still lay around. Most of these had been taken to a place for identification, but I was able to find the children's vaccination certificates lying around the site. The ground was flat and dry with no vegetation, but on top of the baked clay was a layer of powdery sand several centimetres deep. The wreckage was scattered over a wide area, but Lucy and Sophy had been picked up some hundred feet in front of it, hurled there by the force of the disintegrating aircraft, the soft powdery sand helping to break their fall.

Their boarding passes had been found so I knew that they were sitting in row 7, which must have been where the aircraft had broken up, allowing them to be flung clear. It would seem that they were not wearing seat belts at this time as there were no marks on their bodies, and this might have saved them. Most people were preparing for landing so were either hurled forward, still strapped into their seats, or incinerated in the rear part of the aircraft. I tried to work out why Bridget was not with the children and concluded that she had probably made the seat into a bed for the two of them and then moved to another seat herself.

The plane crashed in the early evening, onto the bank of a canal that workmen were building. The foreman of the work gang found Lucy, crying for her mother and picked her up and comforted her.

Dalip Singh had been working in the fields at the time and when he saw the plane crash rushed over to find Sophy lying in front of the wreckage. He put both Lucy and Sophy in his truck and started taking them to hospital when he met an ambulance dashing to the scene. This then took them to the All India Institute of Medicine in Delhi. It was one of the most remarkable events of this whole tragic story that in India, this country of chaos and confusion, both children had been admitted within two hours of the crash to one of the best hospitals in the country. Sophy required blood transfusion to save her life, so if it had not been for this very prompt action she would have died.

A Swedish girl, a few years older than Lucy was the only other survivor. Two women, one a stewardess, had lived for a few days, but their injuries were so great they did not survive. In all 86 people died in the aeroplane, and three workmen who had been constructing the canal. It just seemed miraculous that out of the only three survivors two of them should be my children. Indeed they became known as the miracle children by the press, who followed their progress with the greatest of interest.

It was the first crash ever of Japanese Airlines (JAL) and the nation was devastated, not able to believe that something had gone wrong with one of their aircraft. They were already investigating, as were the Indian authorities and many reasons were given as to why the plane had crashed. There was a problem with the instrument landing system so whether it was because of this or for some other reason, the pilot turned off his instrument landing device and decided to make a visual approach. This was surprising as he had not landed at Delhi many times before and on this occasion the visibility was poor. It was dusk and there had been a heat haze all day, mixed with clouds of dust, making low-level objects indistinct.

Because of the heat during the day much work was done in the late afternoon and evening and to see what they were doing the canal builders lit fires over a large area. The conclusion I reached as to what happened (which differs from what the Japanese decided) was that the pilot mistook the lights lit by the canal workers with the landing lights of the airport and attempted to land. All was quite normal in the voice recording until the very last moment when the last word the pilot uttered was

"Power". He was found at the controls with the stick pulled back, indicating that he was trying to climb again, but too late, the tail slammed against the canal bank and the rest of the plane disintegrated.

The children were saved by their youth, young bodies are pliable and relaxed, and when they were thrown forward with such force they were able to withstand the impact of landing on the powdery ground. I still think of those 89 people who had died, only 3 survived, yet of those three, two were my children.

The week the crash occurred was one of international tragedy. Four days after the JAL disaster a BEA trident crashed on take-off at Heathrow killing everyone on board, another airliner disappeared mysteriously off Vietnam and in France there was a very bad train crash with a hundred dead. In the Solomons a European was drowned, a well known Solomon Islander died in tragic circumstances and a geologist returning to the islands survived an air crash in Ethiopia with a broken back.

The crash had become a major event in India, it was in the news for almost a week, cameramen disguised themselves as nurses to get into the ward to take pictures of the children, who had become the talk of Delhi. The Indian is a very sympathetic person and wherever I went, in taxis or in the hotel, they would be overflowing with genuine sadness and deep emotion. Somehow though life loses its balance, India is a country used to death, and at that time hundreds were dying from drought and in a few months many more would die in floods, but these were accepted tragedies, somehow the air-crash was different.

In all we were a month in India before the consultant agreed to Sophy being moved. JAL took out seats from the first class section of one of their planes to accommodate her stretcher and we all flew back to England. I had been rather worried how the children would respond to being in an aeroplane again and one with the same decor and uniformed staff as their ill-fated flight, but this did not trouble them at all, there seemed to be no memory of the crash itself. Sophy just smiled at everybody in her usual friendly way and Lucy was happy to play with the toys that had been given to her.

The children were in hospital in Hampshire for another month as their bones finally healed and they learnt to walk again. They resented being babies once more and having to learn to walk from the start, but this painful period did not last long and soon they were fully mobile again. They had been miracle children to the Indians and now they were to be the most important people in my life.

CHAPTER SIXTEEN

A chance encounter

It had been a devastating few months and I was totally drained of all emotion. Lucy and Sophy had now left hospital and were in constant demand from family and friends so there was never any problem with somebody to look after them. I needed a break and so decided to go away on holiday. I hardly knew Europe so set off for Scandinavia to see a part of the world I had never been to before.

It was while I was on my way from Stockholm to Uppsala that a tall, pretty blond girl waved me down. As I came to a halt her boyfriend crept out of the bushes, it was the old trick, but I had plenty of room so was happy to give them both a lift. There were the polite formalities and questions as to where they were going, then the girl noticed I was driving on the right, and asked,

"Do you come from England?"

"Yes" I replied, "I am just having a holiday, but will be going back in a few weeks time." She then followed this up,

"I am hoping to come to England to work as an au pair and improve my English."

"But your English is very good." I said.

"No I need to practice more, especially with the pronunciation."

I could hardly believe what she was saying as I needed somebody to look after the children while I did my year's course of further training before returning to the Solomons. I had already started

152

looking for a suitable person before I left and now here was the answer.

"I am looking for somebody to take care of my children while I study in London, would you be interested?"

I explained my situation, the crash and what had happened to Lucy and Sophy.

"Oh yes I would love to do it." Came her reply.

She was very excited about the idea, although I could tell that her boyfriend was not so pleased, so we exchanged addresses and I told her to think it over and then write to me with her decision.

I continued on my journey, crossing into Norway and coming back that way, but I could not forget about my chance encounter, and wondered whether anything would come of it.

It had been just the break I needed, but on my return there was not the letter from Kathy that I had hoped for. So I began interviewing the large number of young women who had answered my advert for a child minder. There was an amazing variety, from the genuine person with experience to one with long manicured nails and elegant hairstyle who had probably never looked after a child in her life. Although it was me that was doing the interviewing, another prospective candidate insisted I sat on the floor and drink wine with her, I wondered quite what was going through her mind? None of them quite fitted the bill, but I realised that I had to make my mind up, when a letter came from Sweden to say Kathy was coming.

Bridget had been dead for almost four months and it had been even longer since I had said goodbye to her in Honiara. There was a big hole in my emotions and my role had changed from supporting her with the children to now being entirely responsible for them. I was desperate for an understanding person to share my charge with and I knew that Kathy could fill this vacuum, but was unsure of how much of herself she was prepared to give. With these thoughts and uncertainties we moved into a house in Bracknell that I had just bought.

This was the first house I had ever owned and perfect for the time and situation we were in. Bracknell was one of the new towns, purposely built to be convenient and a pleasant place to live. Each residential area was designed as a complete neighbourhood with school, shops and protected ways so that you could cycle or walk without having to go on the main road. The children enjoyed having their own house and started school not far away, while I took the train every day to London. Kathy got the children ready for school and looked after them when they came home; we lived as a little family in what seemed an ideal arrangement. She had her own room and went to classes, so was able to achieve what she had come to England for.

Both Kathy and I understood the implications of us living together in this way. I found her attractive and the way she cared for the children only increased my feelings for her, but I was uncertain as to whether she felt the same for me? One night when the children had gone to bed and we were alone in the house I told her of my feelings. She was very receptive, probably knowing in herself what was likely to happen, and in a moment that seemed to last forever, she opened herself to me.

Kathy was only 19 when I met her, rather serious and grown up in her outlook on life. She was tall and slender, with strong blond hair and piercing blue eyes that were both authoritative and kindly. But she had a marvellously lithe and youthful body and with her height and stately grace stood out in a crowd, turning many an eye.

She became devoted to the children, looking after them very well, if not with a certain amount of Nordic firmness. The way in which we had shared our life in those few months made me feel that I might have found the perfect person. However she had planned her life and wanted to train as a nurse so I did not bring any pressure on her to change her mind. We had both done what we wanted and had the additional joy of finding a deep companionship with each other.

Then all too soon the year came to an end, I would be going back to the Solomons and Kathy return to Sweden to start her career. I felt somehow she would be a friend for life, not only for all she did for the children, but for how she had given of herself and helped me live again. It was a parting full of understanding, we were both going our separate ways. What would the future hold?

* * * * *

The agreement for doing the post-graduate course was that I would work for a further two tours in Solomon Islands, which I was happy about. It had been the kind of work I wanted to do and I now had a year's training behind me that I could put into practice. I knew it would have been easier to go back to the Solomons alone, but Lucy and Sophy were my family, they were part of me and I wanted them to have a childhood similar to what I had enjoyed in Zanzibar. This had been one of the happiest times in my life and there was the same opportunity in these islands. I was determined that I should bring them up and knew that in the Solomons I could do this. There were the house-girls that Bridget had trained to look after the children and I saw my future in working overseas, so the three of us returned to the islands that had become so much part of our life.

Coming back to the Solomons was like returning home. Not only had the news of the children's survival been headline news for several days, with the heart-rending picture of Lucy beamed around the world to everyone's television sets, but in the Solomons it had become the island's tragedy. Everyone knew about it, even if they could not read. No television had shown any pictures here, but by word of mouth the story was passed on so that people would stop me in the street or when I went to a village and ask me about it. As for Lucy and Sophy everybody wanted to see them and show their gratitude that they had survived. There were countless offers of help, and everybody invited the children to visit them. It was wonderful to be back to what we felt was our home.

It was even better to return to Gizo, as this was where we had been happiest, but left before we had completed our time. There were the same friendly faces in the hospital and everything was just as it had been before we left to go to Malaita those two years before.

The beauty of this part of the world never failed to impress me and this time we were allocated a house with a grandstand view of all the islands between here and Munda, a view that would command a fortune if it was in a more populous place. I settled down again to work in the hospital and district, and although we had visited all the islands before, there was so much more of interest to see.

The children went to the local school in the morning, then received extra lessons from one of the wives who had started to do this for her own children. They would speak Pidgin to their friends and behave just like Solomon Island children in the morning, then in the afternoon return to a way of life more akin to how they would have to live in the future. I was pleased I had brought the children back with me and not succumbed to leaving them in England with relations.

CHAPTER SEVENTEEN

The Susu Boat and Kolombangara

I had brought back a rigid inflatable boat (RIB) with me on this tour of duty, the first to come to the Solomons. Visiting the many islands became so much easier and faster than by government boat and I could land at all the villages not just the main ones. I would set off loaded down with petrol and return with no fuel left, but equally loaded down with fruit and produce given to me by the villagers.

It was on one of these visits, to the other side of Ranongga, that the boat got its name.

Ranongga was always difficult, there were no sheltered inlets or protecting reef and the full force of the waves broke on the beach. As I came in close to look at the waves breaking on the beach and see whether I could risk a landing, a wave broke over the stern swamping the motor and carrying the boat at a frightening rate towards the rock strewn beach. I could not start the motor again and prepared myself for the inevitable. If we were thrown onto one of the rocks the boat would be wrecked and I would have to jump out in time if I was to be saved.

Despite paddling furiously to try and give the boat some direction, the squat shape of the hull made this difficult and I resigned myself to the fate of the waves. However just then a group of men on the beach saw my plight and without hesitation waded into the sea and picked up the boat bodily with me still inside it. Carrying it though the crashing surf they plonked the boat safely down on the beach. What had been a dangerous situation for me suddenly turned into some fun for them, particularly to see this strange craft.

One of them was carrying the pointed inflatable part as it sticks out behind the stern and looking back at it as it juts out from behind the boat he shouted to the others,

"Im numba wun susu" and they all laughed.

Susu means both breast and breast milk, so translated this becomes, "This is a very good breast". So always after that the boat became known as the Susu boat. The name quickly got round so when I went to the villages the cry would go out,

"Susu boat, dokita come now."

The boat opened up all sorts of benefits both in work and recreation and one of the first outings was to climb the five and a half thousand foot peak of Kolombangara. I had so often looked across at this wonderful mountain, this time I was determined to get to know it better.

It was to be something of a celebration climb as it was the last day of the year. Setting off at the crack of dawn we had started climbing by 7 am. Reaching the campsite where people normally stayed the night only three hours later, we decided to carry on to the summit the same day. The top part was very steep and the undergrowth which was predominantly mountain bamboo, cut into our legs. The final few hundred feet were so steep that we had to use the trees to get to the top. It was almost like climbing the tree as you pulled yourself up from the roots to the trunk and then the branches, to reach out for the next tree and so on to the top. The descent was rapid and easy so that we were down again and had returned to celebrate at the party, instead of seeing in the New Year on the mountain, as we had originally intended.

After the ascent of Kolombangara this great volcano fascinated me, especially its crater. There were stories that a great salt-water lake lay inside, complete with fish from the sea. During the headhunting days people used to live inside the crater so I thought it wouldn't be too difficult to find the way in. However since the threat of attack had now gone the people had no need to venture any further than their gardens on the rich volcanic slopes so all the villages were on the coast. They climbed to the upper slopes to get bamboo and the way to the summit was well known, but nobody had gone into the crater for many years.

I travelled round the island as there were several clinics and an unusually large number of TB and leprosy patients, while at the same time ask if anybody had been into the crater. Eventually I found a man who could show me the path, he was too old to make the journey himself, but said he would tell someone the way.

We arranged a small expedition and when I had some time off set out to go into the crater. Sadly it was raining on the agreed day, flooding the river we were to follow, meaning that we could not walk up the stream. Unperturbed my two companions cut a path along the side of the valley, which in some places was sheer and dropped down to the raging torrent below. After struggling along in this difficult manner for several hours, making progress much slower than anticipated, we were able to make our way down to the river, which in its upper course was less of a torrent. We entered a narrow gorge, to be confronted by a waterfall, but my companions pushed an old tree trunk against it as a ladder, which enabled us to climb to the next level. It was very hard going, we were all tired and I realised that we would not get into the crater that day. By evening we had reached the head of the valley and towering above us was the very steep edge of the outer rim. Here there was a sufficiently level piece of ground, between two branches of the stream, so we made a leaf shelter and stayed there for the night.

After a rather uncomfortable sleep we set off to ascend this steep face and two hours later pulled ourselves to the top. We were now on a knife-edge that we followed round until we could look down into the crater. We could see the river and a pool, but there was certainly no lake and definitely no inland sea with fish in it. The way down into the crater looked even harder than what we had come up and as I did not have the time to carry on, had to be satisfied with the view. We might not have climbed down into the crater but we had been able to look into it and prove that there was no lake there.

When we got back to the village we described our journey to the old man, who said that nobody had looked down into the crater for 50 years, so this compensated for some of my disappointment. He mentioned that he would go up the mountain himself some time when the weather was better and show people the path, but I don't think he ever managed it, so the proper way into the crater is probably now completely lost.

CHAPTER EIGHTEEN

The Queen's Canoe

The Pacific islands were always popular places for visits by the Royal Family as there is less formality and they can genuinely enjoy themselves in one of the most beautiful parts of the world. Following two previous visits by the Duke of Edinburgh, it was probably his enthusiasm for the islands that ensured that such a small part of the Commonwealth should be included in the next Royal visit to the Antipodes.

Although the *Britannia* was not as large a vessel as some of the Bank Line ships that visited Gizo, the passage into the harbour was a difficult one and at least one ship had scraped itself on the reef. Much discussion therefore revolved around whether the *Britannia* should attempt to sail into the harbour or anchor outside, meaning a long journey for the Royal Party by launch, out of site from the waiting crowds on the waterfront. Finally it was agreed that the *Britannia* should come through the passage, assisted by a local pilot.

When the big day came crowds gathered on the hills and waterfront to watch the *Britannia* come into Gizo, led by war canoes and with the backdrop of Kolombangara behind. It was perhaps the most impressive spectacle of the whole visit. The event was talked about for many weeks afterwards, the *Britannia* becoming known as "Canoe blong Queen".

Not only did the visitors include the Queen and Prince Philip, but Princess Anne and Earl Mountbatten as well. It was almost like a family outing and after the formalities, speeches and official welcome the Royal Party freely wandered around the reception ground. Gifts had been presented, but the Western Solomon islanders are particularly good carvers and there were many excellent carvings on display, more for the attention of the many other visitors that had come to Gizo than the Royal Party. However these were soon noticed, particularly by Earl Mountbatten, who decided to add to his list of trophies from around the world. He was clearly enjoying himself as he held up a carved wooden mask against his face and turning to Prince Philip asked if he thought it looked like him. I think the islander would gladly have given him the carving as a present, but Mountbatten insisted on paying for it, so out came the Royal chequebook. The signature on the cheque was probably worth more than the value of the cheque itself, but the humble carver did not consider such things.

Being in such a relaxed mood it was a pity that the Royal visitors did not stay longer, perhaps have a picnic on Olasana, the island from which Lieutenant John F Kennedy and his men were finally rescued. It was a favourite island of ours with its deep-water landing and excellent coral reef. Or, perhaps they could have gone to Simbo, which packs more of interest into its small size than any island in the group. But no, all had been organised, they were to spend just part of the day in this outpost of the diminishing empire, and by afternoon the "Canoe blong Queen" had sailed away.

CHAPTER NINETEEN

Roviana

Travelling from Gizo to Munda you pass through the Wana Wana lagoon, a mass of tiny islands with many different passages, some ending in cul-de-sacs. Munda was the traditional centre for the area but its harbour is formed from offshore reefs and otherwise open to the ocean, making it not suitable for large ships. This was why Gizo was chosen as the government station. Nearby is Roviana lagoon, home to a highly intelligent and good looking people who had dominated all the surrounding islands with their headhunting raids.

Equally keen to obtain souls were the early missionaries who made Munda their base. The best known of these pioneers were the Goldies, who set up a mission hospital and school, which is still the premier education establishment in the West. Then during the war the Japanese built an airstrip, only to be ousted by the Americans, who developed it into one of their main bases. After Guadalcanal had been taken from the Japanese this was the main centre of action and remains of floating harbours and other wartime relics are everywhere to be seen. Fuel tanks from aircraft have been used to make serviceable water tanks and many a house is built on wartime foundations. Although overgrown in many parts, the network of roads and concreted areas indicate the immense size of the base here.

From the airfield huge superfortresses took off to pave the way for the advance to the west and north, while marines congregated in preparation for the next offensive, yet despite the number of troops stationed here there is account of only one liaison leading to a wartime offspring. Perhaps the authorities made sure that there was an abundant supply of condoms available because the Roviana girls are very pretty and many unions did take place.

The best place to stay in Munda was Agnes's Lodge, started by Agnes Kera a well-known character in the West. She was the daughter of an English planter (Norman Wheatley) and Roviana mother (Sambe Vido). Her brother Kitchener Wheatley was one of the first Solomon Island doctors and his daughter, Freda, followed him into the medical field as a nurse. Agnes's other brother Hughie, was also a doctor and served as a Coastwatcher on Bougainville during World War II. Sadly he was captured by the Japanese and died in captivity, probably following torture.

It was Norman Wheatley's marriage to Agnes's mother that almost led to his premature death. He arrived in the Solomon Islands in 1893, before Protectorate had been established and a very dangerous time for any man, white or black. Headhunting was at its peak and a white man's head was regarded as a fine prize, some sixty-two having lost their heads in this way. Wheatley was a shrewd Yorkshire man though and allied himself with Ingava, the powerful chief of the Roviana area. Although this probably saved him from attack by other chiefs, he had offended one of Ingava's warriors who had also taken a fancy to Sambe Vido. The would-be assassin secretly boarded Wheatley's schooner hoping to surprise him but Wheatley was always ready for an attack and shot the killer before he could cast his spear.

Agnes was in Munda during the wartime and was reputed to be the role model for Michener's Bloody Mary in his *Tales of the South Pacific*, popularised as the musical *South Pacific*. Another contender was also called Agnes, Aggie Grey in Western Samoa, who's hotel started off as a hamburger stand in 1942 to serve the U.S. troops stationed there. It appears though that both of these theories are incorrect, for when Michener was invited to Vanuatu as part of their independence celebrations he was asked who the original Bloody Mary was and named her as a Mrs Gardel, living in a village on Espiritu Santo.

Beyond Munda is the Roviana lagoon, a long ribbon of islands enclosing a stretch of water, allowing one to travel for some distance in protected waters. However this is a much shallower stretch of water than both the Wana Wana and Marovo lagoons and in many places even small powered boats cannot travel. At its eastern end it is like a lake with no opening to the sea. The last village in the lagoon is situated by a cliff, with a cave in its base. Within the cave are kept the skulls of powerful chiefs from the headhunting days.

The head is considered the most important part of the individual so when someone dies the body is taken to a small island away from all the others and covered with stones. After about a week the body has decomposed sufficiently for the skull to be disarticulated. This is the only part to be preserved, the rest of the remains being left on the grave island, with those of other individuals. The head is then wrapped in a package of palm leaves and stored in a head-house or cave. These are very sacred places and can only be visited with difficulty and the express permission of the keeper of the skulls. Only men can enter a sacred cave or head-house. We passed this cave by, but I was able to visit several others later on.

On one journey through the Roviana I stopped on an island to shelter from driving rain. When it cleared there was a log floating not far away, but then it seemed to dive down for a while and later come up again, this was no log but a crocodile. Nowadays they are a rare sight in the islands, especially in the West and when they take a person are hunted until they are caught. This one must have learnt what it could safely eat and what to avoid to have survived this long without being hunted.

Roviana also made a significant contribution to the field of sport. Children from a very early age learn how to swim and spend much of their time leaping into the water. They developed their own way of swimming using an over-arm stroke that became known as the "Roviana crawl". Alec Wickham, son of a European planter and Roviana mother was educated in Australia where his prowess in swimming and diving was noticed. In 1910 he set a world record for the 50 yards freestyle with his over-arm crawl. Copied by Australians and now known as the Australian crawl it actually took its origins from Roviana in Solomon Islands.

On the southern flank of New Georgia is an unprotected stretch of coastline, which is generally rough until the haven of Viru Harbour is reached. Going in one passes high limestone cliffs like two great pincers holding back the crashing waves, until the calm of the beautiful harbour is entered. It could be such a perfect place, but the peace was shattered by chain saws and generators, and the harbour clogged up with logs and boats; this was the base for one of the logging companies that have so desecrated the virgin forests of the islands. Like the blackbirders of old the logging companies have set up where they will and pillaged the forest with little regard for the people. The government, hungry for scarce foreign exchange has placed few controls and issued logging licences with hardly any consultation of the people.

Land ownership in Solomon Islands is quite different from the Western model as land is owned traditionally by a tribe, who then apportion it out to be farmed. There are large areas of land which are not used and appear to be owned by nobody and this is where the loggers have taken advantage. This however is not the case and with the population increasing, pressure is now being placed on all the land. Up to comparatively recently the voice of dissent was small and local, but recently there has been a co-ordinated movement against wholesale logging, instead encouraging local felling and small scale saw mills. Solomon Islands has so few natural resources it would be a shame if they allowed themselves to be exploited in the way that so many other countries have been.

My battle with the logging companies was on the living conditions for the workers. These were normally long dormitory blocks and with the simplest form of sanitation. Inspecting these facilities was one of the many duties of the doctor, as well as supporting any health services provided for the workers. There was one particular company in Shortland Islands who refused to improve the facilities of their workers and after many attempts at trying to get them to provide just the bare minimum I was forced to take them to Court. The company put up no defence, but such was the state of the law that they were only fined $30. This was a trivial fine and gave us no support in trying to raise standards in the logging camps.

Shielding the Roviana lagoon and lying not far away across the sea is the beautiful island of Rendova. At its northern end it is very similar to the area around Munda and the people are mostly related to those in Roviana, from inter-marriage and the abduction of women in the head-hunting days. Here also is Rendova Harbour where "The Commander" ran his plantation and the Americans set up a PT boat base during the war. The base was on Kukurana Island and it was here that the then Lieutenant John F Kennedy stayed.

Further to the south at Lokuru, not only does the coast change to one of an exposed shingle shore but also the people are markedly different, with wavy brown hair and a wild appearance. The most exposed part of the island is Baniata on a point facing the full force of the prevailing wind. When the sea is rough the only way to get to it is to trek overland from Lokuru, but on this occasion it was sufficiently calm for me to reach it by boat. Here the people have interesting ethnic origins, speaking a language quite different to other parts of the Solomon Islands. One can only surmise that when the waves of migrating peoples passed down the islands this isolated part of Rendova was never over-run. They might well be some of the original inhabitants of the islands.

Tragically Baniata and the surrounding area was devastated by a Tsunami in 2009. It originated from an undersea volcano and being exposed to the full force of the sea caused terrible damage to this part of Rendova, while fortunately the rest of the island was protected.

The difficult terrain of Rendova also gave rise to rumour of a hidden Japanese village. In the last days of World War II groups of Japanese became isolated from their colleagues and hid away in the jungle, still thinking that the war continued. Ingrained into the Japanese psyche is the disgrace of surrender, so there are accounts of lone Japanese who succeeded in hiding away until long after the war finished. Sightings of Japanese in Rendova continued for some time and it was said that a village had been established deep in the uninhabited interior, but whether this was just speculation or the Japanese did not survive, the village site has never been discovered.

Rendova is formed by two volcanoes, the almost perfectly shaped peak that is visible from Munda and a second more rugged mountain in the south. From it there is a long tail of volcanic outpouring that continues towards the neighbouring island of Tetepare, a wild and mysterious place that is uninhabited except for a small plantation at the extreme western end. Tetepare is generally regarded as a taboo island, full of devils so that if you try to live there you will not survive for long. At one time it supported a substantial population, but this was devastated by headhunting raids, probably the reason it is now considered taboo. However this might not just be due to devils as nowhere is there a decent anchorage or good village site. On the surface the Solomons appear to have considerable space for expansion of the population, so different from other Pacific Island nations, but much of the land, such as that on Tetepare, is not productive.

CHAPTER TWENTY

Valery

When we first met Valery it was with some apprehension. Arriving first in Honiara we had asked around for help with the children as Bridget wanted to work again. Somebody's house-girl knew somebody else who knew somebody who knew of two girls looking for work. From this rather roundabout recommendation we met the girls, they were intelligent, spoke good English and were entirely dependable. We could not believe our luck.

They were with us for a month, then quite suddenly told us that they had to go back to school. We hadn't realised they would only be with us for a short time, but one of the girls told us she had an auntie who was good with children, so we agreed to see her.

On the appointed day Valery arrived, barefoot and wearing a dress that had seen better days. Her hair looked like she had been dragged through a hedge backwards and an aroma of eau-de-sweat surrounded her. She was like a wild woman who had just emerged from the jungle onto the streets of Honiara. At first we were unsure about taking her on, but as she had been recommended we decided to give her a trial. Bridget was patient and taught her how to manage the children. Soon she settled into domestic life and even began to smarten herself up a bit.

Solomon Islanders have a natural way with children and Valery was no exception. She was always there for them and they were never too much trouble. Some times I used to feel that she was too soft with Lucy and Sophy, but this did not have the same effect as not disciplining a child in Britain. Although it seemed that the children could do what they liked, they didn't take advantage of the situation and respected the freedom they had been given. Lucy and Sophy played with the Melanesian children and fitted in as though they were exactly the same as them.

Children are common property in Melanesia and often when I asked Valery where Lucy and Sophy were she would say they were in such and such a house, or playing with some particular friend. I should have been worried but there was never any need, they always came back at meal times and there was always somebody keeping an eye on them, wherever they were.

Valery was never a substitute mother because of this community sharing of children, but one day I noticed that she was getting a little plump and when I enquired she said she was pregnant. I asked her who the father was, she told me his name, but then followed it up by saying that she did not want to marry him. Having children before marriage was so common as to be almost the norm. It reminded me of my medical student days delivering babies in the then Liverpool Road branch of the Royal Free Hospital, where there was a large West Indian community. Most of the black mums were in their late teens and unmarried because it was necessary for a woman to prove that she was able to have children before a man would marry her. The paternity of the child was not that important and the husband would have no qualms about accepting his wife's illegitimate offspring.

The pregnancy went smoothly and Valery delivered a baby girl she called Cara, after Lucy's second name. Naming children in the Solomons was always a rather sudden affair, parents never thinking about what to call the child until after it had been born, with the consequence that anything might be used to call the child. I remember one was called "Primus," after a well-known make of pressure stove used in the hospital to boil up the instruments. Popular names were those of former missionaries, so there were lots of Goldies in the Munda area and Wilsons after a former bishop of the Melanesian Mission. Even British hero's name were given, Nelson was one of the favourites. Often the midwife or the doctor's name would be chosen and on a few occasions I was confronted by a namesake that I knew nothing about.

Once when I was on tour a sick child was brought to me which I wanted to take back to hospital, so I asked the mother in Pidgin.

"Wanim nam blong im?" (What is his name?)

The reply came back, "Weba".

So I tried again, "Wanim nam blong im?" with exactly the same result. The nurse then explained that when the child had been born the mother had used my name (it was always pronounced Weba), quite unbeknown to me. I must admit, seeing this malnourished and weedy specimen I was not particularly enamoured with the choice of name for this future citizen.

But perhaps the strangest name I ever came across was "Sandpaper". What was this poor child going to do when it grew up and found out what it was called!

We had actually chosen the name Cara, partly because of its Irish connections, as Bridget had Irish origins, but now this Irish association was to be incorporated into the Solomons. Cara actually means parrot in the Roviana language, but Valery was unconcerned, to her Cara was the name she wanted to call her daughter and this was how she was known.

The arrival of a new baby was a major event and Cara became the focus of attention in the community of mothers and children. She was equally popular with my children, especially Sophy, who despite her young age would struggle to pick up Cara and try and nurse her. Valery, although concerned would never stop her, and fortunately Sophy's uncertain gait, as she struggled with the extra weight, was more secure than it at first appeared.

I thought Valery would have learnt from her first experience of getting pregnant by a man she was not particularly fond of, but no, she was soon pregnant again. This time the possibility of marriage was more likely, but then the man pulled out and Valery had a second illegitimate daughter. She called her Lara, after Sophy's second name.

Valery stayed with us all the time. When we moved back to Honiara she came with us and throughout the ten years of our time in the islands she was the most faithful of house staff. When we finally left I gave her extra money and most of our household things, so that she could be independent with her two daughters.

Later I heard that she had got married, but as with her other two, the choice of partner had not been a good one. She became ill, her husband didn't take care of her and neglected to seek medical attention. I never found out what the illness was, she was always the healthiest of people when she was with us, but so serious was it, that hardly into her thirties, Valery died. The girls and I were quite shocked to receive the news; she had been an important part of our lives and would always be in our memories of Solomon Islands.

* * * * *

A few years later I had the opportunity to go back to the West and hiring a canoe from Munda rode across to Rendova to talk to Valery's family and visit her grave. It was a sad occasion as a group of girls took me along a path right by the shore, to a quiet grove where she had been buried. It was beautifully situated at the old village site, near to where her grandfather was buried. The girls decorated the grave with flowers, and brought a sense of new life to a place where life past was remembered. It was a pleasant spot to be laid to rest, but hard to think that this was where a person who had been so alive when we last saw her, was now in the ground.

I gave my condolences to her parents, but in the society of which she belonged inheritance was matrilineal so it was her maternal uncle who was responsible for her. Matrilineal descent is common in several of the islands of the West as well as on Santa Isabel and parts of Guadalcanal. Inheritance is passed down the female line, but it was the woman's brother who held the power. Valery's uncle was a pastor who had been born with a withered arm. I had met him several times before as he took his responsibilities very seriously and always wanted to make sure Valery was alright. I asked him about her children, they had not stayed in the village as I assumed, but had been adopted by different families, one in Honiara and another the whereabouts I was not told. So on my return to Honiara I found Cara, well cared for and looking like a younger version of her mother.

As to Valery's grave I knew that the custom was to make a proper tomb with cement, so I asked how much it would cost and in a rather utilitarian fashion was told that two bags of cement would be required, as well as some money to make a feast. This was always the traditional way of honouring the dead, but it had not been performed before as Valery's husband, who should have born the responsibility, had abandoned her. The following year I made my final visit to the Solomons and coming across to Rendova there was a new cement grave with "Valery Panda Hite" written on it. Rendova was a beautiful place to be buried, I was just sad that she had died so young.

On this visit I discovered that a family on Kolombangara was looking after Lara. She was the splitting image of her mother, even to her mannerisms; a new Valery had taken her place. It could only happen in the Solomon Islands that these children were so readily looked after and I left the islands content that something of the kind and devoted Valery would continue to live on.

CHAPTER TWENTY ONE

The ancient stones of New Georgia

It was now several years since I had first been to Paradise. As I came this way again I could imagine the mighty war canoes coming out to meet us for the anniversary celebrations, but now on entering the estuary all was quiet. Gone were the throngs of people, the village seemed empty, even more so than on my last visit. The flush of enthusiasm for the CFC church was wearing thin, but the place had not been abandoned and some of the houses had recently been re-thatched. Cornelius the Medical Assistant was still here, and greeted me with a very sick child that required intra-peritoneal transfusion. We visited Jella in the afternoon, I spent the night in the clinic and then the following day took a guide to lead me through the jungle to the Mase terraces. I had been told about these remains of extensive agricultural terracing, so I was intrigued to see them for myself.

We crossed a gentle hill and then went down to the Mase River where straight away the first terraces were visible. Like small walls, completely overgrown with bush, they were not very obvious, but later we came to more substantial ones some 5 feet high, banking up a level area of ground behind them. There were generally only one or two terraces, but occasionally three, not going very high up the hillside and situated near small streams which had fed them. It certainly looked as though they had been built to grow paddy rice, but all the oral evidence from the old people indicated that they were constructed during the 16 and 17ᵗʰ century for growing taro, before the sweet potato had been introduced. Their maintenance was a full-time business, ensuring that the right amount of water fed the plants, draining off the excess to prevent the taro from rotting in the ground. The whole area, called Kusaghe, was in the crater of an extinct volcano, with a narrow gorge entrance that could easily be defended. This was important during the headhunting days, but when this threat diminished and a cash economy developed on the coast, the area was abandoned. Taro was replaced by the sweet potato (an introduced crop from South America) which did not require the labour intensive aquaculture and terracing, so the people moved to the coast.

On a visit to the Cook Islands I saw agricultural terracing climbing up the hillside, very similar to what I had found in Kusaghe. It must have been very ancient, but was still maintained in beautiful condition, with water channels directing the overflow from one level to that below, while rows of sprouting green taro thrived in the rich soil. This must have been exactly how the Mase terraces looked in former times, how impressive it was to find such terracing in its living state.

In several places there were standing stones about a metre or less in height. These were sacred stones and food would have been placed next to them for the spirits. The stones had been shaped, but were not as large or as finely worked as those I was subsequently to visit at old Munda. This was some distance into the jungle from present day Munda and contained large well-worked stones, rectangular in shape.

We followed up the river to the main village site and then climbed to Gegere, where there was a fortified hill and ramparts. This was a defensive position where the people gathered to protect themselves, hurling rocks onto their attackers. Further up and to one side was the most intriguing item of all I had seen, the snake stone. This was a rock about one metre high, etched with the outline of a snake and flower design. It depicted the good snake Nggavovavae, warming himself in the sun. The snake is said to have originally come from Kolombangara, crossing the water and following along the coast until it came to Kusaghe, where it is forever engraved in stone.

We came back to the river and built a lean-to shelter where I spent a very pleasant night under the stars, contemplating all that I had seen. This was the only example of a petroglyph I knew of anywhere in the Solomons, while terraced agriculture has only been found in Kusaghe, on Kolombangara and Rendova. Were the people who had lived here, fortified the hill and made the terraces continuing an ancient culture they had brought with them from somewhere else? One finds stone carving in parts of Indonesia, particularly in Sumatra, Sumba and Flores and terraces are made for growing rice. Could the villagers have been the remnant of a people that had migrated from these parts, or had the ancestors of the present day inhabitants developed a high degree of agricultural practice and an art form by themselves, that has since been lost? The answer was like the sleep that soon engulfed me, a nothingness from which there was no solution.

CHAPTER TWENTY TWO

The skulls of Vella Lavella

Vella Lavella got its Spanish name from the early European explorers, although there is no record of Alvaro de Mendana visiting this part of the Solomons. It praises the beauty of this island, which it certainly has, especially in the northern part. There are numerous long ridges of land jutting out into the sea, with idyllic villages set on strategic positions, looking down on tranquil inlets. In addition it has one of the most amazing natural sites to be found anywhere in the islands.

Walking in from Paraso we followed up a river, which after a while became noticeably hot, so we had to continue across country. From the jungle we had been passing through, it suddenly opened up into a vast cleared area where only Pandanus grew. There was a strong smell of sulphur, with streams of boiling water and mud blowholes. I had been to Rotorua in New Zealand, with its boiling mud and geysers, but this covered a larger area and was virtually unknown except to the islanders in these parts. The star attraction was a boiling cauldron of ever bubbling water some 50 feet in diameter.

Vekalo, the Vella Lavella language is of the Papuan group, quite different from the Austronesian languages of most of the other islands. The ancestors of the present day people probably came to these islands a very long time ago and successfully prevented subsequent invaders from taking over their island. They have a unique verbal history, including one story, which although quite improbable, I found myself almost believing.

A man with a bird's head, known as the Kesoko terrorised the local population, which he killed and ate. His likeness is portrayed on carvings both here and in the Eastern Solomons. I listened to the story, for story telling is an important part of life in the islands, but just assumed it to be another tale, dreamt up to frighten people. Then to my surprise the next day I was taken to a small muddy islet heaped over with stones and littered with skulls. There in the middle was a most peculiar skull; it was about the same size as a child's cranium but had a long bony beak protruding from the front. This they told me was the skull of Kesoko, the birdman.

Apparently the Kesoko had gone unchallenged, capturing and eating unfortunates as they worked their land or paddled around in their canoes. Then the people organised themselves and set about hunting him down. It took a long time, but eventually they succeeded in luring him into a trap, where he was killed. So they brought him to this island and put him here with the skulls of his victims. The island has been a taboo place ever since.

I was intrigued, it seemed so real and here was the evidence, the skull of what looked like a kind of human but with huge beak protruding from the front. I took photographs from all angles and showed them to people in the museum in Honiara, but nobody was able to explain the mystery. Fascinated I made a special visit to the Natural History Museum in London when I was home on leave and went round all the exhibits to see if I could find an explanation for the skull. There were some huge storks that had skulls with something of the same shape, but despite the size of the bird the cranium was considerably smaller. Then quite by chance I walked past the whale and dolphin section and saw it, there it was, the skull of a dolphin! Its cranium is very similar to that of a human, but is drawn out in front to a bony beak. I had solved the mystery, but in many ways this brought an anti-climax to the story, it was not the skull of a birdman, but of a dolphin.

I wondered who had thought to do this and why? Did they want to perpetuate the story and finding a dolphin's skull realised the similarity to the mythical Kesoko, or did they not know that it was the skull of a dolphin and with the story ever in their memory assume that this was of the slain beast? I never went back to this part of Vella Lavella, but even if I had I suspect that I would not be able to find anyone who could tell me. The skull had been there many years and the hoaxer was probably long since dead.

* * * * *

The western coast of Vella Lavella is more exposed and rough seas can make the passage difficult, but the Susu-boat was ideal and I was able to visit the clinics and villages in this part. As well as the mysterious Kesoko I had also heard of sacred places where the skulls of ancestors were kept and so asked around if anybody knew where they were. As the people were now all Christians there was no taboo about visiting them, but similarly they were ashamed to show me, because they felt this had been an unfortunate period in their past when instead of the Christian God they had worshipped their ancestors.

The people showed me two sites on the beach where there were a few skulls but this did not fit with the description I had heard of a large collection in a purpose built site. I asked if there were any more and after some hesitation an old man led me to a hillside, through undisturbed bush, to a place where there was a high ledge covered with skulls. Some were surrounded with customary money and treasures to indicate their importance, while others had fallen out from the ledges built to house them. I was particularly fascinated by some wooden carvings, of a design I had not seen before. It was amazing to see these treasures lying undisturbed in the jungle and I told the old man not to bring anybody else here unless they were from the museum or a government official. So many of the treasures of the islands have been taken by visiting yachts and sold for large sums of money, I did not want these valuables to be lost as well.

CHAPTER TWENTY THREE

The islands next door

It was surprisingly easy to hire a canoe and travel across the channel that separated Shortland Island from Moila point, the southernmost part of Papua New Guinea. I was dropped on rather a dismal beach and began to walk to Buin when along came a truck and stopped next to me,

"Are you Dr Webber?" the driver of the truck enquired.

On the off chance I had sent a letter into the blue, addressed to the medical officer in Buin saying that I would be coming and would be interested to discuss common medical problems with him. I never expected my letter to arrive or even if it did, for him to organise a meeting party, so this was a very pleasant surprise.

Buin had little to offer, but my new found medical colleague was most helpful and offered to send his truck with me to Kieta, the administrative capital of the Province. The rugged road passed through red soil areas similar to parts of Malaita, but on a grand scale, as we climbed into the mountains. The people were that intense black of the Shortland Islanders and it was easy to see how these people had dominated this part of Bougainville and spilled over into the neighbouring islands off the southern coast.

The road became very rough as we climbed above the forest into bare mountains near the 2251 metre peak of Mount Takuan Taki. Soon we came upon the most unlikely of sights, the giant opencast copper mine of Panguna. The top of the mountain had been progressively cut away and huge vehicles that made even a railway engine look small, carried the ore to great holes in the ground, from where it went to the crushers. The contrast between the islanders living in their simple houses, scraping a living from what they could grow on the hillsides, to this monstrosity of modern man's search for wealth was enormous and I was not surprised to find that this became, in time a matter of controversy. Not only was the mine desecrating the heart of the island, but all the proceeds gleaned from the mine went to the foreign company and central government. Even most of the workers were from other islands, housed in the purpose built town of Arawa.

The islanders received very little from this devastation of their island, their complaints falling on deaf ears. Driven beyond breaking point they opposed the mine in every way they could, with in the last resort military action. I was to make another visit to Bougainville some years later, but this was just before the situation got out of control and a state of emergency declared. Fighting took place, but the dispute was never solved, forcing the mine to close in 1989 and the greatest single source of wealth for Papua New Guinea to disappear.

Coming down from the misty peaks of the Panguna mine there was a fine view out over Arawa and Kieta. Arawa was like the suburb of a modern city built in virgin forest with no thought of merging it into its environment. In contrast Kieta, although small, was pretty and a pleasant place to spend a few days. I thought for a while though that I might not have been able to go any further as I had technically entered the country illegally. I went to the immigration who were dismayed at the way I had come. They threatened to deport me for not registering as soon as I entered the country, but I pointed out that there was no immigration in Buin and it had taken me these few days to reach Kieta, the official port of entry. Realising that my intentions were reasonable and I had visited the medical officer in Buin, who was able to confirm my story, they stamped my passport and officially let me in.

* * * * *

At the most eastern end of Papua New Guinea, where the big island comes to a point and a sprinkling of smaller islands looks like they are trying to form another chain parallel to the Solomon, are some small islands north of the Dentrecasteaux, that have risen to international fame. These are the Trobriand Islands, the scene of the first in-depth anthropological study by Malinowski in his famous book, *Argonauts of the Western Pacific.*

Malinowski, born in Poland in 1884 was destined to become a scientist or philosopher but influenced by Sir James Frazer's study of religion and magical practice in his monumental work *The Golden Bough,* came to London to study anthropology. During World War I he was able to realise his ambition and made his way to New Guinea and the Trobriands to study a tribal society in detail. A brilliant linguist he could converse in the local language, undertaking his classic study based on observation and interview. He lived in a tent for the two years he was there, setting a pattern for budding anthropologists of the future. He recorded in detail the Kula cycle that trades red shell necklaces in exchange for white shell bracelets around the islands, special large dugout canoes being prepared for the annual trading cycle.

The Trobriands are flat coral islands, densely inhabited with a strong village structure. Society is centred around the yam and each village has yam houses, which are beautifully decorated in red and white motives and further enhanced with the false cowry shell (*Ovulidae*), adding a pure white lustre to the design. The living houses are made by bending over rows of canes to a central ridge, which is then loosely thatched with Pandanus leaf. These houses are quite small and arranged round the yam houses, which hold the position of importance in the village. Each village consists of only about 20 or 30 houses, separated from each other by a good distance, to avoid land disputes.

The people are small and dark brown with loose curly hair, although you also find some with paler skins and long wavy hair. Life revolves around the growing of the yam and at harvest a great feast is held, which rather like St. Valentine's Day gives licence to the women to court the men, except that it goes further than just declaring their feelings. The women are unusually promiscuous and seek sexual gratification, even going so far as ganging up on a man and holding him down until he performs. It was the annual yam festival that was written about by Malinowski in his *The Sexual Life of Savages in North-Western Melanesia* that became popular reading when it was published.

I had made friends with a local politician so on New Year's day he invited me to go with him to Kuia, a beautiful island with lovely sandy beach in front of the village, where my host held his meeting. It was compact, similar to other Trobriand villages, but in addition there was a large decorated canoe used for the Kula trade. This was a dugout with single outrigger and decorated prow with an especially symbolic prow board. The people were industrially preparing leaf for weaving and were generally in a festive mood. It would soon be time for the yam festival, but I would not be there long enough to find out what my fate, as a single male, might have been.

CHAPTER TWENTY FOUR

A flower in her hair

When she walked into the room all eyes turned to look in her direction, her black skin glistened in the light and there was that smile which could disarm any man. She was not tall, slim but not the thinness of a fashion model; in every way she was beautifully proportioned. Her long sensual fingers, luscious lips and captivating smile were a sensation. She arrived in a tea shirt and short skirt that showed off her fine arms and good legs, and in its simple style put to shame the fancy evening dresses that tried to make the best of a bad job of the other women in the room.

She would stab at her hair with her wooden comb until it stood out in all directions like some headdress, and into it fix a flower, just above her left ear. This was her kind of symbol, she always wore a flower in her hair and would feel undressed without it. Generally it would be a hibiscus, but if she came across an orchid or other exotic flower then this instead would be planted in her big hair.

Born in Munda just before the beginning of the War, she was descended from headhunters and their brides, a combination that produced some of the best looking people in the islands. Perhaps it was this ancestry which imbued the passionate and violent nature of this beautiful woman that I was to later on discover.

Her birth had been something of a harrowing affair as in established labour her mother never got as far as hospital, delivering the baby on the road. This seemed to signify a traumatic early life, for when she was still a young child the Japanese invaded Munda, and made a base there. All the people fled into the forest where they had to live on wild fruit, yams and anything else they could find, while others crossed over to Rendova, which was not in enemy hands.

The American assault on Munda was protracted and difficult, but afterwards the people returned and rebuilt their houses. These however were not far from where the troops had set up base so the children wandered into camp and mixed with them. It was to be a clash of cultures with the friendly, innocent Solomon Islanders and large numbers of single battle-weary men looking for any pleasures that could take their minds off the task in question. The marines were a rough bunch and even young girls fell prey to their lust.

Good looks were not her only asset, for although mischievous she excelled at school training as a nurse at Central Hospital. Like many islanders she had a natural talent for music and joined the hospital band, which amongst its many compositions produced the well known song *Walkabout long China Town*. Music was her soul-mate in which she could get to the depths of her feelings in joy or anguish.

Always an attractive woman she became the focus of many an advance so she decided to take herself away from the social life and volunteered to work with the Gilbertese people who had been settled on Wagina Island. It was here that she found what she wanted to do in life. Hospital nursing had been rewarding but it was in the community that change could be made. Working particularly with the women she became involved in the health of the mothers and their children, realising that family planning was the key to a balanced family unit. As with the population in general there was a very high birth rate, the women had become like baby-producing machines, continuing to have children until their health and that of their offspring suffered. Family planning was a new thing in the Solomons and she became one of its first champions. I had heard about her work and realised that I needed to meet this remarkable woman.

It was in Munda that I first got to know Heti, we were planning a nurses' refresher course and I wanted her to talk about Family Planning and the methods of Health Promotion. She sat on a chair with one leg pulled up, not intending to be provocative, but having that effect anyway. I was greeted with that radiant smile that was enough to entrance any man. I seemed to find an endless source of conversation to keep me in her presence, her magnetic personality encouraging me to continue the encounter for as long as possible. We got up to look at some charts and I found myself moving ever closer to her, it was almost as though we were going to kiss, but this was not the time for such things.

It was April Fools day when the course started and I thought the joke would be on me as I had rashly invited Heti to stay with us. To my surprise she did come up to the house in the evening, rather casually as though she was coming to a hotel. The children were in bed so I showed her the spare room and cooked a light supper. Somehow the easy conversation of our last meeting was lost and she sat there calm and composed, even bored, as I tried to talk to her. I began to get a little disheartened, perhaps I had read too much into our previous meeting, perhaps she was always charming to people, why should I expect it to be any different for me?

After some period of talking without any response I decided to touch her but it was like touching a statue, then without a word she got up and went to the bathroom. I had got the signal, she was not interested and when she came back I began to apologise.

However it was like she had woken out of a dream, she didn't listen to what I was saying and bending over gave me the deepest of kisses. Astonished I pulled her towards me for more. She was now lying down, displaying to the full her remarkable body. It was so beautifully proportioned and as I touched, it had a wonderful firmness, it was like an unexplored paradise that would take an age to discover.

I both blessed and cursed the refresher course, blessed it because it had brought us together and cursed it for the extra work that it involved, when all I wanted to do was be with Heti. We were totally involved with each other, our nights were a series of impassioned delights which seemed as though they would go on for ever. I had never met anybody so sensual before, she took me to the extremes of pleasure, beyond what seemed the realms of possibility. To myself I called her the queen of sex, and now I was her subject, learning an art form that was as mysterious and wonderful as it ever could be.

When she came to stay, she arrived with just a small overnight bag and a month later she was still with me. She had never done it like this before, erring on the side of caution before moving in, but she had already felt deeply about me on our first meeting. We became totally involved in each other and didn't want to do anything else except to be totally as one.

From now on we had a common purpose, I had my medical work and Heti her health promotion, so we travelled together in the susu boat visiting all the villages in detail. The combination of my medical skills and her Solomon Island ways, she a woman and me a man, gave us the perfect partnership for work in the islands. She naturally fitted into village life, and I was happier when I was on tour rather than based in the hospital, so we probably achieved more in those years together than at any other period. There were moments of relaxation as well, when we would find an isolated island and live on only what we could get from the sea. We would dive for shellfish and find local plants, which we barbecued on the beach. We had the stars for our roof at night, washed in the waves and made love on the sand; it was perfect paradise.

Sadly paradise has its opposite and her passion could turn into an irrational and violent rage of incredible tenacity. Her depth of love she took to the absolute extremes, but her upsets and anger were as severe in the opposite direction. She would throw things round the house and drink herself into oblivion.

The next tour I was posted to Honiara and Heti was there waiting for us. We moved into a lovely house on the beach near a Solomon

Island community, she was amongst friends and Lucy and Sophy had a never-ending stream of children to play with, it seemed the ideal arrangement. The first flair of intense passion had died down so we were able to be more rational with each other. I thought we might have found the situation in which we could live a life of peace.

Sadly it did not last long, her jealousy got the better of her once more. Sometimes she would just feel moody and invent a situation to rant and rave about. This was not the life I wanted to lead, eternally trapped in a world not of my making, and thoughts began to develop of an eventual split. I still had a deep and fulfilling time with her, but I knew that sooner or later this time, like the flower that she wore in her hair, which at first was so beautiful and radiant would perish and wither away; and this was what happened.

CHAPTER TWENTY FIVE

Guadalcanal

Central district was the largest of the four districts, encompassing the islands of Guadalcanal, the Gela group, Russell Islands and the outlying Polynesian islands of Rennell and Bellona. The position of District Medical Officer Central became vacant and I was asked if I would go there. I was attracted by the varied islands that would now be my charge and it was time for Lucy and Sophy to move on to a better school, so I was happy to go to Honiara.

In the district there was normally an allocated house for the doctor, but in Honiara one took one's luck in the housing pool, based on your seniority, years of service and number of members of your family. This gave me quite a strong position, but after my previous experience of being pipped at the post by a more senior officer I was expectant of the same thing happening again. There was a lovely house right on the beach, but a little way away from the centre, that I put in for. The house was at Rove where my district headquarters was, so I felt this might give me more reason to be based here. My strongest chance though was from the danger of cyclones. There were several pictures of this house after a previous cyclone had driven most of the beach up onto the garden and done some damage to the roof, so people were frightened of this happening again. Although cyclones are frequent you didn't know where they were going to hit so I decided to take the risk and by good fortune was given this particular house.

To be away from the centre of Honiara, in a small community mainly of Solomon Islanders, not far from my work, and with a beach from which we could go swimming whenever we wanted, made my return to Honiara a pleasant one. We stayed there for the rest of the time I was in the islands and my gamble paid off because there was no cyclone that devastated the north coast of Guadalcanal during those years.

Although other islands were first visited, it was on Guadalcanal that Alvaro de Mendana de Neira landed and erected a cross on 12th May 1568, to take possession of the islands for Spain. After their success in the Americas the Spanish were always looking for new sources of treasure and an Inca story told of islands to the west where gold and silver, as well as black people were to be found. Studying these rather tenuous accounts Sarmiento de Gamboa calculated that these islands lay 600 leagues from Peru in the southern ocean, and persuaded the authorities to mount an expedition. However despite his work Sarmiento found himself on the wrong side of the Inquisition and Mendana, who just happened to be the nephew of the governor of Peru, was given command instead. Setting off with two ships the *Los Reyes* and the *Todos Santos* on 19 November 1567 they followed the calculations made by Sarmiento for one month, but on finding nothing, changed direction to head north. Almost shipwrecked on Ontong Java, they rode out a storm to finally arrive at an island they called Santa Isabel, after the patron saint of the expedition, on 7 February 1568. In order to explore the shallow coastal waters they built a 5-ton brigantine, and sailed round to the southern coast of the island. From here they could see a large land mass in the distance and on reaching it one of the officers, Ortega, called it Guadalcanal after his home village. They returned to Santa Isabel to bring the main part of the expedition back with them.

There was no name given to the islands as a whole and it is curious how they got their biblical name. Having found no gold the expedition was judged a failure when they returned to Peru, but it was the ever optimistic Sarmiento, when writing a report of the expedition, who put on the title page *The Western Islands in the Southern Ocean, commonly called the Isles of Solomon.* A shrewd and gifted man Sarmiento knew how to fire the imagination of the powers-that-be and probably hoped to convince the authorities that they had found the islands of King Solomon. So with no other name put forward they became known as Solomon Islands, which they have kept to this day. Even on independence the name was not changed, as there is no single name that describes the group. A Malaita man says he comes from Malaita, or a person from Munda that they come from Roviana, rather than the Solomon Islands. This is the same with any of the other islands, so being a God-fearing people, the Old Testament name of Solomon was the most acceptable.

Even more unusual is the name Guadalcanal. The Spanish thought the real name of the island was Sabo, but still insisted on giving the island a Spanish name. Guadalcanal is derived from Arabic, when the Moors occupied southern Spain, so by a strange twist of fate the name it is still known by today has its origins in North Africa.

Mendana sailed from Callao (the port of Lima), so on a visit to Peru I went there to see if there was any trace of his voyages and sure enough, on the wharf of Callao, there is a plaque commemorating his voyages to the Solomon Islands. He inaccurately recorded their position on his maps so it was not for a couple of hundred years that Western navigators found them again. Amongst these was Lieutenant John Shortland, who visited the islands that bear his name and surveyed the coast of Guadalcanal in 1788, a prelude to Britain declaring a Protectorate over the Solomons in 1893.

Guadalcanal at 5,302 sq. km (2,047 sq. miles) is the largest of the Solomon islands and the only one with a sizeable area of level ground. This is situated on the north coast and from which a high ridge rises to the islands' highest mountain (Makarakomburu 2,447 metres or 8,028 feet), then falls again steeply to the south. The narrow stretch of land between the mountains and the sea is known as the Weather Coast because it is on this side of the island that the full force of the prevailing winds blow. Despite this there is a sizeable population on the Weather Coast. Most people though live in the north, where the capital, Honiara is situated, a product of the vicious battle that took place here during World War II.

The Japanese in their advance south towards Australia built an airfield on the plain of Guadalcanal, which they had just finished when the Americans invaded. With only a small occupying force little resistance was offered and the island easily taken. The Japanese then landed troops in considerable numbers further up the coast to make a remarkable trek through the jungle and surprise the Americans with an attack from inland, rather than from the sea. There were some prominent hills overlooking the airfield that they set out to capture, but the Americans had fortified them already. A ferocious battle took place at what was to become known as Bloody Ridge, from the slaughter that took place there. This was one of the most desperate struggles of the whole war and resulted in huge numbers of Japanese dead.

Realising the importance of the situation, both sides brought in reinforcements to support their positions, leading to a number of naval battles. The result was that the strait between Guadalcanal and the Gela islands became known as Iron Bottom Sound from the number of ships sunk there. In all there are 48 warships resting on the bottom, 24 from each side, including 2 Japanese battleships and 8 Allied cruisers. Up to now what had been a little known island became one of the most famous battlegrounds of the war, and the turning point in the Japanese advance.

Before the war the colonial headquarters had been on the small island of Tulagi, mid-way between Guadalcanal and Malaita, but with an airfield, roads and military buildings from the American base, a new capital Honiara, was created. This was largely due to the work of David Trench the District Officer, who had worked with the American forces during the War and was responsible for restoring life to normal after the devastation had passed on. Although there is a good airfield and plenty of room for the expansion of a town, the north coast of Guadalcanal lacks a good harbour, an unusual feature for the islands. Mendana landed at a promontory he called Point Cruz and it is around this that Honiara is centred. With in-filling the reef and construction of deep water docks it is now suitable for large ships, but can be rather exposed, especially when a cyclone threatens. The derivation of the name Honiara, from *Naho-ni-ara*, "Facing the Ara," which are the E and SE Trade Winds, explains this.

Large Quonset huts left after the war formed warehouses and stores for the early town and it was not until the 1980's that the last one was replaced by purpose built structures. The Mataniko River divides the town into two halves, while most of the better housing is built on ridges that rise up behind the coastal strip. These were formerly fringing reef beneath the sea, witness to the rapid rise of Guadalcanal as it was (and still is) forced upwards by tectonic plate movement.

Potent reminders of the war still remain, including the original control tower at Henderson airfield and the fox hole of Colonel William J. Fox, after which all other fox-holes are named. Most of the war junk has now been collected up into small museums, but the odd bullet can still be found on the ground and the main ammunition dump is still sealed off. One curious hangover from the war is Number Nine, the section of the original base where the hospital was situated and to go to hospital, people still say they are going to "Number Nine."

The British Administration continued to function during the war, although the Japanese occupied most of the islands. The Resident Commissioner and the Bishop moved to Malaita, which was never invaded, while the remainder of the administrative staff became Coast Watchers. They set up bases behind the enemy lines and reported on shipping movements, giving the Americans advanced warning of impending attack. Many Solomon islanders were involved in these covert operations, acting as scouts and guides. Three of the best known were Solomon Dakei, Hugo Gigini and Silas Sitai who were at school in Fiji when the war broke out. The Americans brought them to the islands to act as interpreters and guides, but they wanted to be more involved in the war and persuaded their commander to give them instruction in the use of weapons. With their natural abilities in the jungle and intimate knowledge of the islands they distinguished themselves in many skirmishes.

The trio returned to school in Fiji at the end of 1942 with many tales to tell. Completing their education they became key members of the post-war government, Solomon Dakei joining the Medical department in charge of the x-ray in Central Hospital. But Solomon had many strings to his bow, including a love of music, so he formed a medical band and made the first recordings in the Solomon Islands. His most famous is the pidgin *Walkabout long Chinatown*, which is still perhaps the best known song in the islands. Solomon's deep base voice contrasting with the soprano voices of the nurses produced a melodious harmony.

Silas Sitai followed a distinguished administrative career, firstly in Eastern District then in Central. Here he rapidly rose through the layers of Government to become the first Chairman of Governing Council. It is likely that he would have continued to take a leading role in Solomon Islands as it progressed towards independence, but Silas was a chain smoker which probably led to his death from a heart attack at the early age of 52.

The Guadalcanal plains are a drier part of the island and has seen most development in recent times. Ideal for growing coconuts there are several plantations, while much of it has now been sown with oil palms, a foreign but successful tree. Through these trees, particularly the coconuts, fly some of the most colourful parrots to be found anywhere in the world, the Cardinal Lory (*Eos (Chalcopsitta) cardinalis*), the Palm Lorikeet (*Charmosyna palmarum*) and the Coconut Lory (*Trichoglossus haematodus*). There is a blaze of emerald greens and dazzling red as they chatter amongst the tops of the trees, then all rush off together for no particular reason. The noisiest of the birds though is the cockatoo (*Cacatua ducorpsi*) being unique to Solomon Islands. This pure white bird is a favourite pet and I remember one difficult voyage where a retired administrator, returning as a guest of the government, insisted on bringing his two birds with him on the ship. They would fly about all over the place, screeching with their raucous voices and nibbling the paint work, much to the consternation of the crew. One of these birds finally mistook its landing and fluttered into the sea, where I thought the annoyed captain would leave it to his fate. But instead he leapt from the bridge, plunging some 20 feet into the water, scooping up the pathetic bundle of feathers and beak with his huge black hands. Swimming back to the ship he brought it on board, much to the relief of its grateful owner. When we arrived in port the captain told me that he had filed a complaint about the cockatoo damaging his paint-work. If it had been any other bird it would probably have been hunted down or at least left to the sharks, but as the captain of his ship he had responsibility for all his passengers, even if they had wings and were gnawing away at his vessel.

As well as the many beautiful birds, Guadalcanal is home to one of the largest frogs in the world *Rana guppyi*. They are found in the lowland river areas of the larger islands, often hiding in caves where they feed on the dark-adapted insects found there. They can reach a weight of 1.5 kilos and are hunted by the islanders for food.

* * * * *

There were still many memories of the war and when I was in the western end of Guadalcanal, checking leprosy patients, I heard several stories of what had happened during those troubled times. The coastline in this part of the island is heavily indented and very attractive, especially around Fox Bay, with the Catholic mission station at Tangarare the main health facility. While working with the Sisters they told me about their wartime experiences.

The Japanese troops were advancing and the Sisters knew they had to escape, so they came up with a clever plan. Receiving word that they were being hunted down and knowing that they would be chased even if they went into the jungle, they spread a story around that an American submarine was rescuing people. At the dead of night they made false tracks down to the beach, walking backwards as they came back up so it looked like they had only gone one way. They then went into the jungle and hid there until the danger had passed.

The Marist missionaries had hoped to remain neutral, but the Japanese were no respecters of convention and made a point of attacking the mission at Ruavatu. There they tried to persuade the priests, Fathers Duhamel and Oude Engbrink to go through the American lines and spread tales that a large Japanese force was gathering to attack, while Sisters Sylvia and Odile were to be held as hostages. They refused to do as requested so after a week of torture and deprivation they were killed. It was actions like these and the wanton destruction of the islanders' gardens and villages that soon persuaded the Solomon Islanders which side they wanted to be on.

There was a heroic escape for the masters and pupils of Maravovo School after the Japanese landed not far away. Taking what rations they could they fled into the jungle, but these did not last long and their only hope of survival was to make their way to the American lines. It was a long and difficult journey, made more hazardous by the number of Japanese troops in the area. Several times they had narrow escapes, especially as they neared the front line. Try as they may they kept on running into Japanese patrols, then finally they took a chance and crossed through some barbed wire carrying a white handkerchief tied to a stick. To their relief this now rather exhausted group of school children and their teachers had crossed the right lines to safety.

There are many stories of bravery by Solomon Islanders during the war and their help was instrumental in defeating the Japanese. Although the Japanese had shown their prowess as jungle fighters in Burma and

Malaya, they could not compete with a people who found the jungle as natural as walking along the road. Islanders served as scouts to the American forces and assisted the Coast Watchers in reporting on enemy action. The Coast Watchers were mainly British or New Zealanders who had worked in the islands prior to the war. They served as an advanced intelligence network playing a crucial role in the Allied victory. D.C. Horton, who had been in the British Administration when war broke out stayed on as a Coast Watcher and wrote about their exploits in *Fire Over the Islands*. The western end of Guadalcanal where I was travelling was one of the most valuable Coast Watcher areas, its many rocky promontories providing good views out over a part of the sea where much of the shipping movements took place.

One of the most famous Solomon Island scouts was Jacob Vouza, who served with the American forces throughout the campaign. He was captured by the Japanese and interrogated in an attempt to find where the American troops were situated. In their efforts to extract information Vouza was bayoneted twice in the chest and through the neck, being left for dead. Remarkably he survived and crawled back to the American lines to give what information he had on the Japanese forces. After 12 days in hospital he was back fighting, decorated by both the British and Americans for his bravery. After the war he became a notable figure and the Vouza Bridge to the east of Honiara is named after him. Built by the Japanese they asked him to officially open the bridge, which he did with a long speech recalling his wartime exploits. Never one for tact or the careful use of words Vouza spared no sentiments on what the Japanese did to him at that time. Fortunately his speech was in pidgin so the Japanese delegation did not understand much of what was being said.

CHAPTER TWENTY SIX

Moro and the mountains

There were several inland villages that could only be visited by walking to them, but Guadalcanal seemed better than Malaita as the paths were more distinct and followed ridges wherever possible, although the heights one climbed to were much greater.

Much of the plain area could be visited by car, something I was not used to, but no road rounded the island because at either end steep promontories presented formidable engineering problems. So to visit the Weather Coast I flew to the small airfield of Babanikira, at the western end and walked for a week to Marau Sound at the extreme east. At Makaruka I planned to visit Moro the head of a semi-religious movement that held sway along much of the Weather Coast.

The Solomon Islands and neighbouring Vanuatu seem to have given rise to some amazing religious cults. I had already met one in the Western Solomons, while here on Guadalcanal was a practice that had no Christian basis. It tapped the religious devotion that Christianity has engendered, but emphasised the traditional ways and customs that had been handed down through the generations. Moro had set himself up as chief, living a simple life style, going almost naked, ignoring Western influence and using traditional medicines. There were many laudable ideas in what he wanted to achieve, but his lack of acceptance of any form of administration brought him into conflict with the authorities. All western medicine was refused and this was what I wanted to discuss with him. They would not allow their children to be vaccinated or their pregnant women to be checked prior to delivery. However not all their practices were bad for when I cut my leg they covered the wound with a particular kind of leaf that was as good as any sticking plaster.

I spent two nights at Makaruka waiting for Moro to return from visiting another village, but by the second day he had still not come. I subsequently learnt that he had gone right past and not called in, despite me leaving many messages for him. So the next morning I got up early and surprised him where he was staying before he was able to go off somewhere else. He clearly did not want to discuss these matters with me, but we had lost several children in his villages and I was determined to try and reach some compromise on health issues. I found him smaller and less fearful than the person that had been described to me and he listened intently to what I had to say. We had a useful discussion and with follow-up I thought I could make progress, but I was detecting that he was no longer the leader of what he had started, the power had been taken from him by his lieutenants, who were now manipulating the movement. It was going to be a more difficult task than just convincing Moro to bring any improvement in health care to his people.

In contrast to the Moro Movement the people of Tetekanji, inland from Marau Sound, had absorbed the benefits of Western civilisation, without loosing their traditional ways. They saw no need to revert to the ancient practices and had developed an enviable lifestyle that I could only but admire. Unlike anywhere else I had walked they sent their own person down to the coast to meet me, to carry my bag and take me the best way to the village. This meant that everybody knew I was coming so when I arrived all the people from the surrounding area and their medical problems were waiting, but they had prepared a good supper first.

Na Bakua was a beautiful village set on the curve of a river. Although it is the coast that at first seems the more attractive I could see why these people had chosen to live in their pleasant valley inland. It had abundant fertile land, was a little cooler than the coast and had less malaria.

The same superior organization continued for the next two days, a runner went ahead to tell the people, then the two carriers, the medical assistant and myself followed on behind. This was to Nauli and Narasi, but the following day there was an immense climb, almost straight up a sheer cliff side, until after two hours we staggered to the top and a momentous view. We had crossed from the well-organised area of runners and good meals to the real bush people of Guadalcanal. They lived in simple houses and wore skirts made from palm fronds as the people had done before the introduction of cloth. They depended entirely on the forest that surrounded them on all sides and had no need for cash or the goods that it brought. The main village was Kakendakena, the end of an exhausting day's journey.

Set high in the mountains it was a cool and wonderful place, a perfect retreat if it had not been so difficult to get to, however this was undoubtedly why it had remained so unspoilt. The old chief accommodated us in his house and was a mine of information on the old ways of the people. He showed us some stone tools that had been used before the ubiquitous bush-knife was introduced and cast aspersions on the trumped-up custom ways of Moro. I felt I had met a person who knew the real customary ways of the people, with the usual Solomon Island welcome, not the secretive falsehoods of the Moro Movement. He said that no doctor had visited the area since the war, although by the scarcity of medical problems they showed me I realised that the medical assistant, John Tagabosoe, who accompanied me, had done a good job. He knew the area and it was a tribute to his care and attention that they were so well looked after.

The following day was an easy walk, but interesting in that we passed through three villages where several of the women had goitres. Like many inland areas there is a shortage of iodine and the women with their greater needs during menstruation and pregnancy are the first to show goitres. Fish and other produce from the sea are rich sources of iodine, and although I had come up from the coast and it was no great distance away, this indicated to me the complete isolation that these bush people experienced. On a subsequent visit we gave all the women depot iodine injections which were most effective in shrinking their goitres, but it was to change their diet that I tried to convince them would be the long-term cure.

This was a very depressed area and at the last village, Vaasi, there were just two men and only one of them strong enough to act as our guide for the next part of the journey. I thought how I would have reacted if a stranger came into my village and asked me to be a guide, so I quite expected him to refuse, but remarkably he agreed to take us on, and what a journey that was. There were two immense climbs, both above the 1000 metres mark, where the vegetation changes, red orchids appear and the trees hang with old-mans-beard. We continued going upwards until we entered the clouds as we skirted round Vatupochao Mountain. Dropping down into a fertile basin, where people from the lower levels come to make their gardens, we climbed up once more into Chimiu.

The rains came in earnest and turned the path into a mud slide, so progress was slippery and exhausting as we struggled up the steep valley side to Salamarao. We stayed here for the night, but the rain continued unabated so when we came down to cross the Bokokimbo river it was in flood, a rushing mass of white water through which I could see no way across. But Asa, my guide, was not perturbed, he cut a way up the riverside and coming to a widening of the stream declared that here we could cross. I was sceptical, but followed him into the torrent as he balanced my rucksack on his head. He went down and down until the water came up to his shoulders, but he still kept going. Fortunately it got no deeper and after a brief struggle against the current, we were across.

* * * * *

Guadalcanal has the highest mountains in the Solomon Islands with two peaks, Popomanaseu and Makarakomburu surpassing in height anything in the far bigger continental land mass of Australia. For many years Mount Popomanaseu, which is visible from Honiara, was thought to be the highest peak, but after a more accurate survey Mount Makarakomburu at 2447 m, was found to be higher. It is on the Weather Coast at the head of the magnificent Koloula River where the steep sides of the valley cut right into the mountain. A powerful river, it rushes down between great boulders, icy with mountain water, such a contrast to the heat of the tropical lowlands.

There had been one expedition to the summit that the people knew about, but this had been some time ago and they had no reason to ascend to the heights. They normally only went to the lower slopes to cultivate so there was a path only this far up. I had a few spare days before my next tour so arranged for three people from the village to guide me and take it in turns to cut a path.

The four of us set off early the next morning not knowing how long we would take, as we climbed steadily upwards to the place where the previous expedition had camped. It was still early in the day and we were all quite fresh so decided to continue. From here though it became difficult as at this height a thin-stemmed mountain bamboo grew in such profusion that any path was soon overgrown. We spent a long time cutting a way through, it seemed to be never ending, but eventually we were able to crawl along a small tunnel we had made. Once through we entered an area of stunted trees covered with hanging lichen and I knew we were near the top. Surfacing from the undergrowth we came onto a ridge where the previous expedition had reached, but there was clearly a higher one across a small valley. This we crossed and cut our way up through the trees, using the roots and branches to pull ourselves from one tree to the next, until emerging at the highest, I could see nothing above.

Looking across the valley was the other peak Popomanaseu and I knew that we had reached the highest point in the islands. According to my guides we had been the first to get to this particular spot, but I could only relish my success for a short time as the clouds came across and covered us in mist so that we started to shiver with cold. We returned to the bottom the same day and the warmer temperature I was more used to.

Valearanisi was a small village and my ascent of Makarakomburu had used up the main supply of guides and carriers so there were no other men left to take me across the island. As on the previous occasion when there were only two men in the village and one became my guide the people came up with another solution, this time two rather well built boys were detailed to lead me.

I thought the climb up the mountain would have been difficult, but that across the head of the valley was even steeper. The pass was over 2 thousand metres (the highest in Guadalcanal) so we all collapsed on the top exhausted. For our pains though we were rewarded with a fine view of the twin peaks of Makarakomburu and Popomanaseu rising out of a sea of clouds. Although so close to the Weather Coast this was the highest part of the island and from here there was a steady descent onto the central plateau.

Still far away, I was keen to reach a famous old village at the foot of sacred Mount Tatuve by that night. This mountain has always been held as the abode of the spirits and when a party from a visiting Austrian ship (*Albatross*) set out to climb it in 1896 they were all killed to prevent them from transgressing the custom. The area is now less populated and the custom not so strong, but out of respect for the ancient ways I did not consider trying to climb it, even in these days.

The next day we crossed the ridge that led up to the summit of Popomanaseu, from where we could look down on the great Sutakama Valley. The river curved round the side of Tatuve, then in the far distance broke through the last ridge of mountains to meander across the plains to the sea. We dropped down to the bottom of the valley and following along the side of the rushing river, climbed up to the last ridge, where there was an unexpected amount of activity. People had come here from various parts of the island and built new houses, as this was the scene of Guadalcanal's gold rush.

Gold had been found on what had become known as Gold Ridge, but in such small quantities that mining it was never considered a viable proposition. However a few people had stayed, digging out their own patch of ground and panning the soil in the river. There had been no great finds, but people were being more successful than previously and the Chinese merchants were offering reasonable prices so more people were moving into the area. Sadly though all effort was concentrated on the search for gold to the neglect of fields and family, so instead of spending time growing sweet potatoes and greens, the gold seekers bought polished rice, which they fed to their children. Rice is far less nutritious than the sweet potato, with the result that I saw some of the worst malnutrition that I have ever seen in any of the islands.

It has popularly been thought that the reason the Solomon Islands were called as such was because of the discovery of gold on Guadalcanal. However Gold Ridge is some distance inland and there is no evidence that the Spaniards came this far into the interior or found any gold. It was just the wishful thinking of Sarmiento, without any evidence to back-up his fanciful name.

Medically Guadalcanal was an interesting island because the two main chronic diseases of leprosy and tuberculosis were neatly stratified; TB was common in the coastal villages, while leprosy was predominantly inland. This was fortunate in many ways as the coastal villages, where the more serious problem lay, were easy to visit by ship, while the only way to get to the leprosy villages was to walk. Because of this leprosy had been rather neglected and one of the objectives of my series of walks was to evaluate the situation. What was even more interesting was that once the diagnosis of leprosy had been made people would become concentrated in certain villages where everybody either had leprosy or were the children or helpers of people who had. My last few walks were particularly planned to go to these leprosy villages.

Flying to Avu Avu on the other side of the island I followed up a comparatively easy ridge to Verakelia, where I was met by a guide who took me to Betimeleni, a delightfully situated village overlooked by high cliffs and ribbon waterfalls. People had collected here from surrounding villages, but after attending to their problems I was still not allowed to rest, instead being taken on to Haimbau. Here the medical assistant and a much larger crowd were waiting for me, I was back in Chimiu where the organization and hospitality of the people had so impressed me on my last visit here. They plied us with much food and gave us more to carry, which surprised me, as there was always plenty wherever we stayed. It seemed unnecessary to load ourselves down with having to carry food and I wondered why my helpers were so keen to take it?

We soon left the gentle slopes of Chimiu behind, entering Goragana (Horohana) where we had to climb steeply into this more mountainous part. At the new village of Pau Pau I met quite the smallest man I had ever come across; fully grown, the top of his head hardly came up to my chest, he was the same height as my 8 year old daughter. He showed no signs of malnutrition or any abnormality and I wondered whether there had once been a tribe of diminutive people, similar to pygmies. There were certainly stories of a small race of people, but I never met any more.

Charles Fox, the famous missionary recounted that there were very small people on the high hills, called different names in different islands. They did not know how to make fire, cultivate a garden or build a house. They danced in the moonlight and spoke languages that were not Melanesian. I was also told that about a hundred years ago there were very small people living in the mountains, so perhaps there is some truth in the stories and this man was one of the few that were left.

There is also a possible link with Papua New Guinea, as in his wanderings treating people for hookworm, Dr Lambert, working for the Rockefeller Foundation, came across a very small people called

Kunis, in the hills surrounding the Popo valley in Papua. He described them as fully-grown, but of midget size and fully adapted to climbing up and down the hills. They had pretty little faces, powerful thighs, short legs, pigeon breasts and sway backs. They could carry loads over hills with the greatest of ease, but when they came to level ground they had a clumsy waddling gait. They could possibly be descended from the Orang Asli in Malaysia who are also of a small size, being perhaps the original inhabitants of the Melanesian chain of islands.

The most famous leprosy village was Nata, but this had been partially abandoned and most of the people moved to a new village that they had called New Nata. Here was a large concentration of leprosy cases but to my relief they were mainly burnt out with no signs of any new ones, especially amongst the children. Leprosy, in a strange way seems to bring out the best in people and here was a model of community life; everybody shared what they had and helped each other. Although they had isolated themselves from a society from which they felt cast out, the people lived a better life here than their unscarred neighbours.

They tried to persuade us to take the usual road to Nata, but I saw what looked like a much more interesting way from further up the river. I began to regret my insistence though as we seemed to be forever climbing, the track was narrow and rocky and at one place we had to cross a deep chasm by a dilapidated log bridge that was in the process of collapsing. There was no way round, and to fall would have been fatal. We gingerly made our way across, trusting to the loya cane handrail as our safety line, should the bridge collapse. Safely on the other side we had to climb up a rocky screed which made hard work on our ankles. In fact we had climbed so high that we were above Mount Tatuve and could look down on its forbidden summit.

One of our guides had lugged a shotgun for the last three days without spotting anything, then suddenly we all had to stop as he crept forward, there was a bang and down came a small pigeon. It was such a small carcass I could not understand whey he had wanted to kill it, I thought it might just have been for sport, but anyway he carried it along with us.

The descent was as bad as I had dreaded, I really hated going down, the strain on my knees and ankles and sliding all over the place told on me more than climbing up hill. Finally I resorted to going barefoot, which made it easier to gain some grip, but still it was a long time before we reached the bottom. We followed down the river through spectacular mountain scenery, then by a short sharp climb ascended to the most amazingly hidden place I have ever seen. From the valley floor all sides were very steep, going up to sharp peaks and steep ridges with no sign of any inhabitable place, but after climbing 1,000 feet from the valley floor we suddenly came across a flat table of land. What a remarkable place, a completely hidden fortress of rugged peaks protecting this area of habitable land. Nata must have been a highly sought after village site in the past, with probably a large population, but now it was in a pathetic state, with few people and the houses in a poor state of repair.

It was that night that I realised why we needed to bring food with us. Our precious pigeon was stewed with one tiny taro and shared between the family of our host and the four of us. I didn't sleep well that night, partly from hunger and because I was disturbed by the crying of a child. In the morning the guides asked me if I had heard the crying. They said that the child was asking for food, but its parents or perhaps they were its grandparents, had told it that there wasn't any. This was the first time I had ever come across such hunger in all the time I had been in the Solomons and I wondered why this famous village, which had supported such a large population in the past, was now in such a pathetic state?

When one comes into a village in the afternoon there are normally just a few old people and children, and it is not until after dark or the next morning that you meet all the adults who have been away cultivating their crops. But in this village I realised that there were no young adults, the village consisted solely of old people and a few young children that they were looking after. What had happened was that all the able bodied had been attracted by the Moro movement and gone to Makaruka, leaving the old people to fend for themselves as best they could. It was a sorry state of affairs and clearly the customary ideas of Moro did not include looking after the elderly members of the family. The Moro movement may have had some grand intentions, but in the treatment of its children and the elderly it had certainly failed.

There was only one way out of Nata, and that was down the same way we had come. We followed up a narrow ridge on the side of Mount Tatuve, where it seemed we had come very close to the summit, but then our ridge, which had narrowed to a knife edge, ended in a sheer drop, so we were forced to take another way, winding down the other side to Nuhu.

It was here that we came across the site of a major planning blunder. A magnificent concrete walled clinic, had been built here, complete with corrugated iron roof and glass in the windows. It was hard enough for my guides and me to just walk through this difficult terrain, but the thought of the human effort required to haul all the materials required for its construction, filled me with amazement. Yet for all this labour the clinic had remained unused due to the simple fact that it was sited in the wrong place and no medical assistant would work here. Rather than build it in a main village it had been placed mid-way between the two, with the thought that it would equally serve both, but what had been forgotten was that any staff working here would not be living in either village so would not have the support of a community. The clinic had stood like this for 11 years and now all the people had moved away from the area. This was a sad waste of resources that could ill be afforded.

We had planned to stay at Nuhu that night, but finding just one family there, and with the thoughts of a repeat hungry stop we continued on across the deep clear Suta and climbed the other side of the valley to Parina. We were more than in luck, because the people had given up their brief following of the ideas of Moro and returned to build new houses, plant fresh crops and start life again on their ridge top village. We told them about our previous night's stay and they recounted all that had happened to them down on the coast. I was encouraged that people were returning again to the hills and questioning the philosophies of Moro.

CHAPTER TWENTY SEVEN

Murder in the jungle

It was early one Sunday morning when the telephone rang,

"Doctor, there has been a murder, can you do the post-mortem."

"Take the body to the hospital and I will come and do it later." I replied.

"No, the murder took place near Aola and we need to go there."

The policeman said they had chartered a ship for a journey that I knew would take about 6 hours, so I anticipated being back that night.

"How was the man killed?" I asked after they told me more about what had happened.

"He was hit on the head by a bush knife."

On the way to the ship I went to the hospital to pick up a clamp and saw so that I could open the skull.

We set off for Aola and it was while we were on the ship that they explained the murder had taken place some distance away in the bush and the victim had already been buried. I was not prepared for a long trek into the jungle and even less to stay overnight in the village, but still I was amazed at the inability of the police to walk any distance in this kind of terrain. With their heavy boots and gentle life in the city they were much less adapted for walking than I was and our party of some 20 persons, soon became a long trail of floundering policeman. In fact the relatives had almost finished digging up the body by the time the police finally arrived on the scene.

It was a very small village with no more than two or three families and a sense of complete shock and dismay hung over the place. Nothing like this had ever happened before and the people did not know what to do. It took some time for the police to be informed so as the body was already beginning to putrefy it had been buried just outside the village. When we arrived the people dug it up and I had to do my post-mortem at the side of the grave. There were huge lacerations on the head so I opened the skull to reveal the deep cuts into the brain that had been the cause of death. I was appalled at the brutality of the assault, considerable force would have been required to cut so deeply into the skull, and as the lacerations were on the back the attack must have come from behind.

By the time I finished it was dark so we prepared to spend the night there, but with the absence of any bedding, little food and the knowledge that the murderer was still at large, I didn't get much sleep. The police made a half-hearted search for the accused the next day, but with their abilities in the jungle I didn't rate their chances of success very highly. We returned to Honiara, but I later heard that the murderer had given himself up to the police patrol that had been left behind to search for him.

Everybody knew who the suspect was so no detective work was required by the police. This man had come from another place and was tolerated, but not liked when he took some land and began to farm it. The situation became acute however when he then persuaded one of the young women from the village to come and live with him. This was strictly against the custom and the father of the girl went and brought his daughter back and forbade her to marry the man.

On hearing this the man sought vengeance and waited for the father at a place where he knew he would come along the path. He did not have to wait long and jumping out on the father set to with his bush knife (machete). The old man would have had no chance, probably being felled by the first blow.

When I was called as a medical witness in the murder trial I pointed out that all the lacerations were on the back of the head and the level of force that would have been required to inflict the wounds must have been considerable. This was a deliberate chopping action as with an execution, not the result of a fight. However the expatriate judge was a lenient man and tried to find reason why he could pass only the minimum sentence. He asked if the body had been formerly identified to me, which I could not confirm. It seemed to be rather stating the obvious, there were no more that 20 persons in the village, they all knew each other, so I could see no way in which they might have presented me with any other body with those injuries than the victim of the murder. However this fact and a trumped-up story by the accused that it was the result of a fight (when the attack had clearly come from behind), led to a sentence of manslaughter.

It was a strange trial as there was no jury and the judge was both the defence and the presiding judge. The prosecuting lawyer was a Solomon Island trainee, learning his skills from the judge so in effect all the proceedings were controlled by the one person. It was a formative time in the Solomons and perhaps the full judicial system that we have become used to as British justice could not be practiced but in such an important case one felt that more could have been done to produce a better trial. There were certainly enough educated people to form a jury and another lawyer could have been flown up from Vanuatu to have acted for the defence.

Although there was no death sentence, life imprisonment for such a vicious attack would have been accepted as sufficient punishment, but with the crime reduced to manslaughter the sentence was only for a few years. When news of this reached the village there was shock and dismay; justice had not been seen to be done and resentment remained for a judiciary out of touch with the people's customs and rights.

CHAPTER TWENTY EIGHT

Taboo mountains and flooded rivers

Not long after the murder I needed to do another journey to the eastern part of Guadalcanal so set off from Aola, following up the river. The place where the old man had collapsed from his wounds was now evil ground so a new path had been made to avoid the area. We spent the night at Bubunuhu, one of the few clinics in the interior, and then continued on to Bubukembe, a pretty village with a superb view. It was situated on the side of Mount Vatupochau, a taboo mountain. No one dared climb it for it was said to be the haunt of devils and the place where all illness came from. During the geological surveys a helicopter had landed on the summit, but the pilot and guide were chased by flying dogs and when they tried to take off something seemed to be holding the helicopter down. This story made me even more intrigued by the place and I tried to persuade someone to show me the way, but try as I may nobody would take me and I knew I would get lost if I attempted to climb it myself.

Leaving Bubukembe we then had to walk round Vatupochau and along a narrow faulted ridge, from where we could look down over a vast area that had been destroyed by an earthquake. Previously a hill, it was said to have fallen down and blocked a river to form Lees Lake. This was the only inland lake in Guadalcanal; indeed lakes were unusual in any of the islands. I had acquired another infected sore and my leg was swollen, so I went down to the lake to soak it in the water.

I floated around on a simple log raft, watching the cormorants and other birds in this unique paradise in the middle of the jungle, not realising that later on I would witness a catastrophe similar to what had happened here.

In the afternoon we started walking again, I thought it would not be far to the next village, which would give us a good chance of completing the crossing of the island by the next day, but whether it was the terrain or my leg the walk became sheer hell as I dragged myself up and down the side of a steep valley. I arrived in a raging fever, collapsed on the floor of the first house we were shown into and remained there until the next morning. Fortunately I was better after a night's sleep so we continued on up the steady climb to the summit from where we were rewarded with one of those rarities of walking through the jungle, a good view. It was then a steep descent to Avu Avu on the other side of the island, and with the rain that greeted us it became more a case of sliding down, rather than a gentle walk. We crossed the river just in time, as it was we had to half swim, but later it became a raging torrent, impossible to get across. There was a road as far as Makaruka, so we had no difficulty getting that far, but beyond there were more rivers, and with the deluge they would all be in flood. There was nothing else we could do but sit and wait for the rain to abate.

Rather depressed we were preparing to spend a second night at Makaruka when a breathless and soaking man arrived with a note from the Medical Assistant at Marau. He had delivered a woman, but the placenta was retained, could I please come quickly. We set off at once, although it would soon be dark, I was walking fast, prepared to keep going all night, as I knew how quickly a retained placenta can bleed a woman to death. It was very dark as we got to the river, which was running fast and there seemed no way to get across. Our guide said he had managed on the way up, so plunged into the river only to be swept down stream at an alarming rate. He somehow managed to get back to the bank and when he found his way back to us said he had tried too low down. He went a few yards further upstream and plunged in again, only to be swept off once more. I admired the courage of the man for no sooner had he recovered than he said he would try again. I told him he could have one more go and if not successful we would have to wait for the river to subside a little, as it was just too dangerous. He went further upstream and to our surprise did not disappear this time. We followed him into the water, it was like plunging into the unknown, bad enough in daylight, but in the dark angry night one felt very much alone.

We continued until the village of our guide as this was where the Medical Assistant had come in his canoe and left the message. The MA could not wait for us however as he could see the storm coming and needed to return to look after his patient. I was all for going on, but our guide told us of an even bigger river that we needed to cross, so I knew it was impossible that night.

We were up at first light, the day was fine and the rivers had gone down as suddenly as they had come up. Half way there we met the Medical Assistant who reassured me that his patient was still satisfactory. We got to Marau by late morning and I was able to remove the placenta without much blood loss, so all ended well.

CHAPTER TWENTY NINE

The hill that boomed

I continued my walks on Guadalcanal, going right round the island for the second time and including villages I had not visited on my previous tours. It was while on the last of these walks, from Totongo into Tetekanji, that the most unexpected event of all my years in the Solomons occurred.

The Medical Assistant John Tagabosoe and myself started out from Totongo, went across to Kuvamiti and reached Luguvasa that evening. John was one of the best Medical Assistants there was, knowing his area like no other and commanding the respect of the people. As arranged, all the Tetekanji people came down to meet us so we held a big clinic, and as before we were well looked after that night. The next day we followed down the river for a short distance and then turned up a small tributary. An old, but very agile man was leading us and two young boys, who tagged on for fun, were following far behind. Landslides had taken away the bush and the valley was full of stones making walking difficult, so when we got to the head of the valley we rested. There was a waterfall at one end and altogether it was a most attractive place.

We stayed there for some 10 minutes, the others wanting to hang around longer but I decided that we should move on. The old man went first, then the boy carrying John's rucksack, then me, then John and my carrier last of all. It was a very steep climb and after a short while we came to a rock face made slippery by an ooze of water, with no bushes or tree roots to give any handholds. Fortunately somebody had tied a loya cane on which I entrusted all my weight as I pulled myself up. The path continued on upwards, then went over to the left for a while and finally upwards again, but was always very steep. We could see straight down into the valley from where we had just come, hundreds of feet below us.

I was on the final upward stretch, closely behind the old man and John's carrier, while John and my carrier had lagged behind, when there was a most unusual sound. A tremendous "Boom," like a gun going off, came from the mountains over to our left. We all stopped in our tracks, the old man having enough time to say he had never heard anything like it before, when quite unprepared, we felt it. The ground started shaking with long rhythmic undulations. These became more violent, everything was shaking, and there was no stability anywhere. I didn't know what was happening, but flattened myself against the hillside, hanging on for all I was worth. I didn't dare move, but noticed that the old man and the carrier had taken the risk of being shaken off and rushed to get to the top.

After noticing that they had gone I looked over to the left and not far away I saw all the trees and bushes buckle over and tumble down the mountainside. I looked to the right of me and saw the same thing happen there. It was an earthquake, which had started landslides, and from where I was precariously perched it looked as though the whole hillside was about to fall down.

By some fluke I was on a reasonably stable island of rock and vegetation, but soon that would go as well. A tremendous sadness came over me, I was not concerned about the act of death, but thought of Lucy and Sophy loosing their father as well as their mother, why did it have to happen? So many thoughts went through my mind in those brief moments, I was not sure whether I was still alive or already in some dream world of the dead.

Then suddenly I realised the shaking had stopped, the piece of

217

ground on which I was precariously perched had not fallen down, I was still alive. I scrambled to the top, fuelled on by a burst of energy that could only have occurred in a situation such as this, to a small valley and comparative safety. As I rounded the top I noticed deep cracks in the path, certainly it was a near thing that our piece of ground had not fallen, but if there was another tremor, as there always is, then it certainly would go.

A feeling of despair came over me as I realised that John and my carrier must have been where I saw the land fall on my right. I felt they must have been killed, but optimistically and unexpectedly for me, I shouted for all I was worth,

"John come up quickly, the ground is breaking."

I waited at the top, looking down, expecting only silence to answer me back, then a head popped up, and another. I could see from their movements that they were exhausted and frightened, but I implored them not to rest, but come up to the top as quickly as possible. They wasted no time and as they got to the top I dragged them over the edge as though I was pulling them into a boat from the sea. We left the edge of the cliff quickly and rushed down into the little valley. We were just in time for no sooner had we reached it than there was a second and even larger tremor. The ground moved like a shaking jelly, the immense trees swayed like tall blades of grass in the wind, there was a tremendous din of cracking, breaking, falling, birds screaming, it was a terrifying experience.

It was a long shake and when you have no point of stability anywhere it is a most unnerving experience. Then it stopped, but the din of tons of stone and rock falling down the hillside continued. I could see the relief on John's face as he realised how close he had come to being taken by the second tremor; then he recounted his story.

When the quake came, he just hung on to the hillside, but had the presence of mind to look up and to his horror saw a boulder some four feet in diameter tumbling straight towards him. He quickly moved to one side, the boulder just catching his leg and bruising it. Another slightly smaller rock followed the first, cutting the other man's leg. These were followed by earth and rubble, which suddenly stopped just a short distance above them. John had thought that the path curved back again and I had fallen down with the landslide so he started digging around in the earth with his hands to see if he could find any part of me. As he colourfully explained,

"Me lookim for some part blong dokita, maybe me findim, hand or foot or somting alsam."

It was while he was digging that he heard my shout and came rushing to the top. We both laughed at each other, him searching for my lifeless body and me thinking he had been swept down the cliff. It made a good story that circulated round the bush for many years after, and John was the best of storytellers.

The tremors continued and I became increasingly concerned. We would wait for 5 to 10 minutes; there would be the same "Boom" and then that awesome shaking. The islands are on the edge of a tectonic plate, earthquakes occur frequently, but I had never known one with so many after-shocks and I realised that it must have been a big one.

Our little valley had high mountains on either side and if a slide should develop on one of these and fall our way and not into the main valley, we would be covered. Also the trees swayed alarmingly and I was always looking up to see that they did not break and fall on us. The same horrific roar of tons of stone falling down the valley side gave us considerable doubt about the safety of the two boys who had followed us at a distance. If they had started climbing up the hill they would certainly have been killed. We also recounted our good fortune at not having delayed longer for our rest, if we had been on the steep rock face, or hadn't reached the top by the second tremor, then we would certainly have been killed.

But what concerned me now was where was the earthquake coming from, was there any specific cause and what damage had been done? The booming noise was not like the earth tremors we were used to, which sounded more like an express train passing through a station.

They had a directional element and the sound increased in intensity with the strength of the tremor, but his one was different.

Many of our tremors before had been associated with eruptions of Mount Bagana on Bouganville island, could this one be due to a volcano nearer to us, was this the much feared eruption of Savo? If it was Savo, this was extremely serious as Honiara would have been devastated, and that was where Lucy and Sophy were.

Still the tremors, accompanied by the booming sound, continued. I was thankful I was amongst Solomon Islanders, I could sense tension in everyone, but there was never any hint of panic. Only the old man gave the occasional whimper as he guessed the inevitable fate of the two boys who had been following us.

After the relief of our escape, the continuing tremors started to increase my alarm again. I wondered if we were really going to survive, was a levelling process going on until even our little piece of land would slide down into the valley below? Would a big shake knock down trees that would kill us? And if we survived all these perils, how were we going to get out of this predicament? We knew we could not go back the way we had come and our path ahead was steeply down the other side, where we had heard stone and rubble falling, so we presumed we could not go that way either.

We waited there for an hour and a half with tremors coming all the time. Eventually I had to make a move, I was beginning to get anxious about many things, including our present position, and so we started to reconnoitre the path down. We had only gone a short way when we found another path leading up the hill to the left. We had a short conference and decided that although it went upwards, when we really needed to go down, it was liable to be safer than a steeply descending path.

We had chosen correctly for it took a gentle route in the direction we wanted to go, along the side of the hill to a small village. Just before the village a large section of the path had been undermined and looked like it would fall at any minute, so we went across one at a time, hoping there would be no tremor while we were in the middle. The village was intact, but deserted; everybody had gone down to Nabakua to wait for us there.

It was here that the old man left us. He wanted to get back somehow and see what had happened to the two boys. We were sad to see him go.

It seemed that the path down to Nabakua had no difficult places, so we set off again hoping our luck would hold. Once we reached the valley, we were amazed at the scene that greeted us, rocks, trees, gardens, everything had come slithering down the hills. In one place there was a landslide that reached right up to the top of a hill, so we rushed across to the other side, as there was danger that more rocks would start falling down.

In the valley were two routes, one a quick way down to the coast which we decided to try, but as we followed up a stream we came to a huge heap of fallen earth and rock, which when we climbed over, discovered it was a temporary dam. This had just formed and the river was building up behind it, likely to break through at any moment, so we beat a hasty retreat back the way we had come. The other way posed no problems and we eventually arrived at Nabakua.

Everyone had collected there as planned, but they were waiting outside in the open, rather frightened. Our arrival coincided with another tremor and I was amazed at how much the houses moved, swaying first one side and then the other, but finally finishing upright, none had fallen down. I realised that although they seemed flimsy, thatch houses on their flexible stilts were in fact perfect for earthquakes, and as a consequence nobody was killed. Death due to earthquakes in so many other parts of the world is from falling masonry, but here no one in the whole island was killed due to this cause.

We attended to our patients and then had a discussion as to what to do. The villagers tried to persuade us to spend the night there and look for a new way the next day, but I was worried about the situation in the rest of the island and had to try everything in order to find a way to the coast. We set off up the hillside where they had planted their gardens. The ground was badly cracked, but we kept on going until we came to the ridge at the top, here landslides had taken away ground on both sides making it impossible to cross, there was no alternative but to go back again.

I wanted to follow down the river, but the villagers said that there were some steep gorges and the river was bound to be blocked. There was only one other way and that was to go back to Kuvamiti, where we had come up the day before. I didn't want to go this way and the people said it was a difficult path, but I knew this might be the only way out, so reluctantly we tried one last time.

I was getting depressed, we had been expending much energy climbing up, only to have to turn back the way we had come, were we going to do the same again here? It was a hard climb and still we were going higher, I couldn't face having to go back again, I was determined we should get through somehow. Once we reached the top, the path cut across the ridge and followed the other side, which fortunately was intact. A landslide had taken away a large section of the path, but the slip had not started from the top of the hill, so we were able to cut a new track above it. Finally we started to go down, the ground was horribly cracked, and I feared the worst, but the roots of trees were so intertwined they held everything together. It was while we were going down this path that another large aftershock came. We were in a precarious position and I was beginning to wish we had taken the villagers advice and stayed at Nabakua. We just stood still and waited, everything shook and moved alarmingly, but did not fall down, we were alright. Our descent from here was rapid, eventually reaching the wide valley, we had made it, from here on there would be no problem, we were safe.

I had noticed while we were coming down that there seemed to be less damage on this, the northern side of the island, and as we got closer to the coast there was no damage at all. I began to realise that it could not be Savo that had erupted, something else must have happened. We spent the night at Kuvamiti; we were too exhausted both physically and mentally to go any further. Sadly there was no radio in the village, but next day we came across somebody who had one and they confirmed that it was not Savo, but a powerful earthquake, measuring 7.5 on the Richter scale, centred off the coast not far from where we had been. Thursday 21 April 1977 was certainly a day I would always remember.

The island is on a fault line known as the Benioff earthquake zone, caused by the Australian tectonic plate, tending to push up the island of Guadalcanal. There had been earthquakes before, but never as violent as this. A moderate one in 1934 or 1935 was centred in the bush area, when Lees Lake was formed, but it did not seem to affect the people very much.

It was an easy walk to the coast and by good fortune our arrival coincided with the return journey of the ship that had taken me to Totongo, so I was able to go back with it to Honiara, arriving that evening.

When I walked into the house everyone gasped in surprise. I had the feeling they thought they were seeing a ghost. They knew I was in danger, but had no way of finding out what had happened. We hugged each other and compared stories, I was so glad they were alright.

The tremors had been quite strong in Honiara, but fortunately nobody was hurt. People went out into the streets and the school children were led outside to wait for the shaking to stop. There had been no tidal wave on the north coast and there was only minor damage to the buildings. The roof over our veranda had fallen down and many of our ornaments were broken. I knew though that the situation in the interior was more serious and there could have been damage from a tsunami on the Weather Coast.

When we were making our way out of Tetekanji we had seen an aircraft flying over the area, so as soon as I got back I went to the District Commissioner and asked him.

"What are you doing about the earthquake?"

"We flew over in a plane and saw a few landslides, but otherwise not much damage," was his reply.

Very few of the administrative staff had been into the interior of the island and didn't really know what the situation was like there. Looking down from an aircraft all you see is a homogenous sea of trees and the villages are hard to spot.

"I went with a geologist and came to the conclusion that apart from blocked rivers, all was all right," he continued.

But I knew he had never walked into the interior himself and I don't think realised how many people lived there. A cursory flight in a plane would probably have missed most of the villages anyway.

"I was nearly killed and felt sure that others had not been so fortunate," said I, as I told him the full story of our escape.

"Whole villages will be cut-off and all of them will be short of food." I continued. As not only had the landslides taken away many of the people's crops, but the ground had been so shaken that where it was still intact the plants would have been too damaged to continue growing.

"What can we do about it?" He then asked me.

"We need a helicopter," I replied. I could see him look at me as though I had been too long in the jungle, because there were few aircraft in the islands and certainly no helicopters.

"And how are we going to get a helicopter?" He asked, not expecting to get an answer.

"What about the Australians, they have a large commercial interest in the soon-to-be-independent Solomon Islands and have just opened a High Commission, so would probably be delighted to be seen doing something for the islands?" He was rather taken aback by this suggestion and contemplated it for a while, then replied.

"I am going to a party this evening when the Australian High Commissioner will be there, I will ask him."

The helicopter arrived within a couple of days in a huge transport plane of the RAAF. We organised three teams each consisting of a medical assistant and a policeman to be dropped off at strategic places, while I went on the first flight to show the pilot where all the villages were. It was an amazing experience to skim over the jungle that I had trudged through for days, climb steep ridges in an instant and drop effortlessly onto high tables of land that had taken hours to struggle up. In two hours of flying I covered all the villages that had taken me over a year to visit on foot. It was rather like Sophy's concept of "Bush Walking" where she imagined that when I went on tour I literally walked on the top of the bush, like some mythical giant.

In all my walks I had tried to keep accurate maps because villages were always being moved and maps rapidly went out of date. These were what we used in the helicopter, so I was pleased to find that all the villages were where I had marked them. This was particularly important as with the jungle cover you did not see a village until you were right above it and with the limited range of a helicopter we had no time for searching around.

The scene was devastating, huge faces of exposed rock, immense mounds of tumbled earth, seemingly whole hillsides had fallen down to block the rivers, now running thick with mud. Amazingly though all the villages were intact, some slides had come very close, others had damaged houses, but nobody had been hurt in the villages we visited. The most serious problem though were the peoples' gardens, these had either slipped down the hillside, or the growing crops shaken so violently in the ground that they were all damaged. I knew that there would be a serious problem of hunger if we did nothing, but was loath to use food aid as it would have substituted rice for the traditional diet of sweet potatoes. This could have long term consequences so I discussed this with the Council members who arranged for any spare food to be collected from undamaged villages by the shipping runs.

Another priority surprisingly was drinking water. This is traditionally from springs or small streams, but all had been disrupted and would take months to run clean again. Fortunately there is never any shortage of rainwater so somebody had the ingenious idea of supplying lengths of galvanised iron, plastic sheeting and a bucket, so that a simple method of collecting drinking water could be constructed.

I asked the party that had been dropped off in Tetekanji to enquire about the fate of the two boys who had followed us on our last walk. I later learnt that they had fooled around in the valley and never started to climb up the steep part, so when the tremors came they ran back down the valley to safety. Our guide had found his way back to his village and reported on what had happened to us, but 12 people had not been so lucky. Five were killed at Ghorobau and one old lady at Raevu, while six died on the way to work in their gardens. The landslide that killed them was so massive it completely blocked the valley, forming a new lake. The interior of Guadalcanal was never to be the same again.

Several of us had learnt a lesson on what to do when caught in a landslide. Contrary to one's natural reaction, the avoiding action is to face the landslide and climb up the hillside, rather than run down. A landslide starts from a small area near the top and then fans out, rocks fall first, slowly to start with, but rapidly increase in speed, bouncing and breaking up as they near the bottom. The ground is also comparatively slow moving near the top and sides, but as it progresses downwards it gathers momentum. By facing up the landslide one can see rocks falling and by going upward you stand a greater chance of getting above its origin. Certainly one group of fatalities panicked and ran down the hill, not seeing the landslide that killed them, whereas two boys from the same group ran up the hill to safety. Many other groups of people caught in their gardens also had the sense to climb upwards (six women even spending the night on top of a hill), so saving themselves.

It had been a devastating experience for the people living in the interior. They had preserved a traditional way of life that had become increasingly more difficult to maintain as the new concept of a cash economy had attracted young families down to the coast, leaving the old to continue the best they could. This was therefore the final blow for many of them and they asked to be moved out of the interior, to new village sites nearer the coast. It was a sad time for me as I had grown to admire their independence and preservation of a traditional method of jungle living. Some of the most beautiful places I had ever been to were deep in the middle of the island, now they were to be abandoned. Famous village names, such as Nata, were to disappear forever from the map of Guadalcanal.

The damage was not only in the interior though, the epicentre of the earthquake had been a few miles offshore from the southernmost part of Guadalcanal, near Avu Avu. What had actually happened was visible in the amazing site of the reef off Lauvi Lagoon, which just a few days ago had been fully submerged, but was now some 2 metres above the surface of the sea. The whole of Guadalcanal had been raised up and tilted, especially the southern end of the island, such was the force of nature. Over the next few years I watched this exposed reef become colonised and a new island form. When I returned in 1989 it was a well established island, so much vegetation had grown it looked as though it had been like that for thousands of years.

The tsunami had struck the coast from Avu Avu westwards, but most of its force had been dissipated up the rivers. The bridge at Avu Avu had been carried some 200 metres upstream, whereas the Alivagheto river had no vegetation along its banks for 100 metres inland. The salt water had scorched all the ground and nothing would grow here again for several years. Fortunately most of the villages on the Weather Coast had large shingle banks, built up by the often-rough seas, and this had been a sufficient barrier to protect all but the few houses close to the shore. However landslides had threatened villages built close to the hills and Ghorobau, where five people died, was completely abandoned. A sea of mud from the massive landslide now covered most of the village.

There was a remarkable escape in one of these villages where a woman had been lying on her bed with her baby. When the tremor came she picked up the baby and ran outside, moments before a huge boulder came rolling through the wall completely shattering the bed where she had been lying just moments before.

As with the interior villages some needed to be moved to safer places, while others refused to go even though there was a danger from rivers bursting through the temporary dams that blocked their way. In one place the inland people wanted to move down but the coastal people would not let them. Meetings were arranged to get together all the influential people to try and work out an acceptable solution.

I suddenly found myself in higher social circles due to the work for the earthquake. The Governor called me to his office to recount my story and the Australian High Commission, which before had been an unknown office in a small road in Honiara, was now elevated to a place of considerable importance. The helicopter had become famous, there were songs composed about it, and tea-shirts printed, the Australians were delighted with what this small act of mercy had achieved.

CHAPTER THIRTY

Savo and Gela

Just off Honiara and an ever-present threat to the north coast of Guadalcanal is the small volcanic island of Savo. It contains a Mount Pelée type of volcano, meaning that it could erupt with little warning in a most violent way.

The original Mount Pelée volcano is on the island of Martinique in the Caribbean, which erupted with such ferocity in 1902 that it destroyed the town of Saint-Pierre and its entire population of 30,000 people. Because of its explosive nature it has given its name to volcanoes of this type, but the name Pele is actually that of a Hawaiian goddess who lives in the continually active craters of Kilauea on the island of Mauna Loa.

When Mendana sailed past Savo it was pouring out steam, while eruptions have occurred in 1800 and again in 1845. The second eruption was particularly violent, killing many people and covering the whole area in a thick layer of ash. It was still active in 1880, but has remained quiet ever since. Regular temperature recordings are made to detect the first signs of increased activity, while an evacuation plan for Savo is ready in case of need.

With its rich volcanic soils and an unexpected bonus of the megapode bird it has attracted a surprisingly large population. The megapode (*Megapodius freycinet*) is the same as that found on Simbo in Western Solomons, but on Savo it is exploited to a much greater extent. The people mark out the beach where it comes to lay its eggs and claim any laid on their lot. There is such constant digging for eggs that it seems impossible that any are able to hatch to continue the colony, but somehow they succeed and this careful balance between man and bird is sustained.

Savo can be walked round in a day and to cross it, including climbing the volcano, is equally easy. A small stream flows from the crater, providing the best access, the water becoming warmer as the crater is reached. Inside the ground is hot with several fumaroles belching hot steam. It is only when you are in the crater that the threat of this pretty little island is realised. It has been estimated that if the volcano did erupt, not only would the population on the island be in grave danger, but Honiara and other coastal places would be swamped by a tsunami and possibly a pyroclastic cloud as well.

The people of Savo speak a Papuan language, quite different from other languages in the islands, but similar to the Russell islands, to which they might have some ancient connections.

* * * * *

Florida was the name given by Mendana to the group of islands that lie midway between Guadalcanal and Malaita, but they are now more commonly known as Gela (or Ngella). Mendana's chief pilot Hernanado Gallego described the people, "They go naked with nothing on at all, and are tattooed. They dye their hair red, eat human flesh and build their houses over water." Over 700 men in 20 canoes attacked Mendana's ships, but with their greater fire power the Spaniards drove them back and burnt their villages.

The Florida Islands are in a strategic position for any conquering power, the British making them into their pre-war base. The first Resident, Charles Woodford, chose the island of Tulagi, just off Big Gela, to establish his headquarters. This has a superb harbour, and is easily defended, rather than being on a larger island where one is more vulnerable. During World War II the Japanese occupied the islands, turning Tulagi into a marine base. Despite the Japanese being driven out of the islands in their first retreat in the war, they were invited back again in more recent times to set-up a fishing industry, choosing Tulagi again to base their fleet and build a canning factory.

The Anglican mission established its main centre at Siota at the northern end of Small Gela and from there sent missionaries to all the other islands. A boarding school was established in 1896, which was later converted into a theological college. At Taroaniara the mission school taught carpentry, engineering, navigation, shipbuilding and printing. It was to these mission stations that my step-grandfather had come in the 1930's, both as a teacher and to help with the construction of the mission buildings. I asked around if anybody remembered him and was able to find his house-girl, now an old lady.

Taroaniara was named after one of the first Solomon Islanders to be converted to Christianity, dying a martyr's death at the same time as Bishop Patteson. He was waiting in the ship's boat while the Bishop went ashore, but as soon as the signal was given that Patteson had been killed people in canoes shot at the occupants. Stephen Taroaniara was struck in the chest by six arrows, dying soon afterwards, uttering the famous phrase "The Bishop and I," forever linking him to Bishop Patteson.

The language of Gela was studied by the famous missionary Charles Fox, who composed a dictionary and collected folk stories. He mentioned that it bore a similarity with the language of the people of Nias, an island off Western Sumatra, both in grammar and vocabulary. Nias is a particularly interesting island because of its megalithic culture that is still practised to this day. But such similarity of language would suggest that there must have been some link in ancient times, perhaps it was people originating from Nias that travelled down the island chain of what is now Indonesia to arrive many years later in this part of the Solomons.

Land ownership is fundamental to Solomon Island life, it being collectively held by the clan and farmed by individuals for the duration of their life. Likewise the reef was also owned and anybody fishing on it, not of the clan, had to pay for the privilege. The reefs around Gela are a particularly good sources of the *arca* shell that is used to make shell money by the Langa Langa people of Malaita. They would paddle the 25 miles across to Gela and after diving for the shell, pay the owners of the reef for all the shell they had taken.

Crocodiles used to be common in these islands, but people seemed to have a special way with them and there was said to be one at Siota that provided a ferry service across the mile of water between the Gelas. A Belaga man, (that is one of the people of the crocodile) could call it, then sit on its back to be taken to the other side.

The Solomon Islands might have been a very different place after World War I as it was at the same place as the crocodile ferry that Admiral Jellicoe made a visit and proposed a large naval base to be built. Fortunately this was not realised, but the harbour (called Purvis Harbour) showed its potential by holding over two hundred American and allied warships during World War II. In the hills that border the Boli passage, which forms a deep water channel from Purvis Harbour between the Gelas, are wonderful limestone caves that are yet to be properly explored.

Sandfly Island was given its European name not from the insects that plagued the populace, but after H.M.S. *Sandfly*, which suffered the loss of its commanding officer and four sailors at the hands of headhunters in 1880. The main village is Leitongo from where I was able to walk to the other side. The soil was surprisingly poor, on which only a ragged grass grew, but the lack of any jungle meant that there were fine views, especially on the descent to Boroni bay. It is probable that the land here was originally jungle covered, but intensive cultivation had drained the soil of all its nutrients and it cannot support tree growth anymore. From here it is a short canoe journey across to Sambani Island, more commonly known by the name given it by its Spanish explorers, Buena Vista. This is perhaps the most appropriate name as from here there are fine views back over all the islands as far as Santa Isabel.

CHAPTER THIRTY ONE

Santa Isabel

Santa Isabel was the first of the main islands to be reached by Mendana. He arrived on 7th February 1568 and gave the island this name because it was on Santa Isabel's day (19th November) that he had set sail. They anchored in the bay of Ghene, Gallego describing the people as, "Tawny and with crisp hair, going naked, except for short aprons of palm leaves". He suspected they ate human flesh, which was later shown to be correct when they brought him a quarter of a boy, including his arm and hand. After an initial friendly meeting the Spaniards then used force in an attempt to get food, so beginning the conflict with the white man that was to blight these islands for centuries. Worse though was the disease they left behind, a terrible sickness that wiped out whole villages in the area where they had been, forever leaving that coast under-populated.

Although the island is now very strongly Christian the first attempts to convert the island by the Catholics ended with the martyrdom of Bishop Epalle. In 1845 the Bishop and his party were travelling round in a chartered schooner, going ashore in Astrolabe Bay where a large crowd of people had gathered. The people were normally friendly because this was not the first contact they had made, but on this occasion they turned on their unarmed visitors and Bishop Epalle was repeatedly hit on the head with an axe. His companions managed to rescue him, but his injuries were too great and he died two days later.

Santa Isabel was itself one of the favoured haunts of headhunters from Roviana, who made so many raids that the population on the southwest coast was almost exterminated. To protect themselves the people built houses in the trees, with an ever ready pile of stones that they could hurl down on their attackers. Others moved to the area around Buala for protection as there was a powerful chief there called Bera, who had built up a formidable armoury from trade with European ships. Due to all this conflict and killing the missionaries considered they were witnessing the extinction of a dying race, but fortunately this was not to be the case, as was the impression I had when I visited.

Santa Isabel is one of the most beautiful of all the islands with a very attractive people. It is the longest of the Solomon Islands, breaking up into an archipelago at its western end, with small islands stretching almost as far as Choiseul. Buala, the capital is situated on the north coast, near the eastern end of the island, and it was to here that I first went. This was where the majority of the population lived, but filled with my experience of walking across Malaita and Guadalcanal, I wanted to cross the island to visit the few villages in the interior.

Above Buala the cultivated slopes were free of forest and provided impressive views of the coast as we climbed to Bara, quite one of the most well constructed villages I have ever seen. Like a national monument its houses were decoratively made, and arranged around the slopes of the hill on which they stood in perfect harmony. It was such a lovely place I was tempted to stay here but we continued on to the next village, situated in a trough, parallel to the main line of peaks. Then came the climb across the mountains, but after Guadalcanal it was a comparatively easy walk to the top, from where we followed a long ridge all the way down to Siligodu. There were impressive views over San Jorge Island and the Kaipito valley, but still I was not allowed to stop and enjoy them. We reached the first village in the evening, my guide suggesting that we go on to Koge, as all the climbing was over. We had virtually walked across Santa Isabel in the one day.

I soon discovered why my guide was so keen to get as far as Koge as it is one of the most impressive villages I have ever been to. The houses were some of the largest I have ever seen in the Solomons, built with stout poles and using a very closely fitting leaf, they had been made to last for ages. A unique feature was the rounded extension at each end, giving the central room immense proportions. Coffee was grown on the slopes, while peanuts were in abundance in the valley, no wonder the people could afford to make such grand houses. The valley had a wide flat floor and silt was constantly brought down by the meandering river, making it a very fertile place, able to grow many different kinds of crops.

A tractor road led to the sea where there was a clinic and the next morning a canoe waited to take us back round the coast to the other side. The prevailing wind was blowing on the northern side so we had a comparatively calm sea as we visited all the villages on this stretch of the coast. Rounding the headland we stayed at Sigana, quite the tiniest of islands, but completely built on, rather like one of the artificial islands found on Malaita, with the exception that this was not artificial. We called in at a few more villages the next day, but the sea was getting rough with huge waves, so we struggled into Lingo, soaking, bruised and tired. We had to climb up to the village from the beach, but when we reached the top the most delightful sight greeted my salt filled eyes. Here was the greenest grass I had ever seen, crossed by a network of pleasant streams, with neat paths and tastefully arranged houses. We all lay on the grass, it was so soft and inviting.

The village seemed quiet and empty, but as we lay there people gradually emerged, their manner was peaceful and subdued, as befitted the atmosphere. The headman of the village had been in charge of Sibu leprosarium and his kindly daughters had also been afflicted with the disease. They made us very welcome, fussing round to make sure everything was just so. A further delightful surprise awaited me when I went to wash. A pretty hibiscus lined path led down to a big pool with a cliff at the far side, over which a small waterfall provided a perfect natural shower. A stream left the pool and then went on a few yards before dropping straight down into the sea, providing a ready made flushing toilet. Nature had provided the perfect village site and the people had turned it into a fairytale place.

Santa Isabel has so much beauty, not only in the countryside and its neatly arranged villages, but also in its people. They are slender with fine features and a lovely brown skin. Not as pale as Malaita people, they however have the same bleached highlights to their hair, some even verging on being blond. This is coupled with the nicest of manner, always smiling and welcoming, and with an intelligence that has taken several of them to high office in the government.

CHAPTER THIRTY TWO

Russell Islands

Between Guadalcanal and the Western Solomons are the Russell Islands, rather different from most other islands as they are not mountainous, but have a gentle undulating terrain more similar to Europe. This makes them ideal for plantations, particularly coconuts.

The Russell Islands are owned almost in their entirety by Levers Pacific Plantations, producing much of the Solomon Island copra. Levers arrived in the Solomon as a consequence of the Pacific Islands Company, which had originally exploited the phosphate deposits on Ocean Island. The Company secured large tracts of land intending to start coconut plantations, but before they were able to realise their ambition they were bought out by Levers Pacific Plantations. In the early days of Protectorate the revenue from these plantations was sufficient to keep the beleaguered administration in financial balance.

Occupied by the Japanese during World War II, the islands were evacuated before the Americans made their advance. An airstrip was built which formed an advance base for fighters taking off to support the assault on New Georgia and other islands in the West. As in many of the islands these wartime airstrips became the peacetime airports for the Solomon Island air services.

The Solomons seem to have inspired visiting Americans to write books about their wartime adventures and one of these inadvertently took place in the Russell Islands. I say inadvertently because it was not until some time after the book had been published that the link with the Russell Islands became known.

The story is of Patsy Lee, a girl of Chinese origins, and of how the young Patsy floated on wreckage from her torpedoed ship all the way from Singapore to the Solomon Islands. On her arrival in the islands she was adopted by US marines and subsequently taken back to America by the Forces chaplain, having been looked after in the interim by nuns in Vanuatu (New Hebrides as it was then). After a long search the chaplain located some relatives in Singapore, which seemed to substantiate the story. Patsy subsequently became a nurse and got married, the chaplain later on writing a book about her remarkable story.

In time the book came to the Solomons and was read by a Chinese woman who had been brought up by friends following the tragic murder of her parents. She had lived on the Levers plantation in the Russell Islands with her family during the War, her father having a small store. He refused to be evacuated prior to the Japanese invasion and continued to trade, although supplies were running short. The people had no money but needed the few provisions remaining in the store, so a desperate situation developed resulting in one enraged worker murdering all the family, except for the two little girls. One of the girls was wounded in the attack and the other was unhurt because she was staying with friends at the time.

The wounded girl was cared for by villagers, who handed her over to the marines when they made their advance on the Russells. They jokingly said she had floated all the way from Singapore, which with no sign of her family or any other Chinese on the island seemed a sufficiently plausible story for the chaplain to believe. However knowing the fate of her family the Chinese lady realised that Patsy Lee might be her sister, so she contacted Archbishop Stuyvenberg in Honiara, who in turn contacted the chaplain who had written the book. The lady went to America, where the two sisters were re-united and the real story came out.

CHAPTER THIRTY THREE

Rennell and Bellona

The main inhabitants of the Solomon Islands are Melanesian peoples, but on the more remote coral islands Polynesians are the principal inhabitants. It is a curious fact that the Polynesians probably originated in the Eastern Solomons, travelling to Samoa and Tonga, from where a second wave of migrants went to most of the other islands of the Pacific. They were very successful at colonising remote islands, not only surviving the long sea journeys, but increasing in number to such an extent that new islands were looked for. It was probably in this last phase of migrations that the remote coral islands of the Solomons were settled. The closest of these Polynesian islands to Guadalcanal are the raised coral atolls of Rennell and Bellona, some 100 miles to the south.

The major tectonic plate boundary that passes through Guadalcanal and which had successively lifted the weather coast of this island, as I was so traumatically made aware, also raised any reefs south of it. Rennell and Bellona were once coral reefs, but continuous raising of the Pacific Plate has pushed them high above the sea, so instead of being just a few metres above the surface, they now have cliffs and are some distance above the level of the ocean. Rennell is the larger of the islands with at its eastern end an inland lake, however Bellona is the more fertile and supports a greater population.

The Polynesians differ from island to island and the Bellonese and

Rennellese are quite distinctive. They are a very intelligent and outgoing people so have taken every opportunity to expand their influence and are found in quite large numbers in Honiara. They are in Government service, in business or carry out any trade they can to advance their own interests and expand their horizons. Some have become sailors, travelling the world and many of the girls have married expatriates and now live happily in distant lands.

I had met many Bellonese in Honiara and was interested to visit their home island, but all my attempts to get there ended in frustration. The first time the boat had to turn back because they discovered that it was pumping water in along the propeller shaft, the second time it was cancelled, then on my third attempt there was a series of trivial delays. When we eventually arrived at Bellona the Captain said I only had an hour in which to do my work.

With the cancelled and delayed ships there was a build up of patients, with more like a days work for me to do, so by a supreme effort I managed to rush through everybody in three hours. The Captain then tried to save time by ordering that we all return to the ship in one dinghy load when it was quite obvious that this would be too many. The wind was strong and the waves breaking so I was very worried when everyone did jump in the small dinghy as the captain had commanded. With hardly any freeboard the top-heavy boat was pushed out into the crashing surf. The Bellonese are a happy-go-lucky people so with most of my fellow passengers there was a mood of gay abandonment, while I sat quietly clutching my precious bag of patient records and medical instruments, anticipating disaster. We wallowed through one wave then a really big one loomed up, the dinghy was too heavy for the crew to manage, the wave picked us up and elegantly up-ended it, hurling everyone into the sea. Fortunately islanders all learn to swim from a young age, so we all made it back to the shore, I swimming with one hand held above the water as I tried to keep my bag dry. The next time we divided into two groups and successfully reached the ship, so for all the captain's impatience, we had taken much longer than if we had followed the safer strategy from the beginning.

We then travelled on to the sister island of Rennell where we spent the night, so there was time for me to walk to the lake after finishing my clinic. Lakes in the Solomons are unusual and this one was especially so because it had started off as a sea lagoon, but after the island had been raised by tectonic activity, it had become a fresh water lake. It is home to a particular kind of sea snake that is found nowhere else in the world. The snake is called Tugihono (*Laticauda crockeri*) and lives on a unique fish *Eleotris fusca* that is also found in the lake. It must have evolved into this endemic species as the lake changed from salt to fresh water, as sea snakes are found only in the sea. However, also found in the lake is a sea krait, unchanged from its relatives in the sea, so is this a recent introduction, and if so how did it get there? Is there some subterranean passage with the sea or did it somehow find its way overland, where it would have had to climb the cliffs before it could get into the lake?

The unique features of Rennell Island as the largest raised atoll in the world and with Lake Tegano and its endemic fauna have caused it to be inscribed on the World Heritage List (number 558). As it mentions the site is a true natural laboratory for scientific study.

Rennell has more endemic species of birds than any other island in the Solomons with a starling, a fantail, shrikebill and two species of white-eye found nowhere else. Sadly the people did not appreciate the unique wildlife of their island, as I was to find from a rather roundabout observation.

For the size of the island and the distance by sea from any other land there seemed to be a surprising absence of canoes. I asked people why this was and the explanation was tragically simple. Canoes were made from a large straight tree that the people called a canoe tree. It had succulent berries that were eaten by a particular kind of pigeon that transferred the seeds around the forest in its droppings. However when the first gun came to the islands the people had a means to kill and eat this pigeon, so in a surprisingly short time all the pigeons were killed off and as a consequence no more canoe trees grew!

Rennell was perhaps the last of the unknown islands as it intrigued the explorers of the 1920's and 30's. Lambert was fired with a desire to visit it in his hookworm campaigns and describes the initial contacts he made with the people, full of suspicion and mistrust. The people stopped any ship from visiting the islands for more than a day or two and a rivalry between the lake people and those of the beach meant that access to the interior was virtually impossible. However the lure of iron objects, particularly axes and knives weakened their resistance and finally bought a way to overcome these difficulties.

The Rennell people trace their origins through many generations from the island of Uvea in the Wallis Islands. They didn't come there directly though, first going to Rotumah, before making the long journey to Rennell.

I had arranged to fly back from Rennell so was glad to leave the unhappy ship with its unreasonable Captain and walk across the island to the airfield and my last clinic. After making me rush through my patients, the Captain wasted time at an intervening port where all the crew messed about on the beach, so despite it being dark when we arrived I set off walking straight away. I continued by the light of my torch and slept in a deserted village half way to my destination. However when I woke the next morning my foot was swollen from a small scratch that had become infected. I limped on until I could go no further, racked with fever, it was agony to put my foot down. Fortunately an early riser, on his way to the fields found me, so he went back to the village and got the only vehicle on the island, a tractor, picked me up and took me to the airfield. After a while the penicillin I had given myself began to work, so I saw all the patients that were waiting for me and then flew back to Honiara.

Any small scratch can rapidly become infected in the damp moist climate of the islands and one needs to be obsessional in covering every minor abrasion of the skin. This was not the first time this had happened to me, so I knew what to do, but infection must have taken place in the short interval between me scratching myself and getting back to the ship to cover it up. Cellulitis can quickly develop, with the infected limb rapidly swelling up and systemic fever making you feel awful. Fortunately the acute infection is still susceptible to penicillin, but the chronic ulcer that nearly always develops can take months to heal.

Sometime after my visit, the islands of Rennell and Bellona were to suffer a major tragedy. As a means of administering the islands, council members would come to Honiara for their meetings. There were only small aircraft and on this particular flight, all the places were taken up with the island members, the most respected and dynamic leaders of the two communities. As the plane neared Guadalcanal there was a huge storm overhead and the pilot thought he would not be able to find the airfield so he turned round to return to Rennell. However as he approached the islands they disappeared under a bank of cloud so he turned back again to try Honiara once more, but the plane ran out of fuel before it reached the coast. A major search was mounted both with aircraft and by sea, but the remains of the plane or any of its occupants were never found. For these small communities to loose all their leaders at one time was a devastating blow. It took them a very long time to recover.

CHAPTER THIRTY FOUR

A voyage into history: Makira and the Eastern Outer Islands

The one part of Solomon Islands I never really got to know like the others, were the Eastern Islands. I had managed to be District Medical Officer for three of the four districts that there were before the re-organizations that came during independence, but I never worked in the East. Finally the opportunity came when I was promoted to Chief Medical Officer, which gave me licence to visit any part of Solomon Islands.

The most southerly island in the chain of main islands is Makira, also known as San Cristobal, from the name given it by Mendana. The capital is Kira Kira where I stayed in the Government Resthouse, which is meant to be haunted. There are many stories of its ghost, but it did not reveal itself to me while I stayed there.

The ghost is that of a girl of Santa Ana who was born in 1796. When she was 13 she was bought by a group of eight bachelors to be their common mistress. Thinking she was common property another man tried to sleep with her, but on being repeatedly rejected he went to a sorcerer to cast a spell. The girl developed a distressing illness and subsequently died, her spirit ascending into a tall tree near where she used to live. Due to the way she had been treated she hated all bachelors, particularly Solomon Islanders and would haunt them if they stayed near her tree. When the Resthouse was being built it was considered necessary to cut down the tree despite warnings from the local people that she would then haunt the Resthouse. As prophesied this is exactly what happened and many a bachelor, European as well as Solomon Islander will testify to the strange opening of doors, or more particularly her special form of terror, to awaken the sleeper by whispering in his ear.

As well as the large island of Makira, there are also several smaller islands nearby and the ship first went to Ulawa, which is actually closer to South Malaita than to Makira.

It was to Ulawa in the late 19th century that the sweet potato was first introduced from the mission school on Norfolk Island. The sweet potato has now replaced the yam as the staple crop in most of the islands, except those occupied by Polynesians, where taro is the main food. In ancient times Ulawa was a rich source of stone adzes which were traded to other islands of the Eastern Solomons.

Excavations indicate that Ulawa was settled more than 1000 years ago, the people, ancestral to the present-day inhabitants manufacturing adzes and a range of other tools for export and their own use. They made gardens that they surrounded with stone boundary walls, similar to what I had seen on the island of Vao, off Malakula, in Vanuatu. Remnants of these garden walls are found around Haradewi village.

The ship returned to Ugi (or Uki) island to spend the night, another place where archaeological excavation has found continuous occupation for at least 500 years. Many fragments of worked shell have been discovered, indicating that Ugi is where the famous carving style of shell inlay bowls probably originated. This style is now largely confined to Santa Ana, Santa Catalina and the Star Harbour area, that I was soon to visit.

On the Weather Coast is the magnificent harbour of Arosi. I had not expected Makira to be so beautiful, with its misty hills and many inlets this gave it a special kind of attractiveness. It has however a shadowy past as recorded by Charles Fox in his *Story of the Solomons*. In about 1875, John Still, an Anglican Missionary was sitting with some people when a group of men brought a captive bound hand and foot and threw him on the fire. The fire burnt through the man's bonds so he tried to escape, but they caught him again and put him back on the fire until he was well cooked, after which they ate him. Cannibalism was part of the way of life and if there was to be a feast then human bodies were required. These were often obtained by professional murderers who would make a living out of supplying them. They would use all kinds of methods to obtain bodies, purposely befriending people and killing them when their confidence had been gained. Sometimes visitors to a feast were put on the menu.

Early missionaries recorded seeing many bodies cooked and prepared for feasts. This was the fate of the first Catholic attempts to missionize the islands in 1852. Three priests were eaten and the rest became ill from malaria, signalling the end of their attempt.

Makira also has interesting links with Indonesia in their death rituals, particularly with the Taraja people in the highlands of Sulawesi. The Taraja have very elaborate ceremonies, as they believe that life on this earth is just a preparation for the greater life after death. For somebody to have lived a full life and then be sent to the next world with the grandest of feasts and sacrifice was the ultimate achievement. However if a young child died they had not fulfilled life on this earth and were given a special burial in a tree. A hole is cut in a growing tree and the small body placed inside. In time the tree will grow round the hole and only the scar will show where the burial was. This seems to be a very unique form of burial, but also occurred in Makira before Christian burial completely replaced this practice.

Charles Fox also mentions that a chief would be buried in a truncated pyramid, called a *heo,* made from undressed blocks of stone going up in steps to a height of some thirty feet, with a large flat top. In his day (he was in Makira between 1908 and 1923) there were only two or three *heos* remaining as earthen mounds, on the top of which dolmens had been built. The dolmen is a very interesting monument that had its heyday in Western Europe in Neolithic times. It is found in other parts of the world, such as North Africa and Korea, but the nearest site to the Solomon Islands is in the Kelabit highlands of Sarawak on the island of Borneo. In the same way that ancient practices found in present day Indonesia may substantiate the link with people migrating from this part of the world, so to could a link be made with Sarawak in Malaysia. The only trouble is that this is a very remote part of the island and the Kelabit people do not have any history of travelling from their highland valleys, as they are not a sea-going people.

Arosi was also home to a shark people similar to those found in the Langa Langa lagoon on Malaita. They would exchange their souls with a shark and so in effect became the shark. They could call the shark using their family name and if they had a grievance against someone, send it to kill them when they were swimming or out in their canoe. The shark would overturn the canoe and bring the hapless individual to its master who would then perform the coup-de-grace. When the shark died so would its master and Charles Fox mentioned that when he shot a shark from his boat the shark man died at the same time. He was therefore accused of murder.

We covered the Weather coast the next day, reaching Santa Ana by nightfall. Here there is evidence of continuous occupation of the island by the same people for the last 1000 years. There is also a much earlier layer of excavation indicating that there were people living on this island 3000 years ago, but a break in the archaeological sequence suggests that they were not the same people. The present day occupants of Santa Ana and Santa Catalina have many features of both Polynesian and Melanesian; perhaps there was a mixing of earlier and later peoples, as the Polynesians may well have originated from this area (see Annex 2).

Star Harbour has a pleasant setting and the rocky eastern coast was most impressive. It is famous for its carvers, specialising in carved house posts and decorated canoes. Excavations have found a few Trochus (*Trochidae*) shell fragments and other decorated items indicating that this style of decorated carving, in common with remains found in Ugi, is at least 500 years old.

On the north coast of Makira, at Pamua, there used to be a pottery industry, but this died out before the white man came to Solomon Islands. Ancient pottery is known from sites both here and in other parts of the Solomons, but seems to have died out a long time ago, which is curious. There must always have been a need for pots to carry water and for cooking before the arrival of the metal pot that is used today, so why the people lost the skill is a mystery. Bamboo makes a reasonable substitute for carrying water and when green can be stuffed with sweet potatoes and placed on the fire until it goes black, when the potatoes inside will be ready. The traditional Pacific method of cooking, called *motu* is used for feasts, where packets of food are wrapped in banana leaves and placed on hot stones within the ground. By these means it would be possible to do all the cooking one required and also carry water, so perhaps the necessity for making pots was found to be too laborious.

Far to the east of Makira are the Eastern Outer Islands which are as close to Vanuatu, with which they share much in common. The main island is Santa Cruz (Ndeni), which is like a smaller version of the larger islands to the west, made of rock and bush, but on a much smaller scale. It does however have two very unique features, one medical and the other archaeological.

Santa Cruz is the only place in the islands where scrub typhus (Tsutsugamushi fever) is found. This can vary from a very mild illness to a debilitating condition with occasionally fatal consequences. Fortunately here it is a mild infection and pupils at the mission school who come from other islands, often complain of a flue like illness when they first start. Once they have had it though they are immune from further infection.

Different from the main islands to the west, a characteristic decorated pottery called Lapita ware (dated to between 1500 and 600 BC) has been excavated in Santa Cruz and the nearby Reef Islands.

Similar pottery has also been found in Vanuatu, New Caledonia, Fiji, Tonga and Samoa. However the pottery in the Polynesian islands shows a transition from classic Lapita style to Polynesian, so tracing this back it can be hypothesised that the origin of this trend started in the Santa Cruz islands in the Solomons and the Torres and Banks Islands in Vanuatu. There is also evidence of trade over long distance by canoe, indicating that these people had the knowledge to travel considerable distance into Polynesia. So it seems that although the present day islanders are of Melanesian type some 2 to 3 thousand years ago a people, who subsequently became the Polynesians, originated from here (see Annex 2).

On another visit I had flown to Santa Cruz to await the ship. Our first stop was the Reef Islands, most appropriately named from the extensive raised coral reef from which they are made. Although much smaller in size than Santa Cruz the people have considerable influence throughout the Eastern Outer Islands. I found them unusually aggressive, very demanding and self opinionated, with not much to offer except the excess of their numbers. They have infiltrated most of the islands and although the gentler Santa Cruz people hold their own on their own island most of the opinion and influence in the district is from the Reef Islanders. They are mainly Melanesian, but in one of those strange quirks of history, Polynesians have back-migrated to the tiny islands of Nifiloli and Pileni.

The sight that greeted us the following morning was one of the most impressive I have seen in any of the islands. I was used to the usual coastal strip and line of coconut trees, or the bush laden hills of the bigger islands, but instead there were huge jagged rocks, rising straight out of the sea. These are the Duff islands. Only one is inhabited, the village being on a small piece of level ground at the southern end and an artificial island they have built up on the nearby reef, on the largest of the islands. Towering above the village is an impressive rock that features significantly in their custom stories.

There are only some three hundred people in the Duffs, there being a limit to how many they can support on their rocky islands, but despite their number these people provide the best example of how the Polynesian islands were colonized. They trace their ancestry, in common with the people of Sikaiana and Ontong Java from Tuvalu (formerly the Ellis Islands). They are very skilled as sailors and used to build huge canoes for inter-island travel. These consisted of a large sea going canoe with single outrigger and platform joining the two, on top of which was built a small house. The single sail was made of palm fronds in the shape of a large stylised spade. Sadly these large canoes are no longer made, but the tradition is maintained, with the construction of models that faithfully copy their larger originals.

The Duff islands may have been the crucial staging place for the colonization of Polynesia as recent archaeological finds suggest. Digging down through old burial sites a succession of graves were found ranging from typical vertical mounds of the Polynesian manner of burial, to Melanesian style. The lowest level is some two to three thousand years old. Could they have been the original transition population that outgrew their little island and were forced to venture further into the Pacific to find new islands to inhabit?

I was sorry to leave these beautiful islands but ahead lay a 36 hour journey to Tikopia so we were obliged to leave by mid-day. The sea was gentle for most of that day, but during the night the wind increased so that by the following morning there was a heavy swell. We floated around in the lea off Tikopia, then transferring to the dinghy, waited for the right wave to surf in over the reef to calmer water inside.

If the Duff islanders are a transitional community, the Tikopians are one of the most traditional Polynesian communities that still survive today. Most Polynesians, like those in Hawaii or Tahiti have become so mixed with other races that it is difficult to decide who is of the original type, but the Tikopians have rigorously maintained their traditional way of life, uninfluenced by the 20th century. They were the subject of early anthropological research by Raymond Firth in his monumental work *We the Tikopia*, so more has been recorded about these people than any others in the Solomon Islands. Not that it was a straightforward progression from the Duff Islands, if this is the way the original Polynesians travelled, for although Tikopia might have been used as a stopping place it was not inhabited until the third wave of migrations. Tonga, Samoa and Futuna were occupied first, from where the second phase of migration proceeded to the surrounding islands and further east. Later on the smaller islands in the Solomons were inhabited, the Tikopians and Anutans tracing their ancestry through fifteen generations from the Wallis islands.

It was the Polynesian's extensive knowledge of the winds and currents, as well as clues from seafaring birds, that allowed them to travel such vast distances across the largest ocean in the world. Although the prevailing winds blow for most of the year, there are times when they reverse, so to set off around this time allowed a voyage of discovery to be made with the opportunity to return should land not be found. Birds migrate from one landmass to another and when they arrived in Polynesia explorers might have set-off to follow them. This is thought to be how New Zealand was discovered as the long-tailed cuckoo migrates from Tahiti and the Cook Islands to take advantage of the southern summer in New Zealand. Similarly the Pacific golden plover (*Pluvialis dominica*) flies from the Marquesas and Society Islands to summer in Russia and North America, stopping off at Hawaii on the way.

Tikopia is a volcanic island with fringing coral reef and the people have made every use of the land, cultivating right up to the mountaintops. The principal crop is taro, a rather inedible root crop when boiled, but by quick frying it can be delicious. Using a similar technique the Tikopians have found that by drying thin slices in the sun, it can be stored for considerable periods, tiding them over times of poor harvest.

There is a crater lake on one side of the island with an impressive path leading to it. The path goes past two large sentinel rocks, the second being particularly difficult to round because the sea side is lashed by waves, while the other drops steeply down into the lake. To overcome this obstacle a magnificent raised path has been constructed from thousands of rocks all carried there by hand, so that the lakeside of the rock can be crossed. Standing on the path gives a fine view up to the volcano crater edge on the far side, curving round to the two rocks and the thin arms of land which separate the lake from the sea. Further round is a natural arch and many fine views of this rugged little island.

I particularly wanted to visit the custom burial place and asking a young man where it was, discovered that this unassuming person was the paramount chief. The grave he showed me was that of his father, and the ancestral chiefly line that extended back many generations. Early explorers calling in at Tikopia mentioned that the chief lived in a large circular house with very small entrance, so that anybody entering was forced to bow their head and crawl on all fours to enter, at the same time paying respect to the chief. I was quite expecting to do this, but such grand houses are no longer to be found and apart from the food stores that all the houses have, they were little different from any on the other islands.

Sadly by the time we got to Anuta, the other Polynesian island not far from Tikopia the waves were huge and the Captain decided it would be far too dangerous to attempt a landing. This was a pity as Anuta plays an interesting part in the link with Polynesia by the discovery of an intermediate type of pottery linking it to the Lapita culture. The first people known to live on Anuta occupied it between 1000 and 600 BC and were not Polynesians. They made plain pots of jar and bowl shapes, which were not elaborately decorated like the Lapita ware. There was no evidence of trade, such as the stone adzes and obsidian found on Santa Cruz and the Reef Islands. However these two pot-making cultures probably had a similar origin, developing quite separately, and then for some unknown reason that in Anuta died out. There is then a break in the archaeological sequence until the ancestors of the present inhabitants arrived, three to four hundred years ago.

We now returned to the other islands in the group Vanikoro (Vanikolo) and Utupua, Vanikoro particularly impressing me with its isolated beauty. A sheer-sided mountain plunged into the fjord like inlet where the ship anchored, while in contrast a narrow strip of land at its base housed lush meadows and the peace and tranquillity of the mission school. The sun set, completing the picture; a blazing red sky setting the mountain on fire, then almost before the magnificent show had disappeared, stars showed through the evening dark and the sky was a mass of delicate lights.

Vanikoro has been the site of more recent history, linking it to the age of discovery of the Pacific by Western nations. La Pérouse, the great French explorer made many discoveries in the southern oceans, visiting Easter Island amongst many others, then disappeared in 1788. What happened to him was not known until many years later when an Irish ship accidentally discovered remains. An expedition subsequently recovered anchors and other parts of the *Astrolabe* and *Bousssole,* La Pérouse's ships. A severe storm had driven the two vessels onto the reef at Vanikoro and the sailors were killed or died from disease.

However Charles Fox, who had a detailed knowledge of the islands, writing in 1967 in his *Story of the Solomons,* gives a different account. After the ships were wrecked, the crew survived and were well treated by the people of Vanikoro. La Pérouse built a ship from the wreckage and with some of the crew sailed away, never to be seen again. The rest of the crew stayed there until they finally died of illness or old age. Bishop Patteson is reputed to have seen sixty European skulls preserved in a head-house, presumably those of the Frenchmen. Perhaps talking to the people would have ascertained the story quicker than a special expedition to find the wreck!

Utupua was gloomy and rain swept as we sailed round it the following morning, taking a long time to find the gap in the reef where an entrance could be made. We did not stay long, returning to Graciosa Bay from where we had started our journey. It was here that Mendana arrived in 1595 to found a settlement, but it suffered bad luck from the very start. A mutiny broke out in the nascent settlement so Mendana went ashore to settle the dispute, executing the camp commander. Mendana then stayed ashore himself but died on 18 October 1595, barely two months after the colony had been established. 47 others died within a month, probably from malaria, and many of the others were sick, so the settlement was abandoned. There was however a curious event that was never explained, until recent archaeological excavations discovered what had happened to Mendana's mysterious fourth boat.

Mendana and his party arrived in four boats, but just as they were coming to Santa Cruz one boat, an almiranta, named *Santa Isabel*, disappeared. The Spanish searched for it, knowing that it was unlikely to have sunk, but they never found it and the mystery of the almiranta and its 182 occupants remained unknown. Chance excavation at Pamua, on the island of Makira, found Spanish pottery identical in type and age to that found at Graciosa Bay. So whether by accident or design, the fourth boat went on to Makira, Ugi and Ulawa, which Mendana had explored in 1568. Curiously Spanish pottery is also found in the uppermost level of the abandoned village site, indicating that it continued to be used for some time. Perhaps this was a successful settlement, some of the Spaniards surviving and mixing with the local population. Alternatively had the pots just been found and subsequently used by the indigenous people? There is no history of part-European descendants, but they might have all tried to sail away and been subsequently lost at sea. The final fate of the fourth boat has still not been completely solved.

Our voyage was not quite over; the ship made a special trip to drop off malaria teams on some of the Reef islands that we had not been to before. On the way we passed Tinakula, the most active volcano in Solomon Islands. The island rises 800m and consists entirely of the volcano. It is continually smoking and ever so often streams of lava and rock roll down its side. Before it became so active it was inhabited, but the entire population was evacuated to the small island of Nupani, when it became too dangerous.

Nupani is such a different island, made of coral and sand rather than the fertile volcanic soil of Tinakula. Still, the inhabitants have made a living from growing taro and coconuts, supplemented by fish and the occasional pig. Water is hard to come by, but the community shows every indication of successfully re-establishing themselves here. There is a graceful coral church and the graves of the early pioneers.

Our last stop was at Nukapu, a very independent little community that had made a name for itself in the early days of missionary activity. Bishop Patteson was evangelising in these islands in 1871 when he was brutally murdered in retaliation for attacks by "Blackbirders". Five men had been taken and it was the father of one of them who killed Patteson. They had normally been friendly islands and Bishop Patteson had good contacts with the people, but he was unlucky to have visited soon after this atrocity took place.

He went ashore alone and unarmed and was welcomed with a new mat, as was the custom. Patteson was a brilliant linguist and had learnt their language so was able to converse with the people, but as he was getting up to leave he was stuck with a club from behind, dying instantly. He was hit on the head again and then on the body, making three wounds, but two more were subsequently made, to symbolise the five men that had been kidnapped. The body was then wrapped in a large mat, fastened at the head and foot, and floated out in a canoe to the waiting ship beyond the reef. Inside on Patteson's chest was placed a palm leaf with five of the fronds knotted, a further indication of the reason for his murder. It was as though a message had been sent to London, for the news of his death reverberated around Whitehall, helping to convince a reluctant British Government of the need to declare a Protectorate over the islands.

CHAPTER THIRTY FIVE

Independence 1978

1975 to 1978 was an exciting time to be in Solomon Islands as the country progressed from a British Protectorate, through self government to full independence. There were many aspects of colonial rule that quite appalled me so I was all in favour of the country progressing to independence as soon as possible. Not that everyone wanted it. I remember talking to one old man about independence and his reply was, "Independence for whom, only those in Honiara want it".

There were concerns about domination by one or other island group; most people feared Malaita domination, while there was a high proportion of Western Solomon Islanders in the government. There were also uncertainties on the form the government should take.

For self-government a very effective system had been worked out called "Governing Council" whereby all elected members chose a Chief Minister and heads of councils (which were like ministries) and then all the members were allocated to each of the councils. For a small island nation with not a large number of suitably educated and experienced people for government this allowed all elected members to take part in the government. However somebody in Britain decided that it would be a good idea if all the Governing Council members could see how governments worked so they were taken to London to see Parliament. The result was that when they got back they decided that they wanted a Westminster system of government with an opposition, rather than a Governing Council. The rivalries that Governing Council was set up to minimise now came out in the open and entered the political arena as parties were formed for the forthcoming elections.

The timetable for independence was first set to be 7 July 1977, a day to remember, but the process took longer than expected and did not happen for another year. It was said that the Governor at that time was so popular that the people hesitated about progressing to independence. He was often seen driving around in his Mini Moke (rather than the official Jaguar) visiting schools and other organisations. With such an amiable administration why did they need to brake from the old colonial master? London however was keen to shed itself of its remaining territories, so it replaced the popular governor, the new incumbent reverting to all the old imperial ways. This had the desired effect of hurrying up the process, so by 1978 all was ready for the independence celebrations.

We were all involved and I was given the job of organising the medical stand. We had designed a unique house consisting of four roundels joined by covered passageways. This we filled with health education posters about important diseases and offered free immunisation to anybody who had not been to their local health centre. Water supply and sanitation were also one of our responsibilities, so to demonstrate how easy it was to have a well, we dug one in the middle of the show grounds so that people could come along and with a few strokes of the pump produce water for themselves. When the Duke of Gloucester, who was representing the Queen in the official proceedings, came to visit our stand, he didn't believe that the water came straight out of the ground and suggested we had a tank of water hidden underneath. I tried to convince him, but short of digging it all up to show him, there was no way we could prove to him that it was that easy in this county of high rainfall to make a well.

The celebrations went on for several days and all worked out well, although in true Solomon Island manner nothing was done until the last minute. It really seemed that everything would not be ready on time, but suddenly all came together and it was a wonderful show. Fortunately the islanders are gifted dancers and musicians so there is never a problem in putting on a show. With all the different islands and ethnic groups there was an amazing range of talent, each was given 15 minutes for their performance, but even so it was almost midnight by the time they had all done their piece.

One of the unique events in the Solomons is the Custom Queen competition, symbolising a marriage, when the girl is decorated with shell money and custom jewellery to the value of her dowry. A girl is chosen by the village and her naked body dressed in the traditional manner, the total value of her shell money far exceeding what she would normally have worn. The contestants are judged on how well they are turned out as well as their beauty. As it is a village affair there was nothing demeaning about such an event and even the girls, who might normally wear Western clothes, did not seem embarrassed to swap them for a loincloth and well draped strings of shell money.

The Independence Ceremony was short and unimpressive. The Union Jack was hauled down at an undignified speed and replaced equally quickly with the new Solomon Island flag. The march past and parade included no traditional warriors, or anything to give it a special Solomon Island flavour, rather it was the last fling of colonial presence. Never again would we see the peaked hat with its ostrich feathers and the starched white uniforms of the Governor and his officials.

CHAPTER THIRTY SIX

The last of the islands

When I first went to Vanuatu the islands were known as the New Hebrides, a name given to them by Captain Cook in 1774. I could see no relation at all with the various islands that lay off the West Coast of Scotland, but Cook must have been thinking of home and the end of his long voyage when he gave them this name. Cook though, was not the first westerner to sight them, the Spanish explorer Quiros (who had sailed with Mendana) arrived at the largest island in 1606 and believing that he had found the fabled southern continent called it Terra Australis del Espiritu Santo. Bougainville subsequently disproved the idea that it was the southern continent, but the name Espiritu Santo (or more commonly just Santo) remained as the name for the largest island.

With the rivalry of the colonial powers to annex all of the Pacific islands, Britain and France, in an effort to forestall Germany, simultaneously appointed Resident Commissioners to the New Hebrides in 1903. It was a time when Britain and France were on good terms with each other rather than fighting for colonial possessions, so the unusual idea of a joint administration, a condominium, was created. The two administrations had different ideas of what was important and promoted their own language and way of life in the islands that came under their control. This neatly divided them into Anglophone and Francophone areas of influence, which led to rivalry and in times hatred. When I visited in 1977 the first seeds of independence had been sown and the Vanuaku Parti (which was English Speaking) had declared provisional government, closing off all their areas to non-party (predominantly French speaking) persons. The opposition had done the same so it was difficult to travel round. I arrived in Vila where John met me at the airfield.

John was the quintessential British administrator with his public school education and correctness of manner so it seemed a little surprising that he had married the vivacious Elian, who pronounced her English in a way only French women can, not meaning to be sexy, but having that effect anyway. They had been friends of ours in Honiara, where Elian had suffered in her attempts to integrate with the stuffy British way of life. She finally persuaded John to request a transfer, so the natural place to go was the New Hebrides, where Elian could live something of the life she had been used to. French territories were directly administered from Paris, rather than setting up self-supporting governments as in the British model, so wherever French was spoken a little bit of France was created.

Due to the twin administrations a degree of rivalry developed and this was particularly pronounced in the medical field. The British hospital was superior to its counterpart in Honiara with the number of its specialists something that we could only dream about. I had been the obstetrician to Central Hospital with only a diploma to back up my appointment, but here they had a consultant with all the requisite qualifications. He was a friend of John and Elian's so it was not long before I was introduced to him and as usually happens when two doctors get talking our conversation soon deteriorated into the subject we knew best. However it soon transpired that Richard and I had another connection and that was East Africa; I had been brought up in Zanzibar when it was a separate country and he had worked in the unified Tanzania. Richard's time in the New Hebrides was coming to an end and he would be going back to Tanzania, so I asked what he would be doing?

"When Barbara Castle met Nyrere she asked him what aid he wanted from the British Government and he had requested a referral hospital in southwest Tanzania. The project has taken many years to develop but it will start next year and Nyrere has asked me to lead it." Apparently Richard had made a big impression on the President when he worked there before and Nyrere had made a personal request for him to be in-charge.

"Who will you have working with you?" I asked.

"I am building up the team at the moment and amongst them will be a Community Health Specialist, would you be interested?" I could not believe my luck as I was wanting to go to Africa next and this was the field in which I had specialised during my year back in England.

"Yes, it is exactly what I want to do so please put me on your list." It was one of those chance meetings that was to have a major influence on my life.

Amongst the other prospective members of Richard's team for the project in Tanzania was another Richard, who was the District Medical Officer for the southernmost islands and he invited me to visit him. The main island was Tanna, which although of quite small size supported a population of 16 thousand on its rich volcanic soil. Many of the people continued to follow their custom ways, especially the Nambas with their unique form of dress, while the women wore long colourful grass skirts, rather than a dress or sarong.

Tanna is home to one of the most approachable active volcanoes in the world, Mount Yasur, so Richard drove me across the island to see it. All around was a sparse lunar landscape, while the volcano rumbled and belched out jets of black smoke. Due to the troubles, the local people had tried to stop anyone from climbing it, but undaunted we waited until it was dark to begin our attempt. It was an uncanny sensation as we struggled up the dusty sides, bumping into boulders which had not so long ago been inside the crater. Every now and then there would be a great roar and bang as hot rocks shot up into the sky.

It was quite an effort to get to the top, fumbling around in the dark and slipping on the uneven surface, but once we reached the crater edge, we were glad that we had made the effort. Two vents were active, sending up tracers of molten rock, then every now and then there would be an immense bang and hot stones would shoot into the sky, higher than the vantage point on which we were standing. We were careful that they did not fall on us as we could see their lighted trail as they fell to earth, but this made us realise that night probably was the best time to view this spectacle; nature's very own firework display.

A curious sect had grown up on Tanna called the Jon Frum (or Jonfrum) movement. It came into prominence after World War II, but probably started in the 1930's with a spirit that helped the people. Nobody will say who exactly Jon Frum was or why this name was chosen, but adherents believe he will bring them all the good things in life, similar to the cargo cult that grew up in Solomon Islands after the War. It is thought that Jon Frum was possibly a black American soldier who unloaded supplies here during the War and for some unknown reason gave them to the islanders. The symbol of the movement, the Red Cross came from another American called John who worked for the International Red Cross, and by a strange twist the people thought this was the symbol of Jon Frum. Its followers erect red crosses and symbolic totems to indicate who are his followers so that when Jon Frum returns he will know who they are.

It was to Tanna that the great missionary of the Pacific, another John, John Williams tried to introduce Christianity. He had been strikingly successful in the Polynesian islands so he now turned his attention to Melanesia. Landing first at Tanna he left behind Polynesian missionaries to learn the language and instruct the people, then he proceeded to Erromanga(o) to do the same. However to the people of Erromanga all white men were sandalwooders, the unscrupulous exploiters of this valuable wood, so landing unarmed he was easy prey. Almost immediately he was clubbed to death; throughout Polynesia he is the most famous of Christians, but it is on the island of Erromanga, in Melanesia, that his grave is to be found. When he arrived in Samoa on his boat the *Messenger of Peace*, amongst the crew was a more deadly threat, influenza. It ravaged the islands and probably supported the evangelizing message of death and retribution to the non-believer. They were not going to let the same thing happen again in Erromanga.

I returned to Vila and flew on to Malakula, the second largest of the islands, the plane landing at Lamap, where Captain Cook had come ashore, but this time it was for another dignitary, the Chief Minister. We therefore had a grand reception on arrival, which slightly handicapped the arrangements made for me by my friends in Vila. As they were fully occupied with the Chief Minister, they delegated their charge to the likeable Tongan John.

How John had come to Malakula from his native Tonga I never found out, but such is the Pacific that you come across the most interesting characters in the most unlikely of places. John was the road builder and took delight in showing me the road he had built in the northern part of the island, while I was more interested in the scenery. It also gave me the opportunity to go across to Vao, a small island off the northeast coast where the people observed a strict delineation of territory, partitioning off the areas around their houses with stone walls, (similar to remains on Ulawa, in the Eastern Solomons). In the centre of the village was a customary meeting place with sacred rocks and slit gongs.

The slit gong is an important feature of inland Malakula, particularly amongst the Nambas further south. These people followed their traditional way of life until comparatively recently, which often meant internecine warfare. One tribe would attack another and any person killed would then have to be revenged, which would in turn lead to a return attack and so on. There are two main groups, the Big Nambas and the Small Nambas, differentiated by the size of the penis sheath (*namba*) they traditionally wear. This is made from rattan wound round the penis and then continued to a point, greatly exaggerating what is hidden inside. Although of considerable interest the nambas were difficult to contact, even cannibalism continuing amongst them well into the 1950's.

The pig is the most important commodity in the islands, in some communities held to be more important than a man's wife. Not only was the pig regarded as wealth to be slaughtered at an important feast to show how rich the person was, but the most prized pigs were those which developed circular tusks. The eye teeth were knocked out of the upper jaw of the young pig to allow the lower canine to grow unhindered, curving back on itself to complete a full circle. This meant that the pig couldn't forage in the normal way and had to be taken care of. A woman would look after it as though it was her own child, even breast feeding it when it was small. These completely curved tusks had great value and were used for buying brides or settling blood disputes. The pigs of Vanuatu seemed to be very special. As well as forming an important part of the life of the islanders, there was a group of pigs that were said to be hermaphrodite.

North of Malakula is the largest island in Vanuatu, Espiritu Santo, where Quiros landed and attempted to set up a colony. He noted that wild oranges grew here which is a curiosity, as they are not found anywhere else in Melanesia. Coates (1970) thought these trees must have originated from Asia probably South China, but if this is the case how did they come to this island? It seems unlikely that migrating peoples brought them, as Quiros noted that they were considered not to be edible. It would be remarkable if they were a mutation as there is no other species of tree that bears any resemblance to the orange.

The main town, situated on the southeast of the island, was called Luganville, although often known just as Santo, as was the whole island. It didn't have the character of the capital Vila and still retained much of its war time origins, with several of the buildings vintage Quonset huts. During the war 100,000 American servicemen were stationed here and much of the war effort in the Solomons was directed from Santo. The most prominent reminder of the war was the wreck of the *President Coolidge*, a luxury liner converted into a troop ship that hit a mine when it tried to enter port without a pilot. This lies on the reef close to "Million Dollar Point", so called because the Americans dumped huge quantities of vehicles and other war surplus here at the end of the war. Apparently the vehicles were offered to the planters for a cut-rate price, but thinking that they would eventually get them for free they prevaricated. Instead the Americans finding no takers pushed the lot into the sea.

* * * * *

I was nearing the end of my time in the Solomons, I had visited all the islands and was now in a more senior position in the Ministry, so only rarely got away from the office into the jungle that I loved. It was perhaps this prospect of a sedentary life and that I had been in the islands for a period of 10 years that made me finally realise the time had come to move on. The offer to go to Tanzania had progressed to a definite commitment and I was to do another course of study to prepare me for it. However I wanted to make one last visit to Guadalcanal, to see how people had recovered from the earthquake and what changes had taken place in the bush.

I returned to Totongo, which I had last been to during the earthquake, but as it was still not late I set off the same evening to walk to Surapau where I was greeted with traditional Guadalcanal hospitality; I knew I was going to miss the life of the interior when I left. The route I had planned to take was still disrupted by earthquake damage, so I had to go a long way round following the river to Kolopau and Luguvasa. There were few people here, but one old man took me to the next village, close to Nauli. The latter part of the walk had been spectacular as we passed through a deep gorge, along shelves of rock, with the bubbling river rushing below. It was still early in the afternoon, I was not yet exhausted, and by my calculations we were close to the mountain ridge, which once across would be plain sailing to the other side. I even thought I might cross Guadalcanal in the same day, which I had never succeeded in doing before, so I tried to persuade someone to take me on. None of the men were willing or in a fit state, then a boy came forward who would lead me, providing I carried the rucksack. We set off again to commence the upward climb, but the additional burden of the rucksack soon began to tell on me. I puffed and panted my way upward, my rests became more frequent, until completely exhausted I collapsed in a cold sweat.

I was feeling quite ill, my heart was pounding in my chest and I realised that I would have difficulty in going on. However this was no place to stop, so my brave little helper shouldered the rucksack and we struggled on. Progress though was slow; I was very weak and had to keep on having long rests to give me enough strength to manage the next uphill stretch. I had completely underestimated the height to which we needed to climb. We soon entered the moss line, where Old Man's Beard hung from the trees and everything was green and damp, but still we needed to go higher, to where the trees were stunted and bent and all was covered with a thick carpet of moss. The mist swirled round us with the encroaching night, and despite our exertions I could feel it was getting cold.

Eventually we reached the top and my knowledgeable companion found a wild succulent plant that I gobbled down, it tasted good and helped to refresh me. Relieved to have completed the exhausting accent I thought my problems were over, but there was worse to come. The way down was very steep, mostly rock and loose under foot. We continued at a perilous rate of descent for over an hour, I was glad we were off that cold summit, but still we had not left the moss layer. My ankles were beginning to buckle under the strain and my guide told me that there were two further descents like this before we even reached the river. I was now in agony as well as exhausted and knew I could go no further. Dark was upon us, so we fumbled through the forest to a small lean-to shelter that my guide knew about. It seemed as though I wasn't the only one to only get as far as this. He cut a few more palm fronds to patch up the roof and some more for us to lie on, then I settled to an uneasy sleep, only half covered by the shelter and competing with tree roots for space on the ground.

With a night's rest, uncomfortable though it had been, I was determined to try and catch up with the long stretch I knew lay ahead. We started before dawn, continuing the agonising descent, made worse by a sprained ankle. It was still two hours of interminable slipping, slithering, scrambling progress before we finally reached the river. I was overjoyed to have completed the difficult mountain stretch; from here it would be easier, even in the state my ankle was in.

We followed down the valley visiting the many villages that would have welcomed us for the night if we had got this far, and soon reached the road. Our way took us to Makaruka, where I rested for a while. Moro was in residence; it seemed better if I arrived unannounced like this. I spent some time trying to persuade him how active health care was important to the welfare of his people and not opposed to his doctrine of self-reliance.

"We would be happy to train up anyone he chose," I said.

He was polite and said little, but I took this as an indication that he was not going to change his attitude. Had Morrow won or would the new realisations that had taken place in the villages I had seen in the interior be a natural end to the movement? I was never to find out.

We reached Avu Avu by nightfall, which before had been our base for organising emergency relief for the earthquake victims. It was now peaceful and Father Percy was away so I was offered the use of his house, which although simple, in my condition was like being given a penthouse suite in a luxury hotel. Next day we made good progress to Kuma, only to be halted within a short distance of our destination by a tremendous thunderstorm. The rain continued with great force, but after two hours it had abated sufficiently for us to go on, only to be faced by a dirty, flooded Kuma river. I took off my trousers and clutched them above my head as we half waded and were half swept down by the current, but managed to reach the other side.

I was surprised at how much damage remained from the

earthquake, now almost two years ago. The landslides still scarred the hillsides, and where gardens had been, was still unusable land. Still some good soil had been brought down on to the flat by the rain and this was now actively cultivated. Life on the Weather Coast was always a struggle, and certainly this had been a harder time than most, but the people had survived.

By a combination of canoe and walking with more swollen rivers to wade through I eventually reached the airfield at Bambanakira in time to catch the plane back to Honiara. It had been a challenging walk and the last I was ever to make in the islands.

* * * * *

It had been a most rewarding time to have been in the Solomons, and now they were going their own way I was pleased I had been able to be a little part of it. However my new job took me away from the people I felt close to, from the smell of the bush and the magnificence of the sea, it was not what I really wanted to do and became the reason for me to leave.

I had visited every island, almost every village; I had lived close to the people and knew how they thought, it was as though I had been one of them. Now I was going I would leave a part of me behind, in those islands I so loved.

The land

There is a strange paradox between Australia and the rest of the land that arches like a shield around this most ancient of continents. Some of the oldest rocks in the world are found in Australia and its great mountain ranges are worn down to little more than big hills, while Southeast Asia and the Western Pacific are young landmasses, with constant volcanic activity shaping them all the time. There are more active volcanoes in Java than any other place in the world, and in the centre of the island of New Guinea is a mountain so high that it is constantly covered in snow, despite being almost on the equator. The highest mountains in the comparatively small sized Solomon Islands are higher than any in the vast expanse of Australia.

These are islands of mountains, smouldering volcanoes and powerful rivers. Rivers that carve out the land, washing its soil far into the sea. Acting like great barriers, the mountains catch the moisture-laden air which descends in constant rainfall, encouraging a prolific growth of jungle. Such is the amount of rainfall that it is jokingly said in the Solomons that there are two seasons, a wet season and a rainy season!

The other island builder is the remarkable coral polyp. It was Charles Darwin who propounded a theory of atoll formation, showing how the fringing coral of a volcanic island continues to grow upwards as the volcano sinks and finally disappears below the surface. This theory was tested in 1896-1898 by a scientific expedition sent out by the Royal Society to take drill samples from the reef at Funafuti, the main island of Tuvalu. However the coral never grows above the low water mark, so how are islands formed? Tuvalu is also a good place to understand how this probably comes about.

Most of the atolls have their islands on the eastern and southern sides of the lagoon, the direction of the prevailing winds, while the other sides remain as low reef. On Funafuti there was a bad cyclone in 1972 and a high shingle bank, the length of the main island, was thrown up. So although the coral never grows above low water level the reef is continually pounded by the prevailing winds and at exceptional times by cyclones, so breaking off pieces of coral and throwing them up on to the top of the reef. After some time, sufficient debris has built up so that any wandering seeds will start the first growth of an island. Once established it does not take long for plant debris to build up to form soil, so supporting trees and a wider range of plants. Another method is by the more violent uplifting of reef by tectonic activity that I had witnessed on Guadalcanal.

While the sea did not present any barrier to the passage of *Homo sapiens* it did to many species of animals and plants, as observed by Alfred Russel Wallace (after whom an imaginary line east of Sulawesi is named). To the west of Wallace's line are large mammals, water buffalo, rhino, and monkeys, while to the east none of these species are found. As one goes further east the number of different species decreases with each barrier of water that has to be crossed. A good example is that of the reptiles. Twenty two families are found in the island of New Guinea, twelve in the Solomons, eight in Fiji, but by the time Samoa is reached there are only four, while two families make it all the way to Tahiti.

Peopling of the Pacific

The eastern islands of Indonesia, Papua New Guinea, Solomon Islands, Vanuatu and New Caledonia are all inhabited by Melanesian peoples. Melanesians were probably the main inhabitants of Southeast Asia and all these islands in ancient times, but remain only in the Western Pacific in any number. This can be seen most clearly in the hinterland of West Malaysia, where Melanesian type people are found in the jungle covered centre of the peninsular. These people, the nomadic Orang Asli share all the same appearances, with a black skin and frizzy hair, but differ slightly in their way of life and customs. There are also Negroid people living in the interiors of several of the Philippine islands who probably arrived from Borneo (where ancient remains have been found in Niah cave). They most likely travelled via the small islands that connect it to Palawan (where the oldest human skull so far discovered in Philippines has been found).

The most ancient human remains in these parts were found in Java, a variety of *Homo erectus* (called *Pithecanthropus* by Dubois, their discoverer) who had reached this part of the world by 1 million years ago (possibly as much as 1.66 million). These were surpassed by ancient *Homo sapiens* originating from Africa (the out-of Africa theory) so that by at least 50,000 years ago *Homo sapiens* appeared in south-east Asia. They crossed into Australia about 46,000 years ago, subsequently migrating via the land bridge that joined it to New Guinea and more slowly passed along the chain of islands of the Western Pacific. A major divergence took place with Papuans, centred on New Guinea and Austronesians in much of Southeast Asia. The Austronesians and their descendants now live in all the Pacific islands, but in the Western Pacific group there are various admixtures of Papuans, as their language type can still be distinguished.

While these are the broad groupings, the islands of the Western Pacific are now inhabited by every variety of tribal type, from the course featured highlanders of New Guinea (Papuans) to the very black, fine featured inhabitants of the Western Solomon Islands. Even within the small island group of Solomon Islands there are the brown skinned people of Malaita and the intensely black people from Choiseul and New Georgia, as different in their appearance as they are in every other way. This would suggest that various migrations have taken place along the island chain, starting from the Indonesian islands or even from mainland Southeast Asia, either displacing the original inhabitants or mating with them, to produce the remarkable variety of peoples that are found there now.

Where there were isolated islands, or parts of islands, such as highland New Guinea, then more ancient Papuan peoples remained, whereas in others, especially coastal areas more admixture occurred. This is particularly noticeable in the islands of Sumba and Flores in Indonesia, where every shade of colour and shape can be seen. There are examples of people, that removed from their background could have come from Solomon Islands or Vanuatu, or others with a Malayo-Indonesian admixture that look very much like Polynesians or Micronesians.

The Orang Asli of Malaysia bear a striking resemblance to Melanesians such that if one was shown a picture of them and another of Solomon Islanders one would be hard placed to tell the difference. They inhabit the jungle-covered interior, leading a simple hunter-gatherer life style. Their houses are constructed from bark and palm thatch, in the same way as many inland Melanesians, while they live on animals that they hunt with blowpipes. The little money that they require is obtained from gathering rattan, which is then traded for other commodities. One of the most interesting similarities is a form of music they invented by striking different lengths of bamboo on the ground, so that the air is forced through the pipe rather like an organ. This method of making music is also found in Solomon Islands, as are panpipes, the other main musical instrument of the Orang Asli.

The island of New Guinea, one of the last to be fully explored by Western man has always been considered to be primitive and under-developed, but 9,000 years ago Papuan peoples had developed early agriculture. (This is at much the same time as the Mesopotamian and Indus Valley civilizations were flourishing). A system of water control was developed over the next 4,000 years to provide year round agriculture, the key to continuous food production and the support of a large population. The pig was domesticated and became an item of great value, being a necessary asset to buy a bride and the ultimate sacrifice on the death of a respected member of society. The early travellers took this custom into Solomon Islands and Vanuatu, where it is still an essential part of the culture to this day.

Wealth and status is determined by how much can be given away, with the ultimate sacrifice being made when somebody dies. A large number of pigs will be slaughtered and the whole village feast on them for several days. This is very similar to the custom practised by the Taraja in central Sulawesi (Indonesia) with the difference being that there it is the water buffalo that is sacrificed. However the pig is the second most valuable animal and will also be sacrificed, so in the Western Pacific islands where buffalo are not found the pig has become the status animal.

All these similarities support the evidence that people migrated in successive waves along the island chain from west to east. As well, present-day genetic testing supports this. However this presumes that early people had developed a means of crossing the sea.

During the last ice age Sumatra, Java and Borneo were joined to mainland Asia by the Sunda shelf, and New Guinea was joined to Australia by the Sahul shelf, but between were still large stretches of water that had to be crossed. So as long as 50,000 years ago man had learnt how to cross the sea in this part of the world, probably long before his western cousin. How this first started can only be speculated.

The simplest form of craft would be to bind logs together and make a raft but there is no tradition of using rafts in this part of the world. While it might have served the very first migrants it was the development of the canoe that was the secret to mans' success. Starting off with a log this must have been progressively shaped and hollowed out until the dugout canoe was perfected. A well made dugout can be extremely sea-worthy and there are many stories of lone paddlers being swept out to sea by storms and surviving to tell the tale. If capsized, they can be baled out and re-boarded so rough seas are not a problem.

However the largest dug-out canoe is determined by the size of the tree from which it is cut and cannot be made too thin walled or else it will not have sufficient support when on the sea. So gradually a new type of canoe developed made from planks, stitched together with creepers or string from the husk of coconuts, and the gaps sealed with a putty like black resin extracted from the nut of the *Parinarium laurinum* tree. It was constructed around a frame, allowing the hull to have some flexibility, and be much lighter than a solid boat. The limitations of size were also overcome so much larger canoes could be built, as found in the Duff Islands and throughout Polynesia.

While the dugout canoe is still the main canoe type to be found in most of the Western Pacific islands, there are good examples of planked canoes in Solomon Islands. These were famously used in headhunting raids from the Roviana lagoon where some specimens are still preserved. Sadly though craftsmen skilled in their manufacture are on the decrease and the construction of large canoes in much of Melanesia is on the decline.

The Melanesians never mastered the art of sail and so most of these early journeys must have been made by paddle. They did however have one great natural asset and this was the coconut. Coconut palms are abundant and the nut easily floats so is carried to any new land where washed up on the beach they start to grow. The coconut is a ready-made store of sterile water and nutritious carbohydrate, so a canoe can be filled with them and nuts opened as required. The husk can be used for making string and the empty shell a water container, bailer, spoon or other utensil.

By this means people started to move from the large island of New Guinea to the smaller islands to the east. The Bismarck archipelago, (now part of Papua New Guinea) was settled 32,000 years ago and people had reached Buka, in the North Solomons by 28,000 to 20,000 years ago. Excavations in Guadalcanal have found remains of a more recent date (1300 to 1000 BC in Poha cave), but because of the large difference in time between the first discovered arrival of man in Buka it would seem that earlier sites still remain to be found. There is a comparatively large stretch of water to be crossed between the Bismarck Archipelago and Buka, whereas between Buka, Bougainville and Solomon Islands there is almost a continuous chain of islands. However, even if man took 10,000 years to get this far then one can anticipate a date of at least 8000 BC for his first arrival in Solomon Islands. As it seems that there was a succession of waves of migrating peoples, the remains found at the Poha River site probably represent a later invasion of people. It was these people, having followed down the island chain that took off from the Eastern Outer Islands of the Solomons and the Banks Islands of Vanuatu to subsequently become a separate people, known as the Polynesians.

The Pacific has always been divided into Melanesia, Polynesia and Micronesia, which is a description of the islands rather than the people. Melanesia being the black islands, Polynesia the many islands and Micronesia the small islands, but these names have become associated with the people as well. On the whole they are distinctive, a Tongan or Samoan is quite different from a Solomon Islander, and a ni-Kiribati (Gilbertese) with his more Mongoloid features, can be separated from a Polynesian, but there are many places where this pure distinction does not apply. Fiji for example has a black people, but in every other way they are Polynesians, while some Polynesians have frizzy hair, like Melanesians.

The Fijians are one of the enigmas of the Polynesian-Melanesian divide. There is no doubt that the people of the main islands are black skinned, but in the large ocean going canoes that they constructed, the Lapita culture of which they were part, and in many of their customs, they are more like Polynesians. Lapita pottery remains indicate that Fiji was first inhabited by 1500 BC. From here groups continued on to Samoa and Tonga.

Similarities in language also support a link between Fiji and Polynesia as Fijian, Polynesian and certain languages of northern Vanuatu were a single language until about 1000 BC. Speakers of this early language then appear to have moved from Vanuatu into Fiji where a dialect developed that subsequently split into Fijian and Polynesian.

There is actually very little difference in the genes of a white and a black person, and a colour change is a very subtle transition for the human body. With the intermixing of the Melanesians with the peoples that migrated down the island chain from Indonesian islands and subsequently gave rise to the Polynesians, this mixture could progress along a black or a non-black line. (This can easily be seen in the offspring of a mixed marriage, where one child can be quite white and the other quite black, although most will be a brown colour). It seems more likely that the Fijians were in fact of the same stock that also went on to Tonga and Samoa, indeed in their build they are very similar, but the Fijians retained the black skin pigmentation, while the Tongans and Samoans became lighter in colour. Polynesians have both straight and frizzy hair, so this is not a determining feature, so in many ways it seems preferable to consider Fijians as Polynesians, albeit with black skins.

Western Samoa and Tonga are in many ways considered the centre of Polynesia, for it was from this area that the major migrations explored the islands of the Eastern Pacific. There is evidence that the ancient Samoans maintained contact with both the Fijians and Tongans, supporting the concept that they had a common origin. However this was not always amicable as Tonga ruled Samoa from 950 to 1250 AD.

Wherever the Polynesians went they introduced new plants, taro, yams, coconuts, breadfruit, arrowroot and sugar cane. Bamboo, the most utilitarian of plants was valuable for building houses, making baskets and for fishing. Ginger was used for culinary purposes and gourds of the *Lagenaria* vine as containers. Even the hibiscus, the flower symbol of the Pacific islands, was introduced more for the value of its wood in making paddles than its magnificent flower. The wild ancestors of all these plants are native to Southeast Asia, adding to the evidence that this is where they originally came from. However they are all found in New Guinea, Solomon Islands and Vanuatu, where they are just as much part of the Melanesian way of life, so it is unlikely that the Polynesians came through the island chain without stopping. More likely it was a gradual process, the people evolving all the time until their final take-off from eastern Solomons and northern Vanuatu.

It was the ability of the people that became the Polynesians to construct sea-going canoes and the use of sail as seen in the models of boats now constructed in the Duff Islands. In Tahiti, Huahine was the canoe building centre of this part of Polynesia. Huge double-hulled vessels over 20 metres in length were constructed. The living quarters was a thatched shelter on the centre of the platform joining the two hulls. Skilled craftsmen from the village would undertake the construction high up on the shore and then the massive canoe would be dragged down to the water on wooden rollers. Human sacrifice was required for the launch so captives would be laid down between the logs.

In several of the Polynesian islands an unexpected finding were the maraes, large stone walled enclosures with often a platform at one end. The typical Tahitian pattern is of a step-like temple platform, often with a central hole containing bones. They are normally of two or three levels, but drawings by eighteenth century visitors show them to be of as many as ten. There is historical record from Captain Cook's visits that the largest of the maraes (Mahiatea) was erected between 1766 and 1767 by the high priestess Purea, in memory of her son Temrere. On Huahine they took on a rather different plan with a long rectangular enclosure formed from slabs of coral, surmounted by a similar one of larger dimensions. I was reminded of the tombs of the kings in Tonga which were of the same plan, but on a larger scale, or the huge statues of Easter Island which were constructed on small stone platforms, in all of these islands there seemed to be a similar need for a higher culture.

Tonga was the only island nation not to be colonised, the colonial powers recognising the line of Royalty, the only kingdom still remaining in the Pacific. This is an ancient institution and centred on the island are the burial mounds of the kings, the *Langi*, constructed from huge limestone slabs. These are massive structures and the effort required to have moved the slabs into position must have taken a large number of able-bodied men. They consist of rectangular platforms three to five layers high, forming a pyramidal shape. Covering the top is a huge stone, concealing a chamber, inside of which the Tui Tonga was buried.

During the reign of Queen Salote she gave permission for one of her relatives to be buried inside one of the *Langi* because he was of Royal line. On raising the immense covering slab that had not been moved for four hundred years, they found a vault some twelve feet by four feet and some three feet deep, walled with finely worked masonry. Inside was not the body of just one person, but three, one lay face downwards and clearly was that of the king, while the other two were crouching by the side. These were probably the bodies of the *Haatafunga* whose duty it was to prepare the body, wrapping it in fine mats, but in so doing they were allowed to take away the precious adornments that had covered the body in the funeral procession. The huge covering stone was lowered by an elaborate mechanical arrangement, which gave the *Haatafunga* just enough time to perform their sacred duties and climb out of the chamber. These ones had been just too slow and were sealed in with their dead master.

Even further afield was South America, which Thor Heyerdahl had famously linked to the Pacific Islands when he made his famous voyage on the Kon-Tiki. This was an alluring theory, especially when on a visit to Peru I found the Incas had red shell necklaces very similar to the shell money made in Solomon Islands. It seemed tempting to add this to the wealth of evidence collected by Thor Heyerdahl in his monumental work, *American Indians in the Pacific*, but this was an exception, modern genetic testing and other data finds no cultural link between South America and the Pacific islands. Rather it was probably the Polynesians, perhaps the greatest sailors of all times, having crossed so much of the Pacific in their voyages of exploration, continued on to the shores of South America. Evidence for this is the sweet potato, a native of South America, but found in Easter Island, Hawaii and New Zealand before Europeans ever ventured to this part of the world.

The other great migration of the Pacific was by a people who later on became known as the Micronesians. The most southern island in the Palau group, Helen Island, is less than 400 kilometres from Halmahera in Indonesia and just over 200 kilometres from the Indonesian islands of Kepulauan Asia. By island hopping people could have made their way from Indonesia to Palau and from there to the other islands of Micronesia. Another theory proposes that they came directly from the Philippines and indeed the people of Palau bear many similar characteristics to Filipinos, but from Mindanao, the closest island of the Philippines it is 820 kilometres, a far greater journey into the unknown than coming up from Indonesia.

It seems more likely that people travelled along the Indonesian island chain, skilled in sailing and navigation, prepared to sail out into the unknown to find new islands. One group travelled through New Guinea, Solomon Islands and Vanuatu, where mixing with Melanesian stock, the Polynesians developed, setting off to explore and finally reach the most easterly parts of the Pacific. Another group took a different route and went north from the area of the Moluccas (Maluku), following the islands to Palau and from there to the rest of Micronesia. Not having mixed with any other races on the way they have a paler skin and more mongoloid features.

While our ancient ancestors took thousands of years to move across the land, these comparatively recent argonauts had been to every island in the vast expanse of the Pacific, making their homes on those that could support them, or travelling on to the next, in an ever continuing voyage of discovery. Their skill at sailing these vast distances never ceases to amaze me and their ability to survive the long sea journeys is a tribute to their tenacity. I had started in Solomon Islands, unaware that there were any connections with the more far flung parts of the Pacific, but found that the ancestors of many of these island people might well have passed through those islands, on their way to found the many nations that are now scattered over the largest ocean on our planet.

Source material and further reading

Allan C. H. (1957) *Customary Land Tenure in the British Solomon Islands Protectorate,* Honiara.

Amherst, L. and Thompson B. (1901) *The Discovery of the Solomon Islands by Alvaro de Mendana in 1568* (two volumes) Hakluyt Society, London.

Armstrong E. S. (1900) *The History of the Melanesian Mission*, London.

Barclay J. (1987) *Travelling Hopefully*, Summer Times Publishing, Singapore.

Beaglehole J. C. (1934) *The Exploration of the Pacific*, London.

Bellwood P. (1978a) *Man's Conquest of the Pacific*, Collins, Auckland.

Bellwood P. (1978b) *The Polynesians, Prehistory of an Island People*, Thames and Hudson, London.

Bellwood P. (1985) *The Prehistory of the Indo-Malaysian Archipelago*, Academic Press, Sydney.

Belshaw C. S. (1954) *Changing Melanesia*, Oxford.

Bogesi G. (1948) Santa Isabel, *Oceania* **18**.

Buck P. (1953) *Explorers of the Pacific*, Honolulu.

Buxton P.A. (1927) *Researches in Polynesia and Melanesia*. (*Memoir Series,* **1 & 2).** The London School of Hygiene and Tropical Medicine, London.

Byrd E.E. & St. Amant L.S. (1959) Studies on the epidemiology of filariasis on Central and South Pacific Islands. *South Pacific Commission Technical Paper Series No. 125*, Noumea.

Coates A. (1970) *Western Pacific Islands*, Her Majesty's Stationary Office, London.

Cochrane G. (1970) *Big Men and Cargo Cults*, Oxford.

Codrington R.H. (1891) *The Melanesians*, Oxford (reprinted 1969).

Crichlow N. (1929) The prevalent diseases of the British Solomon Islands. *Transactions of the Royal Society of Tropical Medicine and Hygiene,* **23**, 179-181.

Cultural Association of the Solomon Islands (1976) *Journal of the Cultural Association of the Solomon Islands*, **4**, Honiara. (See also Solomon Islands Museum Association.)

Cultural Association of the Solomon Islands (1977) *Journal of the Cultural Association of the Solomon Islands*, **5**, Honiara.

Davenport W. and Coker G. (1967) The Moro Movement of Guadalcanal, British Solomon Islands Protectorate, *Journal of the Polynesian Society* **76** (June).

Feldt E. (1946) *The Coast Watchers*, Sydney.

Firth R. (1936) *We, The Tikopia*, Allen and Unwin, London.

Firth R. (1967) *Tikopia Belief and Ritual*, Allen and Unwin, London.

Fox C. E. (1924) *The Threshold of the Pacific*, Kegan Paul, London.

Fox C. E. (1958) *Lord of the Southern Isles*, Mowbery & Co, London.

Fox C.E. (1962) *Kakamora,* Hodder & Stoughton, London.

Fox C.E. (1967) *The Story of the Solomons*, Diocese of Melanesia Press, Taroaniara.

Freeman J. D. and Geddes W. R. (1959) *Anthropology in the South Seas*, Auckland.

Green R.C. (1977) *A First Culture History of the Solomon Islands*, University of Auckland, Auckland.

Guppy H. B. (1887) *The Solomon Islands: Their Geology, General Features and Suitability for Colonization,* London.

Guppy H.B. (1887) *The Solomon Islands and their Natives*, Swan Sonnenschien, London.

Hagelberg E. & Clegg J.B. (1993) Genetic polymorphism in prehistoric Pacific islanders determined by analysis of ancient bone

DNA. *Proceedings of the Royal Society*, **252**, 163-170.

Heyerdahl T. (1952) *American Indians in the Pacific*, George Allen & Unwin Ltd., London.

Hinton A.G. (1972) *Shells of New Guinea and the Central Indo-Pacific.* Jacaranda Press, Sydney.

Honan M. (1997) *Solomon Islands*, Lonely Planet Publications, Hawthorn.

Horton D. C. (1965) *The Happy Isles*, Heinemann, London.

Horton D.C. (1971a) *Fire over the Islands*, A.H. & A.W Reed Ltd., Sydney.

Horton D. C. (1971b) *New Georgia, Pattern for Victory*, Pan/Ballantine, London.

Jack-Hinton C. (1969) *The Search for the Solomon Islands (1567-1838)*, Oxford.

Jennings J.D. (1979) *The Prehistory of Polynesia,* Harvard University Press, Cambridge.

Johnson O. (1946) *Bride in the Solomons*, London.

Jones M. (1974) *Married to Melanesia*, George Allan & Unwin, London.

Keesing R. *Kwaio Religion,* Solomon Islands National Museum, Honiara.

Kennedy P. (1972) *Pacific Onslaught, 7th Dec. 1941/7th Feb. 1943*, Pan/Ballantine, London.

Kent J. (1972) *The Solomon Islands*, Wren Publishing Pty Ltd, Melbourne.

Kenworthy J.C. (1972) *Marine Shells of the Solomon Islands*, Solomon Islands Museum Association, Honiara.

Lambert S. M. (1934) British Solomon Islands health surveys 1933. *Journal of Tropical Medicine and Hygiene.* **37**, 85, 102 & 137.

Lambert S. M. (1941) *A Doctor in Paradise*, J.M.Dent & Sons Ltd., London.

Levine N.D. & Harper F. (1947) Malaria and other insect-borne Diseases in the South Pacific Campaign (1942 – 1945). *American*

Journal of Tropical Medicine, **27**, 119 – 128.

Lawrence P. (1964) *Road Belong Cargo*, Manchester.

Lewis D. (1972) *We the Navigators*, Australian National Press, Canberra.

London, J. (1916) *The Cruise of the Snark,* New York.

Macgregor J. D. (2006) *Colonial Window, A View from the Past,* The Memoir Club, Stanhope.

Macquarrie H. (1943) *Vouza and the Solomon Islands*, Gollancz, London.

Malinowski B. (1922) *Argonauts of the Western Pacific*, Routledge and Kegan Paul, New York.

Malinowski B. (1929) *The Sexual Life of Savages in North-Western Melanesia,* Routledge and Kegan Paul, New York.

Markham C. (1904) *The Voyages of Pedro Fernandez de Quiros, 1595-1606*, Hakluyt Society, London.

Maude H. E. (1968) *Of Islands and Men*, Oxford.

Mayer J.F. (1945) *Birds of the South-West Pacific,* Macmillan, New York.

McCoy M. (1980) *Reptiles and Frogs of the Solomon Islands.* Wau Ecology Institute Publication No. 7, Papua New Guinea.

McCoy M. (2007) *Solomon Islands: A South Seas Journey.* Zipolo Habu.

McCoy M. & Barwick D.I. (1986) *Solomon Islands*, Robert Brown & Associates (Aust) Pty. Ltd., Bathurst.

Michener J.A. (1947) *Tales of the South Pacific*, Corgi Books, London.

Miller J. (1949) *Guadalcanal: the First Offensive*, Washington.

O'Connor F.W. (1923) Researches in the Western Pacific. *London School of Tropical Medicine Research Memorial Series,* **4**, 1-57.

Oliver D. L. (1955) *A Solomon Island Society*, Cambridge, Mass.

Randall W. (2002) *Solomon Time*, Abacus, London.

Randell N. (2003) *The White Headhunter*, Constable, London.

Rentz J. N. (1952) *Marines in the Central Solomons*, Washington.

Rivers W. H. R. (1914) *The History of Melanesian Society*, Cambridge.

Scheffler H.W. (1965) *Choiseul Island Social Structure*, University of California Press, Los Angeles.

Sharp A. (1960) *The Discovery of the Pacific Islands*, Oxford.

Stanley D. (1986) *South Pacific Handbook*, Moon Publications, Chico.

Stevens G.W. and Tedder J.L.O. (1973) *A Honiara Bird Guide*, British Solomon Islands Scout Association, Honiara.

Stevenson A. (1988) *Solomon Islands*, Solomon Islands Tourist Authority, Honiara.

Solomon Islands Museum Association (1972), *Journal of the Solomon Islands Museum Association*, **1**, Honiara.

Solomon Islands Museum Association (1974), *Journal of the Solomon Islands Museum Association*, **2**, Honiara.

Solomon Islands Museum Association (1975), *Journal of the Solomon Islands Museum Association*, **3**, Honiara.

South Pacific Commission. (1946) *Among Those Present,* London.

Tedder J.L.O. *Walks on Guadalcanal*, Solomon Islands Tourist Authority.

Terrel J. (1986) *Prehistory in the Pacific Islands*, Cambridge University Press, Cambridge.

Theroux P. (1992) *The Happy Isles of Oceania*, Penguin, London.

University of the South Pacific (1981) *The Road Out,* Institute of Pacific Studies, Nuku'alofa.

Waterhouse J. H. L. and Jones L. M. (1949) *A Roviana and English Dictionary*, Epworth, Sydney.

Webber R.H. (1975) Vector control of filariasis in the Solomon Islands. *Southeast Asian Journal of Tropical Medicine and Public Health,* **6**, 430-434.

Webber R.H. (1977) The natural decline of *Wuchereria bancrofti* infection in a vector control situation in the Solomon Islands. *Transactions of the Royal Society of Tropical Medicine and Hygiene,* **71**, 396-400.

Webber R.H. (1978) Guadalcanal earthquake, *Tropical Doctor*, **8**, 160-162.

Webber R.H. (1979) Eradication of *Wuchereria bancrofti* infection through vector control. *Transactions of the Royal Society of Tropical Medicine and Hygiene*, **73**, 722-724.

Woodford C. M. (1890) *A Naturalist Among the Headhunters*, George Philip and Son, London.

Zimmerman J. L. (1949) *The Guadalcanal Campaign*, Washington.

Index Page